Advanced Analytics with PySpark

*Patterns for Learning from Data at Scale
Using Python and Spark*

*Akash Tandon, Sandy Ryza, Uri Laserson,
Sean Owen, and Josh Wills*

Beijing · Boston · Farnham · Sebastopol · Tokyo

Advanced Analytics with PySpark

by Akash Tandon, Sandy Ryza, Uri Laserson, Sean Owen, and Josh Wills

Published by O'Reilly Media, Inc., 1005 Gravenstein Highway North, Sebastopol, CA 95472.

O'Reilly books may be purchased for educational, business, or sales promotional use. Online editions are also available for most titles (*http://oreilly.com*). For more information, contact our corporate/institutional sales department: 800-998-9938 or *corporate@oreilly.com*.

Acquisitions Editor: Jessica Haberman
Development Editor: Jeff Bleiel
Production Editor: Christopher Faucher
Copyeditor: Penelope Perkins
Proofreader: Kim Wimpsett

Indexer: Sue Klefstad
Interior Designer: David Futato
Cover Designer: Karen Montgomery
Illustrator: Kate Dullea

June 2022:   First Edition

Revision History for the First Edition
2022-06-14:   First Release

See *http://oreilly.com/catalog/errata.csp?isbn=9781098103651* for release details.

978-1-098-10365-1

[LSI]

Table of Contents

Preface

Apache Spark's long lineage of predecessors, from MPI (message passing interface) to MapReduce, made it possible to write programs that take advantage of massive resources while abstracting away the nitty-gritty details of distributed systems. As much as data processing needs have motivated the development of these frameworks, in a way the field of big data has become so related to them that its scope is defined by what these frameworks can handle. Spark's original promise was to take this a little further—to make writing distributed programs feel like writing regular programs.

The rise in Spark's popularity coincided with that of the Python data (PyData) ecosystem. So it makes sense that Spark's Python API—PySpark—has significantly grown in popularity over the last few years. Although the PyData ecosystem has recently sprung up some distributed programming options, Apache Spark remains one of the most popular choices for working with large datasets across industries and domains. Thanks to recent efforts to integrate PySpark with the other PyData tools, learning the framework can help you boost your productivity significantly as a data science practitioner.

We think that the best way to teach data science is by example. To that end, we have put together a book of applications, trying to touch on the interactions between the most common algorithms, datasets, and design patterns in large-scale analytics. This book isn't meant to be read cover to cover: page to a chapter that looks like something you're trying to accomplish, or that simply ignites your interest, and start there.

Why Did We Write This Book Now?

Apache Spark experienced a major version upgrade in 2020—version 3.0. One of the biggest improvements was the introduction of Spark Adaptive Execution. This feature takes away a big portion of the complexity around tuning and optimization. We do not refer to it in the book because it's turned on by default in Spark 3.2 and later versions, and so you automatically get the benefits.

The ecosystem changes, combined with Spark's latest major release, make this edition a timely one. Unlike previous editions of *Advanced Analytics with Spark*, which chose Scala, we will use Python. We'll cover best practices and integrate with the wider Python data science ecosystem when appropriate. All chapters have been updated to use the latest PySpark API. Two new chapters have been added and multiple chapters have undergone major rewrites. We will not cover Spark's streaming and graph libraries. With Spark in a new era of maturity and stability, we hope that these changes will preserve the book as a useful resource on analytics for years to come.

How This Book Is Organized

Chapter 1 places Spark and PySpark within the wider context of data science and big data analytics. After that, each chapter comprises a self-contained analysis using PySpark. Chapter 2 introduces the basics of data processing in PySpark and Python through a use case in data cleansing. The next few chapters delve into the meat and potatoes of machine learning with Spark, applying some of the most common algorithms in canonical applications. The remaining chapters are a bit more of a grab bag and apply Spark in slightly more exotic applications—for example, querying Wikipedia through latent semantic relationships in the text, analyzing genomics data, and identifying similar images.

This book is not about PySpark's merits and disadvantages. There are a few other things that it is not about either. It introduces the Spark programming model and basics of Spark's Python API, PySpark. However, it does not attempt to be a Spark reference or provide a comprehensive guide to all Spark's nooks and crannies. It does not try to be a machine learning, statistics, or linear algebra reference, although many of the chapters provide some background on these before using them.

Instead, this book will help the reader get a feel for what it's like to use PySpark for complex analytics on large datasets by covering the entire pipeline: not just building and evaluating models, but also cleansing, preprocessing, and exploring data, with attention paid to turning results into production applications. We believe that the best way to teach this is by example.

Here are examples of some tasks that will be tackled in this book:

Predicting forest cover
  We predict type of forest cover using relevant features like location and soil type by using decision trees (see Chapter 4).

Querying Wikipedia for similar entries
  We identify relationships between entries and query the Wikipedia corpus by using NLP (natural language processing) techniques (see Chapter 6).

Understanding utilization of New York cabs
> We compute average taxi waiting time as a function of location by performing temporal and geospatial analysis (see Chapter 7).

Reduce risk for an investment portfolio
> We estimate financial risk for an investment portfolio using the Monte Carlo simulation (see Chapter 9).

When possible, we attempt not to just provide a "solution," but to demonstrate the full data science workflow, with all of its iterations, dead ends, and restarts. This book will be useful for getting more comfortable with Python, Spark, and machine learning and data analysis. However, these are in service of a larger goal, and we hope that most of all this book will teach you how to approach tasks like those described earlier. Each chapter, in about 20 measly pages, will try to get as close as possible to demonstrating how to build one piece of these data applications.

Conventions Used in This Book

The following typographical conventions are used in this book:

Italic
> Indicates new terms, URLs, email addresses, filenames, and file extensions.

`Constant width`
> Used for program listings, as well as within paragraphs to refer to program elements such as variable or function names, databases, data types, environment variables, statements, and keywords.

`Constant width bold`
> Shows commands or other text that should be typed literally by the user.

`Constant width italic`
> Shows text that should be replaced with user-supplied values or by values determined by context.

 This element signifies a tip or suggestion.

 This element signifies a general note.

This element indicates a warning or caution.

Using Code Examples

Supplemental material (code examples, exercises, etc.) is available for download at *https://github.com/sryza/aas*.

If you have a technical question or a problem using the code examples, please send email to *bookquestions@oreilly.com*.

This book is here to help you get your job done. In general, if example code is offered with this book, you may use it in your programs and documentation. You do not need to contact us for permission unless you're reproducing a significant portion of the code. For example, writing a program that uses several chunks of code from this book does not require permission. Selling or distributing examples from O'Reilly books does require permission. Answering a question by citing this book and quoting example code does not require permission. Incorporating a significant amount of example code from this book into your product's documentation does require permission.

We appreciate, but do not require, attribution. An attribution usually includes the title, author, publisher, and ISBN. For example: "*Advanced Analytics with PySpark* by Akash Tandon, Sandy Ryza, Uri Laserson, Sean Owen, and Josh Wills (O'Reilly). Copyright 2022 Akash Tandon, 978-1-098-10365-1."

If you feel your use of code examples falls outside fair use or the permission given above, feel free to contact us at *permissions@oreilly.com*.

O'Reilly Online Learning

 For more than 40 years, *O'Reilly Media* has provided technology and business training, knowledge, and insight to help companies succeed.

Our unique network of experts and innovators share their knowledge and expertise through books, articles, and our online learning platform. O'Reilly's online learning platform gives you on-demand access to live training courses, in-depth learning paths, interactive coding environments, and a vast collection of text and video from O'Reilly and 200+ other publishers. For more information, visit *https://oreilly.com*.

How to Contact Us

Please address comments and questions concerning this book to the publisher:

O'Reilly Media, Inc.
1005 Gravenstein Highway North
Sebastopol, CA 95472
800-998-9938 (in the United States or Canada)
707-829-0515 (international or local)
707-829-0104 (fax)

We have a web page for this book, where we list errata, examples, and any additional information. You can access this page at *https://oreil.ly/adv-analytics-pyspark*.

Email *bookquestions@oreilly.com* to comment or ask technical questions about this book.

For news and information about our books and courses, visit *https://oreilly.com*.

Find us on LinkedIn: *https://linkedin.com/company/oreilly-media*

Follow us on Twitter: *https://twitter.com/oreillymedia*

Watch us on YouTube: *https://youtube.com/oreillymedia*

Acknowledgments

It goes without saying that you wouldn't be reading this book if it were not for the existence of Apache Spark and MLlib. We all owe thanks to the team that has built and open sourced it and the hundreds of contributors who have added to it.

We would like to thank everyone who spent a great deal of time reviewing the content of the previous editions of the book with expert eyes: Michael Bernico, Adam Breindel, Ian Buss, Parviz Deyhim, Jeremy Freeman, Chris Fregly, Debashish Ghosh, Juliet Hougland, Jonathan Keebler, Nisha Muktewar, Frank Nothaft, Nick Pentreath, Kostas Sakellis, Tom White, Marcelo Vanzin, and Juliet Hougland again. Thanks all! We owe you one. This has greatly improved the structure and quality of the result.

Sandy also would like to thank Jordan Pinkus and Richard Wang for helping with some of the theory behind the risk chapter.

Thanks to Jeff Bleiel and O'Reilly for the experience and great support in getting this book published and into your hands.

## CHAPTER 1

Analyzing Big Data

When people say that we live in an age of big data they mean that we have tools for collecting, storing, and processing information at a scale previously unheard of. The following tasks simply could not have been accomplished 10 or 15 years ago:

- Build a model to detect credit card fraud using thousands of features and billions of transactions
- Intelligently recommend millions of products to millions of users
- Estimate financial risk through simulations of portfolios that include millions of instruments
- Easily manipulate genomic data from thousands of people to detect genetic associations with disease
- Assess agricultural land use and crop yield for improved policymaking by periodically processing millions of satellite images

Sitting behind these capabilities is an ecosystem of open source software that can leverage clusters of servers to process massive amounts of data. The introduction/release of Apache Hadoop in 2006 has led to widespread adoption of distributed computing. The big data ecosystem and tooling have evolved at a rapid pace since then. The past five years have also seen the introduction and adoption of many open source machine learning (ML) and deep learning libraries. These tools aim to leverage vast amounts of data that we now collect and store.

But just as a chisel and a block of stone do not make a statue, there is a gap between having access to these tools and all this data and doing something useful with it. Often, "doing something useful" means placing a schema over tabular data and using SQL to answer questions like "Of the gazillion users who made it to the third page in our registration process, how many are over 25?" The field of how to architect data storage and organize information (data warehouses, data lakes, etc.) to make answering such questions easy is a rich one, but we will mostly avoid its intricacies in this book.

Sometimes, "doing something useful" takes a little extra work. SQL still may be core to the approach, but to work around idiosyncrasies in the data or perform complex analysis, we need a programming paradigm that's more flexible and with richer functionality in areas like machine learning and statistics. This is where data science comes in and that's what we are going to talk about in this book.

In this chapter, we'll start by introducing big data as a concept and discuss some of the challenges that arise when working with large datasets. We will then introduce Apache Spark, an open source framework for distributed computing, and its key components. Our focus will be on PySpark, Spark's Python API, and how it fits within a wider ecosystem. This will be followed by a discussion of the changes brought by Spark 3.0, the framework's first major release in four years. We will finish with a brief note about how PySpark addresses challenges of data science and why it is a great addition to your skillset.

Previous editions of this book used Spark's Scala API for code examples. We decided to use PySpark instead because of Python's popularity in the data science community and an increased focus by the core Spark team to better support the language. By the end of this chapter, you will ideally appreciate this decision.

Working with Big Data

Many of our favorite small data tools hit a wall when working with big data. Libraries like pandas are not equipped to deal with data that can't fit in our RAM. Then, what should an equivalent process look like that can leverage clusters of computers to achieve the same outcomes on large datasets? Challenges of distributed computing require us to rethink many of the basic assumptions that we rely on in single-node systems. For example, because data must be partitioned across many nodes on a cluster, algorithms that have wide data dependencies will suffer from the fact that network transfer rates are orders of magnitude slower than memory accesses. As the number of machines working on a problem increases, the probability of a failure increases. These facts require a programming paradigm that is sensitive to the characteristics of the underlying system: one that discourages poor choices and makes it easy to write code that will execute in a highly parallel manner.

How Big Is Big Data?

Without a reference point, the term *big data* is ambiguous. Moreover, the age-old two-tier definition of small and big data can be confusing. When it comes to data size, a three-tiered definition is more helpful (see Table 1-1).

Table 1-1. A tiered definition of data sizes

Dataset type	Fits in RAM?	Fits on local disk?
Small dataset	Yes	Yes
Medium dataset	No	Yes
Big dataset	No	No

As per the table, if the dataset can fit in memory or disk on a single system, it cannot be termed big data. This definition is not perfect, but it does act as a good rule of thumb in context of an average machine.

The focus of this book is to enable you to work efficiently with big data. If your dataset is small and can fit in memory, stay away from distributed systems. To analyze medium-sized datasets, a database or parallelism may be good enough at times. At other times, you may have to set up a cluster and use big data tools. Hopefully, the experience that you will gain in the following chapters will help you make such judgment calls.

Single-machine tools that have come to recent prominence in the software community are not the only tools used for data analysis. Scientific fields like genomics that deal with large datasets have been leveraging parallel-computing frameworks for decades. Most people processing data in these fields today are familiar with a cluster-computing environment called HPC (high-performance computing). Where the difficulties with Python and R lie in their inability to scale, the difficulties with HPC lie in its relatively low level of abstraction and difficulty of use. For example, to process a large file full of DNA-sequencing reads in parallel, we must manually split it up into smaller files and submit a job for each of those files to the cluster scheduler. If some of these fail, the user must detect the failure and manually resubmit them. If the analysis requires all-to-all operations like sorting the entire dataset, the large dataset must be streamed through a single node, or the scientist must resort to lower-level distributed frameworks like MPI, which are difficult to program without extensive knowledge of C and distributed/networked systems.

Tools written for HPC environments often fail to decouple the in-memory data models from the lower-level storage models. For example, many tools only know how to read data from a POSIX filesystem in a single stream, making it difficult to make tools naturally parallelize or to use other storage backends, like databases. Modern distributed computing frameworks provide abstractions that allow users to treat a cluster of computers more like a single computer—to automatically split up files and distribute storage over many machines, divide work into smaller tasks and execute them in a distributed manner, and recover from failures. They can automate a lot of the hassle of working with large datasets and are far cheaper than HPC.

 A simple way to think about *distributed systems* is that they are a group of independent computers that appear to the end user as a single computer. They allow for horizontal scaling. That means adding more computers rather than upgrading a single system (vertical scaling). The latter is relatively expensive and often insufficient for large workloads. Distributed systems are great for scaling and reliability but also introduce complexity when it comes to design, construction, and debugging. One should understand this trade-off before opting for such a tool.

Introducing Apache Spark and PySpark

Enter Apache Spark, an open source framework that combines an engine for distributing programs across clusters of machines with an elegant model for writing programs atop it. Spark originated at the University of California, Berkeley, AMPLab and has since been contributed to the Apache Software Foundation. When released, it was arguably the first open source software that made distributed programming truly accessible to data scientists.

Components

Apart from the core computation engine (Spark Core), Spark is comprised of four main components. Spark code written by a user, using either of its APIs, is executed in the workers' JVMs (Java Virtual Machines) across the cluster (see Chapter 2). These components are available as distinct libraries as shown in Figure 1-1:

Spark SQL and DataFrames + Datasets
    A module for working with structured data.

MLlib
    A scalable machine learning library.

Structured Streaming
    This makes it easy to build scalable fault-tolerant streaming applications.

GraphX (legacy)

GraphX is Apache Spark's library for graphs and graph-parallel computation. However, for graph analytics, GraphFrames is recommended instead of GraphX, which isn't being actively developed as much and lacks Python bindings. Graph-Frames (*https://oreil.ly/p6TYQ*) is an open source general graph processing library that is similar to Apache Spark's GraphX but uses DataFrame-based APIs.

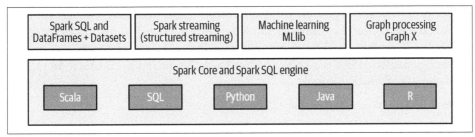

Figure 1-1. Apache Spark components

Comparison with MapReduce

One illuminating way to understand Spark is in terms of its advances over its predecessor, Apache Hadoop's MapReduce. MapReduce revolutionized computation over huge datasets by offering a simple and resilient model for writing programs that could execute in parallel across hundreds to thousands of machines. It broke up work into small tasks and could gracefully accommodate task failures without compromising the job to which they belonged.

Spark maintains MapReduce's linear scalability and fault tolerance, but extends it in three important ways:

- First, rather than relying on a rigid map-then-reduce format, its engine can execute a more general directed acyclic graph of operators. This means that in situations where MapReduce must write out intermediate results to the distributed filesystem, Spark can pass them directly to the next step in the pipeline.

- Second, it complements its computational capability with a rich set of transformations that enable users to express computation more naturally. Out-of-the-box functions are provided for various tasks, including numerical computation, datetime processing, and string manipulation.

- Third, Spark extends its predecessors with in-memory processing. This means that future steps that want to deal with the same dataset need not recompute it or reload it from disk. Spark is well-suited for highly iterative algorithms as well as ad hoc queries.

PySpark

PySpark is Spark's Python API. In simpler words, PySpark is a Python-based wrapper over the core Spark framework, which is written primarily in Scala. PySpark provides an intuitive programming environment for data science practitioners and offers the flexibility of Python with the distributed processing capabilities of Spark.

PySpark allows us to work across programming models. For example, a common pattern is to perform large-scale extract, transform, and load (ETL) workloads with Spark and then collect the results to a local machine followed by manipulation using pandas. We'll explore such programming models as we write PySpark code in the upcoming chapters. Here is a code example from the official documentation to give you a glimpse of what's to come:

```python
from pyspark.ml.classification import LogisticRegression

# Load training data
training = spark.read.format("libsvm").load("data/mllib/sample_libsvm_data.txt")

lr = LogisticRegression(maxIter=10, regParam=0.3, elasticNetParam=0.8)

# Fit the model
lrModel = lr.fit(training)

# Print the coefficients and intercept for logistic regression
print("Coefficients: " + str(lrModel.coefficients))
print("Intercept: " + str(lrModel.intercept))

# We can also use the multinomial family for binary classification
mlr = LogisticRegression(maxIter=10, regParam=0.3, elasticNetParam=0.8,
                         family="multinomial")

# Fit the model
mlrModel = mlr.fit(training)

# Print the coefficients and intercepts for logistic regression
# with multinomial family
print("Multinomial coefficients: " + str(mlrModel.coefficientMatrix))
print("Multinomial intercepts: " + str(mlrModel.interceptVector))
```

Spark Versus PySpark Versus SparkSQL

The distinction between Spark, PySpark, and SparkSQL can confuse beginners. We have introduced the three terms individually. Let's summarize the differences to avoid any confusion going ahead.

Spark
> A distributed processing framework written primarily in the Scala programming language. The framework offers different language APIs on top of the core Scala-based framework.

PySpark
> Spark's Python API. Think of it as a Python-based wrapper on top of core Spark.

SparkSQL
> A Spark module for structured data processing. It is part of the core Spark framework and accessible through all of its language APIs, including PySpark.

Ecosystem

Spark is the closest thing to a Swiss Army knife that we have in the big data ecosystem. To top it off, it integrates well with rest of the ecosystem and is extensible. Spark decouples storage and compute unlike Apache Hadoop and HPC systems described previously. That means we can use Spark to read data stored in many sources—Apache Hadoop, Apache Cassandra, Apache HBase, MongoDB, Apache Hive, RDBMSs, and more—and process it all in memory. Spark's DataFrameReader and DataFrameWriter APIs can also be extended to read data from other sources, such as Apache Kafka, Amazon Kinesis, Azure Storage, and Amazon S3, on which it can operate. It also supports multiple deployment modes, ranging from local environments to Apache YARN and Kubernetes clusters.

There also exists a wide community around it. This has led to creation of many third-party packages. A community-created list of such packages can be found here (*https://oreil.ly/N8ZDf*). Major cloud providers (AWS EMR (*https://oreil.ly/29yh1*), Azure Databricks (*https://oreil.ly/RAShf*), GCP Dataproc (*https://oreil.ly/5i5MT*)) also provide third-party vendor options for running managed Spark workloads. In addition, there are dedicated conferences and local meetup groups that can be of interest for learning about interesting applications and best practices.

Spark 3.0

In 2020, Apache Spark made its first major release since 2016 when Spark 2.0 was released—Spark 3.0. This series' last edition, released in 2017, covered changes brought about by Spark 2.0. Spark 3.0 does not introduce as many major API changes as the last major release. This release focuses on performance and usability improvements without introducing significant backward incompatibility.

The Spark SQL module has seen major performance enhancements in the form of adaptive query execution and dynamic partition pruning. In simpler terms, they allow Spark to adapt a physical execution plan during runtime and skip over data that's not required in a query's results, respectively. These optimizations address significant effort that users had to previously put into manual tuning and optimization. Spark 3.0 is almost two times faster than Spark 2.4 on TPC-DS, an industry-standard analytical processing benchmark. Since most Spark applications are backed by the SQL engine, all the higher-level libraries, including MLlib and structured streaming, and higher-level APIs, including SQL and DataFrames, have benefited. Compliance with the ANSI SQL standard makes the SQL API more usable.

Python has emerged as the leader in terms of adoption in the data science ecosystem. Consequently, Python is now the most widely used language on Spark. PySpark has more than five million monthly downloads on PyPI, the Python Package Index. Spark 3.0 improves its functionalities and usability. pandas user-defined functions (UDFs) have been redesigned to support Python type hints and iterators as arguments. New pandas UDF types have been included, and the error handling is now more pythonic. Python versions below 3.6 have been deprecated. From Spark 3.2 onward, Python 3.6 support has been deprecated too.

Over the last four years, the data science ecosystem has also changed at a rapid pace. There is an increased focus on putting machine learning models in production. Deep learning has provided remarkable results and the Spark team is currently experimenting to allow the project's scheduler to leverage accelerators such as GPUs.

PySpark Addresses Challenges of Data Science

For a system that seeks to enable complex analytics on huge data to be successful, it needs to be informed by—or at least not conflict with—some fundamental challenges faced by data scientists.

- First, the vast majority of work that goes into conducting successful analyses lies in preprocessing data. Data is messy, and cleansing, munging, fusing, mushing, and many other verbs are prerequisites to doing anything useful with it.

- Second, *iteration* is a fundamental part of data science. Modeling and analysis typically require multiple passes over the same data. Popular optimization procedures like stochastic gradient descent involve repeated scans over their inputs to reach convergence. Iteration also matters within the data scientist's own workflow. Choosing the right features, picking the right algorithms, running the right significance tests, and finding the right hyperparameters all require experimentation.

- Third, the task isn't over when a well-performing model has been built. The point of data science is to make data useful to non–data scientists. Uses of data recommendation engines and real-time fraud detection systems culminate in data applications. In such systems, models become part of a production service and may need to be rebuilt periodically or even in real time.

PySpark deals well with the aforementioned challenges of data science, acknowledging that the biggest bottleneck in building data applications is not CPU, disk, or network, but analyst productivity. Collapsing the full pipeline, from preprocessing to model evaluation, into a single programming environment can speed up development. By packaging an expressive programming model with a set of analytic libraries under an REPL (read-eval-print loop) environment, PySpark avoids the round trips to IDEs. The more quickly analysts can experiment with their data, the higher likelihood they have of doing something useful with it.

> A read-eval-print loop, or REPL, is a computer environment where user inputs are read and evaluated, and then the results are returned to the user.

PySpark's core APIs provide a strong foundation for data transformation independent of any functionality in statistics, machine learning, or matrix algebra. When exploring and getting a feel for a dataset, data scientists can keep data in memory while they run queries, and easily cache transformed versions of the data as well, without suffering a trip to disk. As a framework that makes modeling easy but is also a good fit for production systems, it is a huge win for the data science ecosystem.

Where to Go from Here

Spark spans the gap between systems designed for exploratory analytics and systems designed for operational analytics. It is often said that a data scientist is someone who is better at engineering than most statisticians and better at statistics than most engineers. At the very least, Spark is better at being an operational system than most exploratory systems and better for data exploration than the technologies commonly used in operational systems. We hope that this chapter was helpful and you are now excited about getting hands-on with PySpark. That's what we will do from the next chapter onward!

## CHAPTER 2

Introduction to Data Analysis with PySpark

Python is the most widely used language for data science tasks. The prospect of being able to do statistical computing and web programming using the same language contributed to its rise in popularity in the early 2010s. This has led to a thriving ecosystem of tools and a helpful community for data analysis, often referred to as the PyData ecosystem. This is a big reason for PySpark's popularity. Being able to leverage distributed computing via Spark in Python helps data science practitioners be more productive because of familiarity with the programming language and presence of a wide community. For that same reason, we have opted to write our examples in PySpark.

It's difficult to express how transformative it is to do all of your data munging and analysis in a single environment, regardless of where the data itself is stored and processed. It's the sort of thing that you have to experience to understand, and we wanted to be sure that our examples captured some of that magic feeling we experienced when we first started using PySpark. For example, PySpark provides interoperability with pandas, which is one of the most popular PyData tools. We will explore this feature further in the chapter.

In this chapter, we will explore PySpark's powerful DataFrame API via a data cleansing exercise. In PySpark, the DataFrame is an abstraction for datasets that have a regular structure in which each record is a row made up of a set of columns, and each column has a well-defined data type. You can think of a dataframe as the Spark analogue of a table in a relational database. Even though the naming convention might make you think of a `pandas.DataFrame` object, Spark's DataFrames are a different beast. This is because they represent distributed datasets on a cluster, not local data where every row in the data is stored on the same machine. Although there are similarities in how you use DataFrames and the role they play inside the Spark ecosystem, there are some things you may be used to doing when working with dataframes in pandas or R that do not apply to Spark, so it's best to think of them as their own distinct entity and try to approach them with an open mind.

As for data cleansing, it is the first step in any data science project, and often the most important. Many clever analyses have been undone because the data analyzed had fundamental quality problems or underlying artifacts that biased the analysis or led the data scientist to see things that weren't really there. Hence, what better way to introduce you to working with data using PySpark and DataFrames than a data cleansing exercise?

First, we will introduce PySpark's fundamentals and practice them using a sample dataset from the University of California, Irvine, Machine Learning Repository. We'll reiterate why PySpark is a good choice for data science and introduce its programming model. Then we'll set up PySpark on our system or cluster and analyze our dataset using PySpark's DataFrame API. Most of your time using PySpark for data analysis will center around the DataFrame API, so get ready to become intimately familiar with it. This will prepare us for the following chapters where we delve into various machine learning algorithms.

You don't need to deeply understand how Spark works under the hood for performing data science tasks. However, understanding basic concepts about Spark's architecture will make it easier to work with PySpark and make better decisions when writing code. That is what we will cover in the next section.

DataFrame and RDDs

An RDD (resilient distributed dataset) is the most basic abstraction in Spark. It is an immutable distributed collection of elements of your data, partitioned across machines in your Spark cluster. The partitions can be operated in parallel with a low-level API that offers transformations and actions. This was the primary user-facing abstraction at Spark's inception. However, there are some problems with this model. Most importantly, any computation that you perform on top of an RDD is opaque to Spark Core. Hence, there's no built-in optimization that can be done. The problem gets even more acute in the case of PySpark. We won't go into the architecture-level details since that is beyond the scope of this book.

Enter DataFrames. Introduced in Spark 1.3, DataFrames are like distributed, in-memory tables with named columns and schemas, where each column has a specific data type: integer, string, array, map, real, date, timestamp, etc. It is like a table from our point of view. There also exist a common set of operations that allow us to perform typical computations (joins, aggregations). Because of this, Spark is able to construct an efficient execution plan resulting in better performance as compared to an RDD.

We will focus on DataFrames throughout the book. If you want to delve deeper into the differences between DataFrames and RDDs, an excellent resource is *Learning Spark* (O'Reilly).

 When using the DataFrame API, your PySpark code should provide comparable performance with Scala. If you're using a UDF or RDDs, you will have a performance impact.

Spark Architecture

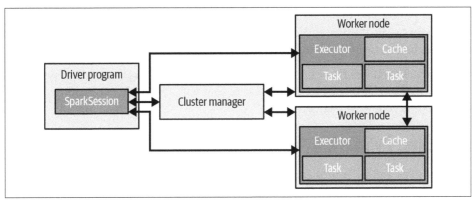

Figure 2-1. Spark architecture diagram

Figure 2-1 depicts the Spark architecture through high-level components. Spark applications run as independent sets of processes on a cluster or locally. At a high level, a Spark application is comprised of a driver process, a cluster manager, and a set of executor processes. The driver program is the central component and responsible for distributing tasks across executor processes. There will always be just one driver process. When we talk about scaling, we mean increasing the number of executors. The cluster manager simply manages resources.

Spark is a distributed, data-parallel compute engine. In the data-parallel model, more data partitions equals more parallelism. Partitioning allows for efficient parallelism. A distributed scheme of breaking up data into chunks or partitions allows Spark executors to process only data that is close to them, minimizing network bandwidth. That is, each executor's core is assigned its own data partition to work on. Remember this whenever a choice related to partitioning comes up.

Spark programming starts with a dataset, usually residing in some form of distributed, persistent storage like the Hadoop distributed file system (HDFS) or a cloud-based solution such as AWS S3 and in a format like Parquet. Writing a Spark program typically consists of a few steps:

1. Define a set of transformations on the input dataset.

2. Invoke actions that output the transformed datasets to persistent storage or return results to the driver's local memory. These actions will ideally be performed by the worker nodes, as depicted on the right in Figure 2-1.

3. Run local computations that operate on the results computed in a distributed fashion. These can help you decide what transformations and actions to undertake next.

It's important to remember that all of PySpark's higher-level abstractions still rely on the same philosophy that has been present in Spark since the very beginning: the interplay between storage and execution. Understanding these principles will help you make better use of Spark for data analysis.

Next, we will install and set up PySpark on our machine so that we can start performing data analysis. This is a one-time exercise that will help us run the code examples from this and following chapters.

Installing PySpark

The examples and code in this book assume you have Spark 3.1.1 available. For the purpose of following the code examples, install PySpark from the PyPI repository (*https://oreil.ly/t0WBZ*).

```
$ pip3 install pyspark
```

Note that PySpark requires Java 8 or later to be installed. If you want SQL, ML, and/or MLlib as extra dependencies, that's an option too. We will need these later.

```
$ pip3 install pyspark[sql,ml,mllib]
```

 Installing from PyPI skips the libraries required to run Scala, Java, or R. Full releases can be obtained from the Spark project site (*https://oreil.ly/pK2Wi*). Refer to the Spark documentation (*https://oreil.ly/FLh4U*) for instructions on setting up a Spark environment, whether on a cluster or simply on your local machine.

Now we're ready to launch the `pyspark-shell`, which is an REPL for the Python language that also has some Spark-specific extensions. This is similar to the Python or IPython shell that you may have used. If you're just running these examples on your personal computer, you can launch a local Spark cluster by specifying `local[N]`, where N is the number of threads to run, or `*` to match the number of cores available

---

on your machine. For example, to launch a local cluster that uses eight threads on an eight-core machine:

```
$ pyspark --master local[*]
```

A Spark application itself is often referred to as a Spark *cluster*. That is a logical abstraction and is different from a physical cluster (multiple machines).

If you have a Hadoop cluster that runs a version of Hadoop that supports YARN, you can launch the Spark jobs on the cluster by using the value of yarn for the Spark master:

```
$ pyspark --master yarn --deploy-mode client
```

The rest of the examples in this book will not show a --master argument to spark-shell, but you will typically need to specify this argument as appropriate for your environment.

You may need to specify additional arguments to make the Spark shell fully utilize your resources. A list of arguments can be found by executing pyspark --help. For example, when running Spark with a local master, you can use --driver-memory 2g to let the single local process use 2 GB of memory. YARN memory configuration is more complex, and relevant options like --executor-memory are explained in the Spark on YARN documentation (*https://oreil.ly/3bRjy*).

The Spark framework officially supports four cluster deployment modes: standalone, YARN, Kubernetes, and Mesos. More details can be found in the Deploying Spark documentation (*https://oreil.ly/hG2a5*).

After running one of these commands, you will see a lot of log messages from Spark as it initializes itself, but you should also see a bit of ASCII art, followed by some additional log messages and a prompt:

```
Python 3.6.12 |Anaconda, Inc.| (default, Sep  8 2020, 23:10:56)
[GCC 7.3.0] on linux
Type "help", "copyright", "credits" or "license" for more information.
Welcome to
      ____              __
     / __/__  ___ _____/ /__
    _\ \/ _ \/ _ `/ __/  '_/
   /__ / .__/\_,_/_/ /_/\_\   version 3.0.1
      /_/
```

```
Using Python version 3.6.12 (default, Sep  8 2020 23:10:56)
SparkSession available as 'spark'.
```

You can run the :help command in the shell. This will prompt you to either start an interactive help mode or ask for help about specific Python objects. In addition to the note about :help, the Spark log messages indicated "SparkSession available as *spark*." This is a reference to the SparkSession, which acts as an entry point to all Spark operations and data. Go ahead and type spark at the command line:

```
spark
...
<pyspark.sql.session.SparkSession object at DEADBEEF>
```

The REPL will print the string form of the object. For the SparkSession object, this is simply its name plus the hexadecimal address of the object in memory. (DEADBEEF is a placeholder; the exact value you see here will vary from run to run.) In an interactive Spark shell, the Spark driver instantiates a SparkSession for you, while in a Spark application, you create a SparkSession object yourself.

In Spark 2.0, the SparkSession became a unified entry point to all Spark operations and data. Previously used entry points such as SparkContext, SQLContext, HiveContext, SparkConf, and StreamingContext can be accessed through it too.

What exactly do we do with the spark variable? SparkSession is an object, so it has methods associated with it. We can see what those methods are in the PySpark shell by typing the name of a variable, followed by a period, followed by tab:

```
spark.[\t]
...
spark.Builder(          spark.conf
spark.newSession(       spark.readStream
spark.stop(             spark.udf
spark.builder           spark.createDataFrame(
spark.range(            spark.sparkContext
spark.streams           spark.version
spark.catalog           spark.getActiveSession(
spark.read              spark.sql(
spark.table(
```

Out of all the methods provided by SparkSession, the ones that we're going to use most often allow us to create DataFrames. Now that we have set up PySpark, we can set up our dataset of interest and start using PySpark's DataFrame API to interact with it. That's what we will do in the next section.

Setting Up Our Data

The UC Irvine Machine Learning Repository is a fantastic source for interesting (and free) datasets for research and education. The dataset we'll analyze was curated from a record linkage study performed at a German hospital in 2010, and it contains several million pairs of patient records that were matched according to several different criteria, such as the patient's name (first and last), address, and birthday. Each matching field was assigned a numerical score from 0.0 to 1.0 based on how similar the strings were, and the data was then hand-labeled to identify which pairs represented the same person and which did not. The underlying values of the fields that were used to create the dataset were removed to protect the privacy of the patients. Numerical identifiers, the match scores for the fields, and the label for each pair (match versus nonmatch) were published for use in record linkage research.

Record Linkage

The general structure of a record linkage problem is something like this: we have a large collection of records from one or more source systems, and it is likely that multiple records refer to the same underlying entity, such as a customer, a patient, or the location of a business or an event. Each entity has a number of attributes, such as a name, an address, or a birthday, and we will need to use these attributes to find the records that refer to the same entity. Unfortunately, the values of these attributes aren't perfect: values might have different formatting, typos, or missing information, which means that a simple equality test on the values of the attributes will cause us to miss a significant number of duplicate records. For example, let's compare the business listings shown in Table 2-1.

Table 2-1. The challenge of record linkage

Name	Address	City	State	Phone
Josh's Coffee Shop	1234 Sunset Boulevard	West Hollywood	CA	(213)-555-1212
Josh Coffee	1234 Sunset Blvd West	Hollywood	CA	555-1212
Coffee Chain #1234	1400 Sunset Blvd #2	Hollywood	CA	206-555-1212
Coffee Chain Regional Office	1400 Sunset Blvd Suite 2	Hollywood	California	206-555-1212

The first two entries in this table refer to the same small coffee shop, even though a data entry error makes it look as if they are in two different cities (West Hollywood and Hollywood). The second two entries, on the other hand, are actually referring to different business locations of the same chain of coffee shops that happen to share a common address: one of the entries refers to an actual coffee shop, and the other one refers to a local corporate office location. Both of the entries give the official phone number of the corporate headquarters in Seattle.

This example illustrates everything that makes record linkage so difficult: even though both pairs of entries look similar to each other, the criteria that we use to make the duplicate/not-duplicate decision is different for each pair. This is the kind of distinction that is easy for a human to understand and identify at a glance, but is difficult for a computer to learn.

Record linkage goes by a lot of different names in the literature and in practice: entity resolution, record deduplication, merge-and-purge, and list washing. For our purposes, we refer to this problem as *record linkage*.

From the shell, let's pull the data from the repository:

```
$ mkdir linkage
$ cd linkage/
$ curl -L -o donation.zip https://bit.ly/1Aoywaq
$ unzip donation.zip
$ unzip 'block_*.zip'
```

If you have a Hadoop cluster handy, you can create a directory for the block data in HDFS and copy the files from the dataset there:

```
$ hadoop dfs -mkdir linkage
$ hadoop dfs -put block_*.csv linkage
```

To create a dataframe for our record linkage dataset, we're going to use the Spark Session object. Specifically, we will use the csv method on its Reader API:

```
prev = spark.read.csv("linkage/block*.csv")
...
prev
...
DataFrame[_c0: string, _c1: string, _c2: string, _c3: string,...
```

By default, every column in a CSV file is treated as a string type, and the column names default to _c0, _c1, _c2, and so on. We can look at the head of a dataframe in the shell by calling its show method:

```
prev.show(2)
...
+-----+-----+------------+------------+------------+------------+-------+------+------+
|  _c0|  _c1|         _c2|         _c3|         _c4|         _c5|    _c6|   _c7|
+-----+-----+------------+------------+------------+------------+-------+------+------+
| id_1| id_2|cmp_fname_c1|cmp_fname_c2|cmp_lname_c1|cmp_lname_c2|cmp_sex|cmp_bd|
| 3148| 8326|           1|           ?|           1|           ?|      1|     1|
|14055|94934|           1|           ?|           1|           ?|      1|     1|
|33948|34740|           1|           ?|           1|           ?|      1|     1|
|  946|71870|           1|           ?|           1|           ?|      1|     1|
```

We can see that the first row of the DataFrame is the name of the header columns, as we expected, and that the CSV file has been cleanly split up into its individual columns. We can also see the presence of the ? strings in some of the columns;

we will need to handle these as missing values. In addition to naming each column correctly, it would be ideal if Spark could properly infer the data type of each of the columns for us.

Fortunately, Spark's CSV reader provides all of this functionality for us via options that we can set on the Reader API. You can see the full list of options that the API takes in the pyspark documentation (*https://oreil.ly/xiLj1*). For now, we'll read and parse the linkage data like this:

```
parsed = spark.read.option("header", "true").option("nullValue", "?").\
        option("inferSchema", "true").csv("linkage/block*.csv")
```

When we call show on the parsed data, we see that the column names are set correctly and the ? strings have been replaced by null values. To see the inferred type for each column, we can print the schema of the parsed DataFrame like this:

```
parsed.printSchema()
...
root
 |-- id_1: integer (nullable = true)
 |-- id_2: integer (nullable = true)
 |-- cmp_fname_c1: double (nullable = true)
 |-- cmp_fname_c2: double (nullable = true)
...
```

Each Column instance contains the name of the column, the most specific data type that could handle the type of data contained in each record, and a boolean field that indicates whether or not the column may contain null values, which is true by default. In order to perform the schema inference, Spark must do *two* passes over the dataset: one pass to figure out the type of each column, and a second pass to do the actual parsing. The first pass can work on a sample if desired.

If you know the schema that you want to use for a file ahead of time, you can create an instance of the pyspark.sql.types.StructType class and pass it to the Reader API via the schema function. This can have a significant performance benefit when the dataset is very large, since Spark will not need to perform an extra pass over the data to figure out the data type of each column.

Here is an example of defining a schema using StructType and StructField:

```
from pyspark.sql.types import *
schema = StructType([StructField("id_1", IntegerType(), False),
  StructField("id_2", StringType(), False),
  StructField("cmp_fname_c1", DoubleType(), False)])

spark.read.schema(schema).csv("...")
```

Another way to define the schema is using DDL (data definition language) statements:

```
schema = "id_1 INT, id_2 INT, cmp_fname_c1 DOUBLE"
```

Data Formats and Data Sources

Spark ships with built-in support for reading and writing dataframes in a variety of formats via the DataFrameReader and DataFrameWriter APIs. In addition to the CSV format discussed here, you can also read and write structured data from the following sources:

parquet
: Leading columnar-oriented data storage format (default option in Spark)

orc
: Another columnar-oriented data storage format

json
: Supports many of the same schema-inference functionality that the CSV format does

jdbc
: Connects to a relational database via the JDBC data connection standard

avro
: Provides efficient message serialization and deserialization when using a streaming source such as Apache Kafka

text
: Maps each line of a file to a dataframe with a single column of type string

image
: Loads image files from a directory as a dataframe with one column, containing image data stored as image schema

libsvm
: Popular text file format for representing labeled observations with sparse features

binary
: Reads binary files and converts each file into a single dataframe row (new in Spark 3.0)

xml
: Simple text-based format for representing structured information such as documents, data, configuration, or books (available via the spark-xml package)

You access the methods of the DataFrameReader API by calling the read method on a SparkSession instance, and you can load data from a file using either the format and load methods or one of the shortcut methods for built-in formats:

```
d1 = spark.read.format("json").load("file.json")
d2 = spark.read.json("file.json")
```

In this example, d1 and d2 reference the same underlying JSON data and will have the same contents. Each of the different file formats has its own set of options that can be set via the same option method that we used for CSV files.

To write data out again, you access the DataFrameWriter API via the write method on any DataFrame instance. The DataFrameWriter API supports the same built-in formats as the DataFrameReader API, so the following two methods are equivalent ways of writing the contents of the d1 DataFrame as a Parquet file:

```
d1.write.format("parquet").save("file.parquet")
d1.write.parquet("file.parquet")
```

By default, Spark will throw an error if you try to save a dataframe to a file that already exists. You can control Spark's behavior in this situation via the mode method on the DataFrameWriter API to either Overwrite the existing file, Append the data in the DataFrame to the file (if it exists), or Ignore the write operation if the file already exists and leave it in place:

```
d2.write.format("parquet").mode("overwrite").save("file.parquet")
```

You can specify the mode as a string literal ("overwrite", "append", "ignore").

DataFrames have a number of methods that enable us to read data from the cluster into the PySpark REPL on our client machine. Perhaps the simplest of these is first, which returns the first element of the DataFrame into the client:

```
parsed.first()
...
Row(id_1=3148, id_2=8326, cmp_fname_c1=1.0, cmp_fname_c2=None,...
```

The first method can be useful for sanity checking a dataset, but we're generally interested in bringing back larger samples of a DataFrame into the client for analysis. When we know that a DataFrame contains only a small number of records, we can use the toPandas or collect method to return all the contents of a DataFrame to the client as an array. For extremely large DataFrames, using these methods can be dangerous and cause an out-of-memory exception. Because we don't know how big the linkage dataset is just yet, we'll hold off on doing this right now.

In the next several sections, we'll use a mix of local development and testing and cluster computation to perform more munging and analysis of the record linkage data, but if you need to take a moment to drink in the new world of awesome that you have just entered, we certainly understand.

Transformations and Actions

The act of creating a DataFrame does not cause any distributed computation to take place on the cluster. Rather, DataFrames define logical datasets that are intermediate steps in a computation. Spark operations on distributed data can be classified into two types: transformations and actions.

All transformations are evaluated lazily. That is, their results are not computed immediately, but they are recorded as a lineage. This allows Spark to optimize the query plan. Distributed computation occurs upon invoking an *action* on a DataFrame. For example, the count action returns the number of objects in an DataFrame:

```
df.count()
...
15
```

The collect action returns an Array with all the Row objects from the DataFrame. This Array resides in local memory, not on the cluster:

```
df.collect()
[Row(id='12', department='sales'), ...
```

Actions need not only return results to the local process. The save action saves the contents of the DataFrame to persistent storage:

```
df.write.format("parquet").("user/ds/mynumbers")
```

Remember that DataFrameReader can accept a directory of text files as input, meaning that a future Spark job could refer to mynumbers as an input directory.

Analyzing Data with the DataFrame API

The DataFrame API comes with a powerful set of tools that will likely be familiar to data scientists who are used to Python and SQL. In this section, we will begin to explore these tools and how to apply them to the record linkage data.

If we look at the schema of the parsed DataFrame and the first few rows of data, we see this:

```
parsed.printSchema()
...
root
 |-- id_1: integer (nullable = true)
 |-- id_2: integer (nullable = true)
 |-- cmp_fname_c1: double (nullable = true)
 |-- cmp_fname_c2: double (nullable = true)
```

```
|-- cmp_lname_c1: double (nullable = true)
|-- cmp_lname_c2: double (nullable = true)
|-- cmp_sex: integer (nullable = true)
|-- cmp_bd: integer (nullable = true)
|-- cmp_bm: integer (nullable = true)
|-- cmp_by: integer (nullable = true)
|-- cmp_plz: integer (nullable = true)
|-- is_match: boolean (nullable = true)

...

parsed.show(5)
...
+-----+-----+-----------+-----------+-----------+-----------+.....
| id_1| id_2|cmp_fname_c1|cmp_fname_c2|cmp_lname_c1|cmp_lname_c2|.....
+-----+-----+-----------+-----------+-----------+-----------+.....
| 3148| 8326|        1.0|       null|        1.0|       null|.....
|14055|94934|        1.0|       null|        1.0|       null|.....
|33948|34740|        1.0|       null|        1.0|       null|.....
|  946|71870|        1.0|       null|        1.0|       null|.....
|64880|71676|        1.0|       null|        1.0|       null|.....
```

- The first two fields are integer IDs that represent the patients who were matched in the record.

- The next nine fields are (possibly missing) numeric values (either doubles or ints) that represent match scores on different fields of the patient records, such as their names, birthdays, and locations. The fields are stored as integers when the only possible values are match (1) or no-match (0), and doubles whenever partial matches are possible.

- The last field is a boolean value (`true` or `false`) indicating whether or not the pair of patient records represented by the line was a match.

Our goal is to come up with a simple classifier that allows us to predict whether a record will be a match based on the values of the match scores for the patient records. Let's start by getting an idea of the number of records we're dealing with via the `count` method:

```
parsed.count()
...
5749132
```

This is a relatively small dataset—certainly small enough to fit in memory on one of the nodes in a cluster or even on your local machine if you don't have a cluster available. Thus far, every time we've processed the data, Spark has reopened the file, reparsed the rows, and then performed the action requested, like showing the first few rows of the data or counting the number of records. When we ask another question, Spark will do these same operations, again and again, even if we have filtered the data down to a small number of records or are working with an aggregated version of the original dataset.

This isn't an optimal use of our compute resources. After the data has been parsed once, we'd like to save the data in its parsed form on the cluster so that we don't have to reparse it every time we want to ask a new question. Spark supports this use case by allowing us to signal that a given DataFrame should be cached in memory after it is generated by calling the cache method on the instance. Let's do that now for the parsed DataFrame:

```
parsed.cache()
```

Once our data has been cached, the next thing we want to know is the relative fraction of records that were matches versus those that were nonmatches:

```
from pyspark.sql.functions import col

parsed.groupBy("is_match").count().orderBy(col("count").desc()).show()
...
+--------+-------+
|is_match|  count|
+--------+-------+
|   false|5728201|
|    true|  20931|
+--------+-------+
```

Instead of writing a function to extract the is_match column, we simply pass its name to the groupBy method on the DataFrame, call the count method to, well, count the number of records inside each grouping, sort the resulting data in descending order based on the count column, and then cleanly render the result of the computation in the REPL with show. Under the covers, the Spark engine determines the most efficient way to perform the aggregation and return the results. This illustrates the clean, fast, and expressive way to do data analysis that Spark provides.

Note that there are two ways we can reference the names of the columns in the DataFrame: either as literal strings, like in groupBy("is_match"), or as Column objects by using the col function that we used on the count column. Either approach is valid in most cases, but we needed to use the col function to call the desc method on the resulting count column object.

DataFrame Aggregation Functions

In addition to count, we can also compute more complex aggregations like sums, mins, maxes, means, and standard deviation using the agg method of the DataFrame API in conjunction with the aggregation functions defined in the pyspark.sql.func tions collection. For example, to find the mean and standard deviation of the cmp_sex field in the overall parsed DataFrame, we could type:

```
from pyspark.sql.functions import avg, stddev

parsed.agg(avg("cmp_sex"), stddev("cmp_sex")).show()
+-----------------+--------------------+
|     avg(cmp_sex)|stddev_samp(cmp_sex)|
+-----------------+--------------------+
|0.955001381078048|  0.2073011111689795|
+-----------------+--------------------+
```

Note that by default Spark computes the sample standard deviation; there is also a stddev_pop function for computing the population standard deviation.

You may have noticed that the functions in the DataFrame API are similar to the components of a SQL query. This isn't a coincidence, and in fact we have the option to treat any DataFrame we create as if it were a database table and to express our questions using familiar and powerful SQL syntax. First, we need to tell the Spark SQL execution engine the name it should associate with the parsed DataFrame, since the name of the variable itself ("parsed") isn't available to Spark:

```
parsed.createOrReplaceTempView("linkage")
```

Because the parsed DataFrame is available only during the length of this PySpark REPL session, it is a *temporary* table. Spark SQL may also be used to query persistent tables in HDFS if we configure Spark to connect to an Apache Hive metastore that tracks the schemas and locations of structured datasets.

Once our temporary table is registered with the Spark SQL engine, we can query it like this:

```
spark.sql("""
  SELECT is_match, COUNT(*) cnt
  FROM linkage
  GROUP BY is_match
  ORDER BY cnt DESC
""").show()
...
+--------+-------+
|is_match|    cnt|
+--------+-------+
|   false|5728201|
|    true|  20931|
+--------+-------+
```

You have the option of running Spark either by using an ANSI 2003-compliant version of Spark SQL (the default) or in HiveQL mode by calling the enableHiveSup port method when you create a SparkSession instance via its Builder API.

Should you use Spark SQL or the DataFrame API to do your analysis in PySpark? There are pros and cons to each: SQL has the benefit of being broadly familiar and expressive for simple queries. It also lets you query data using JDBC/ODBC connectors from databases such as PostgreSQL or tools such as Tableau. The downside of SQL is that it can be difficult to express complex, multistage analyses in a dynamic, readable, and testable way—all areas where the DataFrame API shines. Throughout the rest of the book, we use both Spark SQL and the DataFrame API, and we leave it as an exercise for the reader to examine the choices we made and translate our computations from one interface to the other.

We can apply functions one by one to our DataFrame to obtain statistics such as count and mean. However, PySpark offers a better way to obtain summary statistics for DataFrames, and that's what we will cover in the next section.

Fast Summary Statistics for DataFrames

Although there are many kinds of analyses that may be expressed equally well in SQL or with the DataFrame API, there are certain common things that we want to be able to do with dataframes that can be tedious to express in SQL. One such analysis that is especially helpful is computing the min, max, mean, and standard deviation of all the non-null values in the numerical columns of a dataframe. In PySpark, this function has the same name that it does in pandas, `describe`:

```
summary = parsed.describe()
...
summary.show()
```

The `summary` DataFrame has one column for each variable in the `parsed` DataFrame, along with another column (also named `summary`) that indicates which metric—count, mean, stddev, min, or max—is present in the rest of the columns in the row. We can use the `select` method to choose a subset of the columns to make the summary statistics easier to read and compare:

```
summary.select("summary", "cmp_fname_c1", "cmp_fname_c2").show()
+-------+------------------+------------------+
|summary|     cmp_fname_c1|      cmp_fname_c2|
+-------+------------------+------------------+
|  count|           5748125|            103698|
|   mean|0.7129024704436274|0.9000176718903216|
| stddev|0.3887583596162788|0.2713176105782331|
|    min|               0.0|               0.0|
|    max|               1.0|               1.0|
+-------+------------------+------------------+
```

Note the difference in the value of the `count` variable between `cmp_fname_c1` and `cmp_fname_c2`. While almost every record has a non-null value for `cmp_fname_c1`, less than 2% of the records have a non-null value for `cmp_fname_c2`. To create a useful classifier, we need to rely on variables that are almost always present in the data—unless the fact that they are missing indicates something meaningful about whether the record matches.

Once we have an overall feel for the distribution of the variables in our data, we want to understand how the values of those variables are correlated with the value of the `is_match` column. Therefore, our next step is to compute those same summary statistics for just the subsets of the `parsed` DataFrame that correspond to matches and nonmatches. We can filter DataFrames using either SQL-style `where` syntax or with `Column` objects using the DataFrame API and then use `describe` on the resulting DataFrames:

```
matches = parsed.where("is_match = true")
match_summary = matches.describe()

misses = parsed.filter(col("is_match") == False)
miss_summary = misses.describe()
```

The logic inside the string we pass to the `where` function can include statements that would be valid inside a `WHERE` clause in Spark SQL. For the filtering condition that uses the DataFrame API, we use the `==` operator on the `is_match` column object to check for equality with the boolean object `False`, because that is just Python, not SQL. Note that the `where` function is an alias for the `filter` function; we could have reversed the `where` and `filter` calls in the above snippet and everything would have worked the same way.

We can now start to compare our `match_summary` and `miss_summary` DataFrames to see how the distribution of the variables changes depending on whether the record is a match or a miss. Although this is a relatively small dataset, doing this comparison is still somewhat tedious—what we really want is to transpose the `match_summary` and `miss_summary` DataFrames so that the rows and columns are swapped, which would allow us to join the transposed DataFrames together by variable and analyze the summary statistics, a practice that most data scientists know as "pivoting" or "reshaping" a dataset. In the next section, we'll show you how to perform these transformations.

Pivoting and Reshaping DataFrames

We can transpose the DataFrames entirely using functions provided by PySpark. However, there is another way to perform this task. PySpark allows conversion between Spark and pandas DataFrames. We will convert the DataFrames in question into pandas DataFrames, reshape them, and convert them back to Spark DataFrames. We can safely do this because of the small size of the `summary`, `match_summary`, and `miss_summary` DataFrames since pandas DataFrames reside in memory. In upcoming chapters, we will rely on Spark operations for such transformations on larger datasets.

 Conversion to/from pandas DataFrames is possible because of the Apache Arrow project, which allows efficient data transfer between JVM and Python processes. The PyArrow library was installed as a dependency of the Spark SQL module when we installed `pyspark[sql]` using pip.

Let's convert `summary` into a pandas DataFrame:

```
summary_p = summary.toPandas()
```

We can now use pandas functions on the `summary_p` DataFrame:

```
summary_p.head()
...
summary_p.shape
...
(5,12)
```

We can now perform a transpose operation to swap rows and columns using familiar pandas methods on the DataFrame:

```
summary_p = summary_p.set_index('summary').transpose().reset_index()
...
summary_p = summary_p.rename(columns={'index':'field'})
...
summary_p = summary_p.rename_axis(None, axis=1)
...
summary_p.shape
...
(11,6)
```

We have successfully transposed the `summary_p` pandas DataFrame. Convert it into a Spark DataFrame using SparkSession's `createDataFrame` method:

```
summaryT = spark.createDataFrame(summary_p)
...
summaryT.show()
...
+-----------+-------+-------------------+-------------------+---+------+
|      field|  count|               mean|             stddev|min|   max|
+-----------+-------+-------------------+-------------------+---+------+
|       id_1|5749132|  33324.48559643438| 23659.859374488064|  1| 99980|
|       id_2|5749132|  66587.43558331935| 23620.487613269695|  6|100000|
|cmp_fname_c1|5748125| 0.7129024704437266|0.38875835961628014|0.0|   1.0|
|cmp_fname_c2| 103698| 0.9000176718903189| 0.2713176105782334|0.0|   1.0|
|cmp_lname_c1|5749132| 0.3156278193080383| 0.3342336339615828|0.0|   1.0|
|cmp_lname_c2|   2464| 0.3184128315317443|0.36856706620066537|0.0|   1.0|
|    cmp_sex|5749132|  0.955001381078048|0.20730111116897781|  0|     1|
|     cmp_bd|5748337|0.22446526708507172| 0.41722972238462636|  0|     1|
|     cmp_bm|5748337|0.48885529849763504| 0.4998758236779031|  0|     1|
|     cmp_by|5748337| 0.2227485966810923| 0.4160909629831756|  0|     1|
|    cmp_plz|5736289|0.00552866147434343|0.07414914925420046|  0|     1|
+-----------+-------+-------------------+-------------------+---+------+
```

We are not done yet. Print the schema of the `summaryT` DataFrame:

```
summaryT.printSchema()
...
root
 |-- field: string (nullable = true)
 |-- count: string (nullable = true)
 |-- mean: string (nullable = true)
 |-- stddev: string (nullable = true)
 |-- min: string (nullable = true)
 |-- max: string (nullable = true)
```

In the summary schema, as obtained from the `describe` method, every field is treated as a string. Since we want to analyze the summary statistics as numbers, we'll need to convert the values from strings to doubles:

```
from pyspark.sql.types import DoubleType
for c in summaryT.columns:
  if c == 'field':
    continue
  summaryT = summaryT.withColumn(c, summaryT[c].cast(DoubleType()))
...
summaryT.printSchema()
...
root
 |-- field: string (nullable = true)
 |-- count: double (nullable = true)
 |-- mean: double (nullable = true)
 |-- stddev: double (nullable = true)
```

```
|-- min: double (nullable = true)
|-- max: double (nullable = true)
```

Now that we have figured out how to transpose a summary DataFrame, let's implement our logic into a function that we can reuse on the match_summary and miss_summary DataFrames:

```
from pyspark.sql import DataFrame
from pyspark.sql.types import DoubleType

def pivot_summary(desc):
  # convert to pandas dataframe
  desc_p = desc.toPandas()
  # transpose
  desc_p = desc_p.set_index('summary').transpose().reset_index()
  desc_p = desc_p.rename(columns={'index':'field'})
  desc_p = desc_p.rename_axis(None, axis=1)
  # convert to Spark dataframe
  descT = spark.createDataFrame(desc_p)
  # convert metric columns to double from string
  for c in descT.columns:
    if c == 'field':
      continue
    else:
      descT = descT.withColumn(c, descT[c].cast(DoubleType()))
  return descT
```

Now in your Spark shell, use the pivot_summary function on the match_summary and miss_summary DataFrames:

```
match_summaryT = pivot_summary(match_summary)
miss_summaryT = pivot_summary(miss_summary)
```

Now that we have successfully transposed the summary DataFrames, we can join and compare them. That's what we will do in the next section. Further, we will also select desirable features for building our model.

Joining DataFrames and Selecting Features

So far, we have used Spark SQL and the DataFrame API only to filter and aggregate the records from a dataset, but we can also use these tools to perform joins (inner, left outer, right outer, or full outer) on DataFrames. Although the DataFrame API includes a join function, it's often easier to express these joins using Spark SQL, especially when the tables we are joining have a large number of column names in common and we want to be able to clearly indicate which column we are referring to in our select expressions. Let's create temporary views for the match_summaryT and miss_summaryT DataFrames, join them on the field column, and compute some simple summary statistics on the resulting rows:

```
match_summaryT.createOrReplaceTempView("match_desc")
miss_summaryT.createOrReplaceTempView("miss_desc")
spark.sql("""
  SELECT a.field, a.count + b.count total, a.mean - b.mean delta
  FROM match_desc a INNER JOIN miss_desc b ON a.field = b.field
  WHERE a.field NOT IN ("id_1", "id_2")
  ORDER BY delta DESC, total DESC
""").show()
...
+-----------+---------+--------------------+
|      field|    total|               delta|
+-----------+---------+--------------------+
|    cmp_plz|5736289.0|  0.9563812499852176|
|cmp_lname_c2|   2464.0|  0.8064147192926264|
|     cmp_by|5748337.0|  0.7762059675300512|
|     cmp_bd|5748337.0|   0.775442311783404|
|cmp_lname_c1|5749132.0|  0.6838772482590526|
|     cmp_bm|5748337.0|  0.5109496938298685|
|cmp_fname_c1|5748125.0|  0.2854529057460786|
|cmp_fname_c2| 103698.0| 0.09104268062280008|
|    cmp_sex|5749132.0|0.032408185250332844|
+-----------+---------+--------------------+
```

A good feature has two properties: it tends to have significantly different values for matches and nonmatches (so the difference between the means will be large), and it occurs often enough in the data that we can rely on it to be regularly available for any pair of records. By this measure, cmp_fname_c2 isn't very useful because it's missing a lot of the time, and the difference in the mean value for matches and nonmatches is relatively small—0.09, for a score that ranges from 0 to 1. The cmp_sex feature also isn't particularly helpful because even though it's available for any pair of records, the difference in means is just 0.03.

Features cmp_plz and cmp_by, on the other hand, are excellent. They almost always occur for any pair of records, and there is a very large difference in the mean values (more than 0.77 for both features). Features cmp_bd, cmp_lname_c1, and cmp_bm also seem beneficial: they are generally available in the dataset, and the difference in mean values for matches and nonmatches is substantial.

Features cmp_fname_c1 and cmp_lname_c2 are more of a mixed bag: cmp_fname_c1 doesn't discriminate all that well (the difference in the means is only 0.28) even though it's usually available for a pair of records, whereas cmp_lname_c2 has a large difference in the means, but it's almost always missing. It's not quite obvious under what circumstances we should include these features in our model based on this data.

For now, we're going to use a simple scoring model that ranks the similarity of pairs of records based on the sums of the values of the obviously good features: cmp_plz, cmp_by, cmp_bd, cmp_lname_c1, and cmp_bm. For the few records where the values of these features are missing, we'll use 0 in place of the null value in our sum. We can get a rough feel for the performance of our simple model by creating a dataframe of the computed scores and the value of the is_match column and evaluating how well the score discriminates between matches and nonmatches at various thresholds.

Scoring and Model Evaluation

For our scoring function, we are going to sum up the value of five fields (cmp_lname_c1, cmp_plz, cmp_by, cmp_bd, and cmp_bm). We will use expr from pyspark.sql.functions for doing this. The expr function parses an input expression string into the column that it represents. This string can even involve multiple columns.

Let's create the required expression string:

```
good_features = ["cmp_lname_c1", "cmp_plz", "cmp_by", "cmp_bd", "cmp_bm"]
...
sum_expression = " + ".join(good_features)
...
sum_expression
...
'cmp_lname_c1 + cmp_plz + cmp_by + cmp_bd + cmp_bm'
```

We can now use the sum_expression string for calculating the score. When summing up the values, we will account for and replace null values with 0 using DataFrame's fillna method:

```
from pyspark.sql.functions import expr
scored = parsed.fillna(0, subset=good_features).\
            withColumn('score', expr(sum_expression)).\
            select('score', 'is_match')
...
scored.show()
...
+-----+--------+
|score|is_match|
+-----+--------+
|  5.0|    true|
|  5.0|    true|
|  5.0|    true|
|  5.0|    true|
|  5.0|    true|
|  5.0|    true|
|  4.0|    true|
...
```

The final step in creating our scoring function is to decide what threshold the score must exceed in order for us to predict that the two records represent a match. If we set the threshold too high, then we will incorrectly mark a matching record as a miss (called the *false-negative* rate), whereas if we set the threshold too low, we will incorrectly label misses as matches (the *false-positive* rate). For any nontrivial problem, we always have to trade some false positives for some false negatives, and the question of what the threshold value should be usually comes down to the relative cost of the two kinds of errors in the situation to which the model is being applied.

To help us choose a threshold, it's helpful to create a *contingency table* (which is sometimes called a *cross tabulation*, or *crosstab*) that counts the number of records whose scores fall above/below the threshold value crossed with the number of records in each of those categories that were/were not matches. Since we don't know what threshold value we're going to use yet, let's write a function that takes the `scored` DataFrame and the choice of threshold as parameters and computes the crosstabs using the DataFrame API:

```
def crossTabs(scored: DataFrame, t: DoubleType) -> DataFrame:
  return  scored.selectExpr(f"score >= {t} as above", "is_match").\
          groupBy("above").pivot("is_match", ("true", "false")).\
          count()
```

Note that we are including the `selectExpr` method of the DataFrame API to dynamically determine the value of the field named `above` based on the value of the `t` argument using Python's f-string formatting syntax, which allows us to substitute variables by name if we preface the string literal with the letter `f` (yet another handy bit of Scala implicit magic). Once the `above` field is defined, we create the crosstab with a standard combination of the `groupBy`, `pivot`, and `count` methods that we used before.

By applying a high threshold value of 4.0, meaning that the average of the five features is 0.8, we can filter out almost all of the nonmatches while keeping over 90% of the matches:

```
crossTabs(scored, 4.0).show()
...
+-----+-----+-------+
|above| true|  false|
+-----+-----+-------+
| true|20871|    637|
|false|   60|5727564|
+-----+-----+-------+
```

By applying a lower threshold of 2.0, we can ensure that we capture *all* of the known matching records, but at a substantial cost in terms of false positive (top-right cell):

```
crossTabs(scored, 2.0).show()
...
+-----+-----+-------+
|above| true|  false|
+-----+-----+-------+
| true|20931| 596414|
```

```
|false| null|5131787|
+-----+-----+-------+
```

Even though the number of false positives is higher than we want, this more generous filter still removes 90% of the nonmatching records from our consideration while including every positive match. Even though this is pretty good, it's possible to do even better; see if you can find a way to use some of the other values from MatchData (both missing and not) to come up with a scoring function that successfully identifies every true match at the cost of less than 100 false positives.

Where to Go from Here

If this chapter was your first time carrying out data preparation and analysis with PySpark, we hope that you got a feel for what a powerful foundation these tools provide. If you have been using Python and Spark for a while, we hope that you will pass this chapter along to your friends and colleagues as a way of introducing them to that power as well.

Our goal for this chapter was to provide you with enough knowledge to be able to understand and complete the rest of the examples in this book. If you are the kind of person who learns best through practical examples, your next step is to continue on to the next set of chapters, where we will introduce you to MLlib, the machine learning library designed for Spark.

## CHAPTER 3

Recommending Music and the Audioscrobbler Dataset

The recommender engine is one of the most popular example of large-scale machine learning; for example, most people are familiar with Amazon's. It is a common denominator because recommender engines are everywhere, from social networks to video sites to online retailers. We can also directly observe them in action. We're aware that a computer is picking tracks to play on Spotify, in much the same way we don't necessarily notice that Gmail is deciding whether inbound email is spam.

The output of a recommender is more intuitively understandable than other machine learning algorithms. It's exciting, even. For as much as we think that musical taste is personal and inexplicable, recommenders do a surprisingly good job of identifying tracks we didn't know we would like. For domains like music or movies, where recommenders are often deployed, it's comparatively easy to reason why a recommended piece of music fits with someone's listening history. Not all clustering or classification algorithms match that description. For example, a support vector machine classifier is a set of coefficients, and it's hard even for practitioners to articulate what the numbers mean when they make predictions.

It seems fitting to kick off the next three chapters, which will explore key machine learning algorithms on PySpark, with a chapter built around recommender engines, and recommending music in particular. It's an accessible way to introduce real-world use of PySpark and MLlib and some basic machine learning ideas that will be developed in subsequent chapters.

In this chapter, we'll implement a recommender system in PySpark. Specifically, we will use the Alternating Least Squares (ALS) algorithm on an open dataset provided by a music streaming service. We'll start off by understanding the dataset and importing it in PySpark. Then we'll discuss our motivation for choosing the

ALS algorithm and its implementation in PySpark. This will be followed by data preparation and building our model using PySpark. We'll finish up by making some user recommendations and discussing ways to improve our model through hyperparameter selection.

Setting Up the Data

We will use a dataset published by Audioscrobbler. Audioscrobbler was the first music recommendation system for Last.fm (*http://www.last.fm*), one of the first internet streaming radio sites, founded in 2002. Audioscrobbler provided an open API for "scrobbling," or recording listeners' song plays. Last.fm used this information to build a powerful music recommender engine. The system reached millions of users because third-party apps and sites could provide listening data back to the recommender engine.

At that time, research on recommender engines was mostly confined to learning from rating-like data. That is, recommenders were usually viewed as tools that operated on input like "Bob rates Prince 3.5 stars." The Audioscrobbler dataset is interesting because it merely records plays: "Bob played a Prince track." A play carries less information than a rating. Just because Bob played the track doesn't mean he actually liked it. You or I may occasionally play a song by an artist we don't care for, or even play an album and walk out of the room.

However, listeners rate music far less frequently than they play music. A dataset like this is therefore much larger, covers more users and artists, and contains more total information than a rating dataset, even if each individual data point carries less information. This type of data is often called *implicit feedback* data because the user-artist connections are implied as a side effect of other actions, and not given as explicit ratings or thumbs-up.

A snapshot of a dataset distributed by Last.fm in 2005 can be found online as a compressed archive (*https://oreil.ly/Z7sfL*). Download the archive, and find within it several files. First, the dataset's files need to be made available. If you are using a remote cluster, copy all three data files into storage. This chapter will assume that the files are available at *data/*.

Start `pyspark-shell`. Note that the computations in this chapter will take up more memory than simple applications. If you are running locally rather than on a cluster, for example, you will likely need to specify something like `--driver-memory 4g` to have enough memory to complete these computations. The main dataset is in the *user_artist_data.txt* file. It contains about 141,000 unique users, and 1.6 million unique artists. About 24.2 million users' plays of artists are recorded, along with their counts. Let's read this dataset into a DataFrame and have a look at it:

```
raw_user_artist_path = "data/audioscrobbler_data/user_artist_data.txt"
raw_user_artist_data = spark.read.text(raw_user_artist_path)

raw_user_artist_data.show(5)

...
+-------------------+
|              value|
+-------------------+
|        1000002 1 55|
|  1000002 1000006 33|
|    1000002 1000007 8|
|1000002 1000009 144|
|1000002 1000010 314|
+-------------------+
```

 Machine learning tasks like ALS are likely to be more compute-intensive than simple text processing. It may be better to break the data into smaller pieces—more partitions—for processing. You can chain a call to .repartition(n) after reading the text file to specify a different and larger number of partitions. You might set this higher to match the number of cores in your cluster, for example.

The dataset also gives the names of each artist by ID in the *artist_data.txt* file. Note that when plays are scrobbled, the client application submits the name of the artist being played. This name could be misspelled or nonstandard, and this may only be detected later. For example, "The Smiths," "Smiths, The," and "the smiths" may appear as distinct artist IDs in the dataset even though they are plainly the same artist. So, the dataset also includes *artist_alias.txt*, which maps artist IDs that are known misspellings or variants to the canonical ID of that artist. Let's read these two datasets into PySpark too:

```
raw_artist_data = spark.read.text("data/audioscrobbler_data/artist_data.txt")

raw_artist_data.show(5)

...
+-------------------+
|              value|
+-------------------+
|1134999\t06Crazy ...|
|6821360\tPang Nak...|
|10113088\tTerfel,...|
|10151459\tThe Fla...|
|6826647\tBodensta...|
+-------------------+
only showing top 5 rows
...
```

```
raw_artist_alias = spark.read.text("data/audioscrobbler_data/artist_alias.txt")

raw_artist_alias.show(5)

...
+----------------+
|           value|
+----------------+
| 1092764\t1000311|
| 1095122\t1000557|
| 6708070\t1007267|
|10088054\t1042317|
| 1195917\t1042317|
+----------------+
only showing top 5 rows
```

Now that we have a basic understanding of the datasets, we can discuss our requirements for a recommender algorithm and, subsequently, understand why the Alternating Least Squares algorithm is a good choice.

Our Requirements for a Recommender System

We need to choose a recommender algorithm that is suitable for our data. Here are our considerations:

Implicit feedback

The data is comprised entirely of interactions between users and artists' songs. It contains no information about the users or about the artists other than their names. We need an algorithm that learns without access to user or artist attributes. These are typically called collaborative filtering algorithms. For example, deciding that two users might share similar tastes because they are the same age *is not* an example of collaborative filtering. Deciding that two users might both like the same song because they play many other songs that are the same *is* an example.

Sparsity

Our dataset looks large because it contains tens of millions of play counts. But in a different sense, it is small and skimpy, because it is sparse. On average, each user has played songs from about 171 artists—out of 1.6 million. Some users have listened to only one artist. We need an algorithm that can provide decent recommendations to even these users. After all, every single listener must have started with just one play at some point!

Scalability and real-time predictions

Finally, we need an algorithm that scales, both in its ability to build large models and to create recommendations quickly. Recommendations are typically required in near real time—within a second, not tomorrow.

A broad class of algorithms that may be suitable is latent factor models. They try to explain *observed interactions* between large numbers of users and items through a relatively small number of *unobserved, underlying reasons*. For example, consider a customer who has bought albums by metal bands Megadeth and Pantera but also classical composer Mozart. It may be difficult to explain why exactly these albums were bought and nothing else. However, it's probably a small window on a much larger set of tastes. Maybe the customer likes a coherent spectrum of music from metal to progressive rock to classical. That explanation is simpler and, as a bonus, suggests many other albums that would be of interest. In this example, "liking metal, progressive rock, and classical" are three latent factors that could explain tens of thousands of individual album preferences.

In our case, we will specifically use a type of matrix factorization model. Mathematically, these algorithms treat the user and product data as if it were a large matrix A, where the entry at row i and column j exists if user i has played artist j. A is sparse: most entries of A are 0, because only a few of all possible user-artist combinations actually appear in the data. They factor A as the matrix product of two smaller matrices, X and Y. They are very skinny—both have many rows because A has many rows and columns, but both have just a few columns (k). The k columns correspond to the latent factors that are being used to explain the interaction data.

The factorization can only be approximate because k is small, as shown in Figure 3-1.

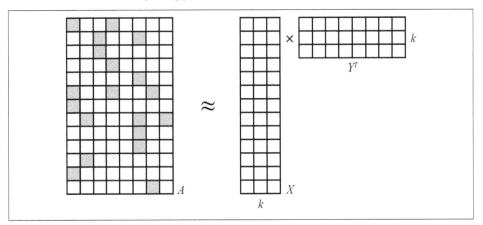

Figure 3-1. Matrix factorization

These algorithms are sometimes called matrix completion algorithms, because the original matrix A may be quite sparse, but the product XY^T is dense. Very few, if any, entries are 0, and therefore the model is only an approximation of A. It is a model in the sense that it produces ("completes") a value for even the many entries that are missing (that is, 0) in the original A.

This is a case where, happily, the linear algebra maps directly and elegantly to intuition. These two matrices contain a row for each user and each artist. The rows have few values—k. Each value corresponds to a latent feature in the model. So the rows express how much users and artists associate with these k latent features, which might correspond to tastes or genres. And it is simply the product of a user-feature and feature-artist matrix that yields a complete estimation of the entire, dense user-artist interaction matrix. This product might be thought of as mapping items to their attributes and then weighting those by user attributes.

The bad news is that $A = XY^T$ generally has no exact solution at all, because X and Y aren't large enough (technically speaking, too low rank (*https://oreil.ly/OfVj4*)) to perfectly represent A. This is actually a good thing. A is just a tiny sample of all interactions that *could* happen. In a way, we believe A is a terribly spotty and therefore hard-to-explain view of a simpler underlying reality that is well explained by just some small number of factors, k, of them. Think of a jigsaw puzzle depicting a cat. The final puzzle is simple to describe: a cat. When you're holding just a few pieces, however, the picture you see is quite difficult to describe.

XY^T should still be as close to A as possible. After all, it's all we've got to go on. It will not and should not reproduce it exactly. The bad news again is that this can't be solved directly for both the best X and best Y at the same time. The good news is that it's trivial to solve for the best X if Y is known, and vice versa. But neither is known beforehand!

Fortunately, there are algorithms that can escape this catch-22 and find a decent solution. One such algorithm that's available in PySpark is the ALS algorithm.

Alternating Least Squares Algorithm

We will use the Alternating Least Squares algorithm to compute latent factors from our dataset. This type of approach was popularized around the time of the Netflix Prize competition by papers like "Collaborative Filtering for Implicit Feedback Datasets" (*https://oreil.ly/3pSzk*) and "Large-Scale Parallel Collaborative Filtering for the Netflix Prize" (*https://oreil.ly/LULpp*). PySpark MLlib's ALS implementation draws on ideas from both of these papers and is the only recommender algorithm currently implemented in Spark MLlib.

Here's a code snippet (non-functional) to give you a peek at what lies ahead in the chapter:

```
from pyspark.ml.recommendation import ALS

als = ALS(maxIter=5, regParam=0.01, userCol="user",
          itemCol="artist", ratingCol="count")
model = als.fit(train)

predictions = model.transform(test)
```

With ALS, we will treat our input data as a large, sparse matrix A, and find out X and Y, as discussed in previous section. At the start, Y isn't known, but it can be initialized to a matrix full of randomly chosen row vectors. Then simple linear algebra gives the best solution for X, given A and Y. In fact, it's trivial to compute each row i of X separately as a function of Y and of one row of A. Because it can be done separately, it can be done in parallel, and that is an excellent property for large-scale computation:

$$A_i Y \left(Y^T Y \right)^{-1} = X_i$$

Equality can't be achieved exactly, so in fact the goal is to minimize $|A_i Y (Y^T Y)^{-1} - X_i|$, or the sum of squared differences between the two matrices' entries. This is where the "least squares" in the name comes from. In practice, this is never solved by actually computing inverses, but faster and more directly via methods like the QR decomposition. This equation simply elaborates on the theory of how the row vector is computed.

The same thing can be done to compute each Y_j from X. And again, to compute X from Y, and so on. This is where the "alternating" part comes from. There's just one small problem: Y was made up—and random! X was computed optimally, yes, but gives a bogus solution for Y. Fortunately, if this process is repeated, X and Y do eventually converge to decent solutions.

When used to factor a matrix representing implicit data, there is a little more complexity to the ALS factorization. It is not factoring the input matrix A directly, but a matrix P of 0s and 1s, containing 1 where A contains a positive value and 0 elsewhere. The values in A are incorporated later as weights. This detail is beyond the scope of this book but is not necessary to understand how to use the algorithm.

Finally, the ALS algorithm can take advantage of the sparsity of the input data as well. This, and its reliance on simple, optimized linear algebra and its data-parallel nature, make it very fast at large scale.

Next, we will preprocess our dataset and make it suitable for use with the ALS algorithm.

Preparing the Data

The first step in building a model is to understand the data that is available and parse or transform it into forms that are useful for analysis in Spark.

Spark MLlib's ALS implementation does not strictly require numeric IDs for users and items, but is more efficient when the IDs are in fact representable as 32-bit integers. That is the case because under the hood the data is being represented using the JVM's data type. Does this dataset conform to this requirement already?

```
raw_user_artist_data.show(10)

...
+-------------------+
|              value|
+-------------------+
|       1000002 1 55|
|  1000002 1000006 33|
|   1000002 1000007 8|
|1000002 1000009 144|
|1000002 1000010 314|
|   1000002 1000013 8|
|  1000002 1000014 42|
|  1000002 1000017 69|
|1000002 1000024 329|
|   1000002 1000025 1|
+-------------------+
```

Each line of the file contains a user ID, an artist ID, and a play count, separated by spaces. To compute statistics on the user ID, we split the line by space characters and parse the values as integers. The result is conceptually three "columns": a user ID, artist ID, and count as ints. It makes sense to transform this to a dataframe with columns named "user", "artist", and "count" because it then becomes simple to compute simple statistics like the maximum and minimum:

```python
from pyspark.sql.functions import split, min, max
from pyspark.sql.types import IntegerType, StringType

user_artist_df = raw_user_artist_data.withColumn('user',
                                    split(raw_user_artist_data['value'], ' ').\
                                    getItem(0).\
                                    cast(IntegerType()))
user_artist_df = user_artist_df.withColumn('artist',
                                    split(raw_user_artist_data['value'], ' ').\
                                    getItem(1).\
                                    cast(IntegerType()))
user_artist_df = user_artist_df.withColumn('count',
                                    split(raw_user_artist_data['value'], ' ').\
                                    getItem(2).\
                                    cast(IntegerType())).drop('value')

user_artist_df.select([min("user"), max("user"), min("artist"),\
                                    max("artist")]).show()
...
+---------+---------+-----------+-----------+
|min(user)|max(user)|min(artist)|max(artist)|
+---------+---------+-----------+-----------+
|       90|  2443548|          1|   10794401|
+---------+---------+-----------+-----------+
```

The maximum user and artist IDs are 2443548 and 10794401, respectively (and their minimums are 90 and 1; no negative values). These are comfortably smaller than 2147483647. No additional transformation will be necessary to use these IDs.

It will be useful later in this example to know the artist names corresponding to the opaque numeric IDs. raw_artist_data contains the artist ID and name separated by a tab. PySpark's split function accepts regular expression values for the pattern parameter. We can split using the whitespace character, \s:

```
from pyspark.sql.functions import col

artist_by_id = raw_artist_data.withColumn('id', split(col('value'), '\s+', 2).\
                                                getItem(0).\
                                                cast(IntegerType())))
artist_by_id = artist_by_id.withColumn('name', split(col('value'), '\s+', 2).\
                                                getItem(1).\
                                                cast(StringType())).drop('value')

artist_by_id.show(5)
...
+--------+--------------------+
|      id|                name|
+--------+--------------------+
| 1134999|         06Crazy Life|
| 6821360|         Pang Nakarin|
|10113088|Terfel, Bartoli- ...|
|10151459|  The Flaming Sidebur|
| 6826647|     Bodenstandig 3000|
+--------+--------------------+
```

This results in a dataframe with the artist ID and name as columns id and name.

raw_artist_alias maps artist IDs that may be misspelled or nonstandard to the ID of the artist's canonical name. This dataset is relatively small, containing about 200,000 entries. It contains two IDs per line, separated by a tab. We will parse this in a similar manner as we did raw_artist_data:

```
artist_alias = raw_artist_alias.withColumn('artist',
                                split(col('value'), '\s+').\
                                    getItem(0).\
                                    cast(IntegerType())).\
                       withColumn('alias',
                                split(col('value'), '\s+').\
                                    getItem(1).\
                                    cast(StringType())).\
                       drop('value')

artist_alias.show(5)
...
+--------+-------+
|  artist|  alias|
```

```
+--------+-------+
| 1092764|1000311|
| 1095122|1000557|
| 6708070|1007267|
|10088054|1042317|
| 1195917|1042317|
+--------+-------+
```

The first entry maps ID 1092764 to 1000311. We can look these up from the
artist_by_id DataFrame:

```
artist_by_id.filter(artist_by_id.id.isin(1092764, 1000311)).show()
...

+-------+--------------+
|     id|          name|
+-------+--------------+
|1000311| Steve Winwood|
|1092764|Winwood, Steve|
+-------+--------------+
```

This entry evidently maps "Winwood, Steve" to "Steve Winwood," which is in fact the
correct name for the artist.

Building a First Model

Although the dataset is in nearly the right form for use with Spark MLlib's ALS
implementation, it requires a small, extra transformation. The aliases dataset should
be applied to convert all artist IDs to a canonical ID, if a different canonical ID exists:

```
from pyspark.sql.functions import broadcast, when

train_data = train_data = user_artist_df.join(broadcast(artist_alias),
                                              'artist', how='left').\
train_data = train_data.withColumn('artist',
                                   when(col('alias').isNull(), col('artist')).\
                                   otherwise(col('alias'))) ❶
train_data = train_data.withColumn('artist', col('artist').\
                                   cast(IntegerType())).\
                                   drop('alias')

train_data.cache()

train_data.count()
...
24296858
```

❶ Get artist's alias if it exists; otherwise, get original artist.

We broadcast the artist_alias DataFrame created earlier. This makes Spark send
and hold in memory just one copy for *each executor* in the cluster. When there

are thousands of tasks and many execute in parallel on each executor, this can save significant network traffic and memory. As a rule of thumb, it's helpful to broadcast a significantly smaller dataset when performing a join with a very big dataset.

Broadcast Variables

When Spark runs a stage, it creates a binary representation of all the information needed to run tasks in that stage; this is called the *closure* of the function that needs to be executed. This closure includes all the data structures on the driver referenced in the function. Spark distributes the closure with every task that is sent to an executor on the cluster.

Broadcast variables are useful when many tasks need access to the same (immutable) data structure. They extend normal handling of task closures to enable:

- Caching data as raw Java objects on each executor, so they need not be deserialized for each task
- Caching data across multiple jobs, stages, and tasks

For example, consider a natural language processing application that requires a large dictionary of English words and has a score function that accepts a line of input and a dictionary. Broadcasting the dictionary means it is transferred to each executor only once.

DataFrame operations can at times also automatically take advantage of broadcasts when performing joins between a large and small table. Just broadcasting the small table is advantageous sometimes. This is called a *broadcast hash join*.

The call to cache suggests to Spark that this DataFrame should be temporarily stored after being computed and, furthermore, kept in memory in the cluster. This is helpful because the ALS algorithm is iterative and will typically need to access this data 10 times or more. Without this, the DataFrame could be repeatedly recomputed from the original data each time it is accessed! The Storage tab in the Spark UI will show how much of the DataFrame is cached and how much memory it uses, as shown in Figure 3-2. This one consumes about 120 MB across the cluster.

Storage Level	Cached Partitions	Fraction Cached	Size in Memory	Size on Disk
Memory Deserialized 1x Replicated	8	100%	120.3 MB	0.0 B

Figure 3-2. Storage tab in the Spark UI, showing cached DataFrame memory usage

When you use `cache` or `persist`, the DataFrame is not fully cached until you trigger an action that goes through every record (e.g., `count`). If you use an action like `show(1)`, only one partition will be cached. That is because PySpark's optimizer will figure out that you do not need to compute all the partitions just to retrieve one record.

Note that the label "Deserialized" in the UI in Figure 3-2 is actually only relevant for RDDs, where "Serialized" means data is stored in memory, not as objects, but as serialized bytes. However, DataFrame instances like this one perform their own "encoding" of common data types in memory separately.

Actually, 120 MB is surprisingly small. Given that there are about 24 million plays stored here, a quick back-of-the-envelope calculation suggests that this would mean that each user-artist-count entry consumes only 5 bytes on average. However, the three 32-bit integers alone ought to consume 12 bytes. This is one of the advantages of a DataFrame. Because the types of data stored are primitive 32-bit integers, their representation can be optimized in memory internally.

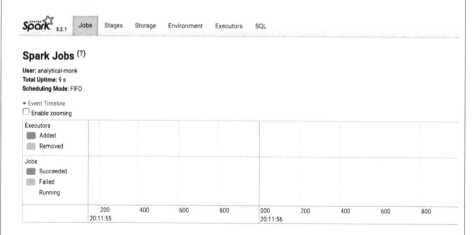

Figure 3-3. Spark UI

The Spark UI comes with the following tabs:

- Jobs
- Stages

- Storage with DataFrame size and memory use
- Environment
- Executors
- SQL

Some tabs, such as the ones related to streaming, are created lazily, i.e., when required.

Finally, we can build a model:

```
from pyspark.ml.recommendation import ALS

model = ALS(rank=10, seed=0, maxIter=5, regParam=0.1,
            implicitPrefs=True, alpha=1.0, userCol='user',
            itemCol='artist', ratingCol='count'). \
        fit(train_data)
```

This constructs `model` as an `ALSModel` with some default configuration. The operation will likely take several minutes or more depending on your cluster. Compared to some machine learning models, whose final form may consist of just a few parameters or coefficients, this type of model is huge. It contains a feature vector of 10 values for each user and product in the model, and in this case there are more than 1.7 million of them. The model contains these large user-feature and product-feature matrices as DataFrames of their own.

The values in your results may be somewhat different. The final model depends on a randomly chosen initial set of feature vectors. The default behavior of this and other components in MLlib, however, is to use the same set of random choices every time by defaulting to a fixed seed. This is unlike other libraries, where behavior of random elements is typically not fixed by default. So, here and elsewhere, a random seed is set with (… `seed=0`,…).

To see some feature vectors, try the following, which displays just one row and does not truncate the wide display of the feature vector:

```
model.userFactors.show(1, truncate = False)

...
+---+---------------------------------------------- ...
|id |features                                        ...
+---+---------------------------------------------- ...
|90 |[0.16020626, 0.20717518, -0.1719469, 0.06038466 ...
+---+---------------------------------------------- ...
```

The other methods invoked on `ALS`, like `setAlpha`, set *hyperparameters* whose values can affect the quality of the recommendations that the model makes. These will be explained later. The more important first question is this: is the model any good?

Does it produce good recommendations? That is what we will try to answer in the next section.

Spot Checking Recommendations

We should first see if the artist recommendations make any intuitive sense, by examining a user, plays, and recommendations for that user. Take, for example, user 2093760. First, let's look at his or her plays to get a sense of the person's tastes. Extract the IDs of artists that this user has listened to and print their names. This means searching the input for artist IDs played by this user and then filtering the set of artists by these IDs to print the names in order:

```
user_id = 2093760

existing_artist_ids = train_data.filter(train_data.user == user_id) \ ❶
    .select("artist").collect() ❷

existing_artist_ids = [i[0] for i in existing_artist_ids]

artist_by_id.filter(col('id').isin(existing_artist_ids)).show() ❸
...
+-------+---------------+
|     id|           name|
+-------+---------------+
|   1180|     David Gray|
|    378|   Blackalicious|
|    813|     Jurassic 5|
|1255340|The Saw Doctors|
|    942|         Xzibit|
+-------+---------------+
```

❶ Find lines whose user is 2093760.

❷ Collect dataset of artist ID.

❸ Filter in those artists.

The artists look like a mix of mainstream pop and hip-hop. A Jurassic 5 fan? Remember, it's 2005. In case you're wondering, the Saw Doctors is a very Irish rock band popular in Ireland.

Now, it's simple to make recommendations for a user, though computing them this way will take a few moments. It's suitable for batch scoring but not real-time use cases:

```
user_subset = train_data.select('user').where(col('user') == user_id).distinct()
top_predictions = model.recommendForUserSubset(user_subset, 5)

top_predictions.show()
```

```
...
+-------+--------------------+
|  user|     recommendations|
+-------+--------------------+
|2093760|[{2814, 0.0294106...|
+-------+--------------------+
```

The resulting recommendations contain lists comprised of artist ID and, of course, "predictions." For this type of ALS algorithm, the prediction is an opaque value normally between 0 and 1, where higher values mean a better recommendation. It is not a probability but can be thought of as an estimate of a 0/1 value indicating whether the user won't or will interact with the artist, respectively.

After extracting the artist IDs for the recommendations, we can look up artist names in a similar way:

```
top_predictions_pandas = top_predictions.toPandas()
print(top_prediction_pandas)
...
      user                                  recommendations
0  2093760  [(2814, 0.029410675168037415), (1300642, 0.028...
...

recommended_artist_ids = [i[0] for i in top_predictions_pandas.\
                                        recommendations[0]]

artist_by_id.filter(col('id').isin(recommended_artist_ids)).show()
...
+-------+----------+
|     id|      name|
+-------+----------+
|   2814|    50 Cent|
|   4605|Snoop Dogg|
|1007614|      Jay-Z|
|1001819|       2Pac|
|1300642|  The Game|
+-------+----------+
```

The result is all hip-hop. This doesn't look like a great set of recommendations, at first glance. While these are generally popular artists, they don't appear to be personalized to this user's listening habits.

Evaluating Recommendation Quality

Of course, that's just one subjective judgment about one user's results. It's hard for anyone but that user to quantify how good the recommendations are. Moreover, it's infeasible to have any human manually score even a small sample of the output to evaluate the results.

It's reasonable to assume that users tend to play songs from artists who are appealing, and not play songs from artists who aren't appealing. So, the plays for a user give a partial picture of "good" and "bad" artist recommendations. This is a problematic assumption but about the best that can be done without any other data. For example, presumably user 2093760 likes many more artists than the 5 listed previously, and of the 1.7 million other artists not played, a few are of interest, and not all are "bad" recommendations.

What if a recommender were evaluated on its ability to rank good artists high in a list of recommendations? This is one of several generic metrics that can be applied to a system that ranks things, like a recommender. The problem is that "good" is defined as "artists the user has listened to," and the recommender system has already received all of this information as input. It could trivially return the user's previously listened-to artists as top recommendations and score perfectly. But this is not useful, especially because the recommender's role is to recommend artists that the user has never listened to.

To make this meaningful, some of the artist play data can be set aside and hidden from the ALS model-building process. Then, this held-out data can be interpreted as a collection of good recommendations for each user but one that the recommender has not already been given. The recommender is asked to rank all items in the model, and the ranks of the held-out artists are examined. Ideally, the recommender places all of them at or near the top of the list.

We can then compute the recommender's score by comparing all held-out artists' ranks to the rest. (In practice, we compute this by examining only a sample of all such pairs, because a potentially huge number of such pairs may exist.) The fraction of pairs where the held-out artist is ranked higher is its score. A score of 1.0 is perfect, 0.0 is the worst possible score, and 0.5 is the expected value achieved from randomly ranking artists.

This metric is directly related to an information retrieval concept called the receiver operating characteristic (ROC) curve (*https://oreil.ly/Pt2bn*). The metric in the preceding paragraph equals the area under this ROC curve and is indeed known as AUC, or area under the curve. AUC may be viewed as the probability that a randomly chosen good recommendation ranks above a randomly chosen bad recommendation.

The AUC metric is also used in the evaluation of classifiers. It is implemented, along with related methods, in the MLlib class `BinaryClassificationMetrics`. For recommenders, we will compute AUC *per user* and average the result. The resulting metric is slightly different and might be called "mean AUC." We will implement this, because it is not (quite) implemented in PySpark.

Other evaluation metrics that are relevant to systems that rank things are implemented in `RankingMetrics`. These include metrics like precision, recall, and mean average precision (MAP) (*https://oreil.ly/obbTT*). MAP is also frequently used and focuses more narrowly on the quality of the top recommendations. However, AUC will be used here as a common and broad measure of the quality of the entire model output.

In fact, the process of holding out some data to select a model and evaluate its accuracy is common practice in all of machine learning. Typically, data is divided into three subsets: training, cross-validation (CV), and test sets. For simplicity in this initial example, only two sets will be used: training and CV. This will be sufficient to choose a model. In Chapter 4, this idea will be extended to include the test set.

Computing AUC

An implementation of mean AUC is provided in the source code accompanying this book. It is not reproduced here, but is explained in some detail in comments in the source code. It accepts the CV set as the "positive" or "good" artists for each user and a prediction function. This function translates a dataframe containing each user-artist pair into a dataframe that also contains its estimated strength of interaction as a "prediction," a number wherein higher values mean higher rank in the recommendations.

To use the input data, we must split it into a training set and a CV set. The ALS model will be trained on the training dataset only, and the CV set will be used to evaluate the model. Here, 90% of the data is used for training and the remaining 10% for cross-validation:

```
def area_under_curve(
    positive_data,
    b_all_artist_IDs,
    predict_function):
...

all_data = user_artist_df.join(broadcast(artist_alias), 'artist', how='left') \
    .withColumn('artist', when(col('alias').isNull(), col('artist'))\
    .otherwise(col('alias'))) \
    .withColumn('artist', col('artist').cast(IntegerType())).drop('alias')

train_data, cv_data = all_data.randomSplit([0.9, 0.1], seed=54321)
train_data.cache()
cv_data.cache()

all_artist_ids = all_data.select("artist").distinct().count()
b_all_artist_ids = broadcast(all_artist_ids)

model = ALS(rank=10, seed=0, maxIter=5, regParam=0.1,
            implicitPrefs=True, alpha=1.0, userCol='user',
            itemCol='artist', ratingCol='count') \
        .fit(train_data)
area_under_curve(cv_data, b_all_artist_ids, model.transform)
```

Note that `areaUnderCurve` accepts a function as its third argument. Here, the `trans form` method from `ALSModel` is passed in, but it will shortly be swapped out for an alternative.

The result is about 0.879. Is this good? It is certainly higher than the 0.5 that is expected from making recommendations randomly, and it's close to 1.0, which is the maximum possible score. Generally, an AUC over 0.9 would be considered high.

But is it an accurate evaluation? This evaluation could be repeated with a different 90% as the training set. The resulting AUC values' average might be a better estimate of the algorithm's performance on the dataset. In fact, one common practice is to divide the data into k subsets of similar size, use $k - 1$ subsets together for training, and evaluate on the remaining subset. We can repeat this k times, using a different set of subsets each time. This is called *k-fold cross-validation* (*https://oreil.ly/DolrQ*). This won't be implemented in examples here, for simplicity, but some support for this technique exists in MLlib in its `CrossValidator` API. The validation API will be revisited in "Random Forests" on page 82.

It's helpful to benchmark this against a simpler approach. For example, consider recommending the globally most-played artists to every user. This is not personalized, but it is simple and may be effective. Define this simple prediction function and evaluate its AUC score:

```
from pyspark.sql.functions import sum as _sum

def predict_most_listened(train):
    listen_counts = train.groupBy("artist")\
                    .agg(_sum("count").alias("prediction"))\
                    .select("artist", "prediction")

    return all_data.join(listen_counts, "artist", "left_outer").\
                    select("user", "artist", "prediction")

area_under_curve(cv_data, b_all_artist_ids, predict_most_listened(train_data))
```

The result is also about 0.880. This suggests that nonpersonalized recommendations are already fairly effective according to this metric. However, we'd expect the "personalized" recommendations to score better in comparison. Clearly, the model needs some tuning. Can it be made better?

Hyperparameter Selection

So far, the hyperparameter values used to build the `ALSModel` were simply given without comment. They are not learned by the algorithm and must be chosen by the caller. The configured hyperparameters were:

`setRank(10)`

> The number of latent factors in the model, or equivalently, the number of columns k in the user-feature and product-feature matrices. In nontrivial cases, this is also their rank.

`setMaxIter(5)`

> The number of iterations that the factorization runs. More iterations take more time but may produce a better factorization.

`setRegParam(0.01)`

> A standard overfitting parameter, also usually called *lambda*. Higher values resist overfitting, but values that are too high hurt the factorization's accuracy.

`setAlpha(1.0)`

> Controls the relative weight of observed versus unobserved user-product interactions in the factorization.

`rank`, `regParam`, and `alpha` can be considered *hyperparameters* to the model. (`max Iter` is more of a constraint on resources used in the factorization.) These are not values that end up in the matrices inside the `ALSModel`—those are simply its *parameters* and are chosen by the algorithm. These hyperparameters are instead parameters to the process of building itself.

The values used in the preceding list are not necessarily optimal. Choosing good hyperparameter values is a common problem in machine learning. The most basic way to choose values is to simply try combinations of values and evaluate a metric for each of them, and choose the combination that produces the best value of the metric.

In the following example, eight possible combinations are tried: `rank` = 5 or 30, `regParam` = 4.0 or 0.0001, and `alpha` = 1.0 or 40.0. These values are still something of a guess, but are chosen to cover a broad range of parameter values. The results are printed in order by top AUC score:

```
from pprint import pprint
from itertools import product

ranks = [5, 30]
reg_params = [4.0, 0.0001]
alphas = [1.0, 40.0]
hyperparam_combinations = list(product(*[ranks, reg_params, alphas]))

evaluations = []

for c in hyperparam_combinations:
    rank = c[0]
    reg_param = c[1]
    alpha = c[2]
    model = ALS().setSeed(0).setImplicitPrefs(true).setRank(rank).\
```

```
            setRegParam(reg_param).setAlpha(alpha).setMaxIter(20).\
            setUserCol("user").setItemCol("artist").\
            setRatingCol("count").setPredictionCol("prediction").\
      fit(trainData)

    auc = area_under_curve(cv_aata, b_all_artist_ids, model.transform)

    model.userFactors.unpersist()  ❶
    model.itemFactors.unpersist()

    evaluations.append((auc, (rank, regParam, alpha)))

  evaluations.sort(key=lambda x:x[0], reverse=True)  ❷
  pprint(evaluations)

  ...
  (0.8928367485129145,(30,4.0,40.0))
  (0.891835487024326,(30,1.0E-4,40.0))
  (0.8912376926662007,(30,4.0,1.0))
  (0.889240668173946,(5,4.0,40.0))
  (0.8886268430389741,(5,4.0,1.0))
  (0.8883278461068959,(5,1.0E-4,40.0))
  (0.8825350012228627,(5,1.0E-4,1.0))
  (0.8770527940660278,(30,1.0E-4,1.0))
```

❶ Free up model resources immediately.

❷ Sort by first value (AUC), descending, and print.

The differences are small in absolute terms, but are still somewhat significant for AUC values. Interestingly, the parameter `alpha` seems consistently better at 40 than 1. (For the curious, 40 was a value proposed as a default in one of the original ALS papers mentioned earlier.) This can be interpreted as indicating that the model is better off focusing far more on what the user did listen to than what he or she did not listen to.

A higher `regParam` looks better too. This suggests the model is somewhat susceptible to overfitting, and so needs a higher `regParam` to resist trying to fit the sparse input given from each user too exactly. Overfitting will be revisited in more detail in "Random Forests" on page 82.

As expected, 5 features are pretty low for a model of this size, and it underperforms the model that uses 30 features to explain tastes. It's possible that the best number of features is actually higher than 30 and that these values are alike in being too small.

Of course, this process can be repeated for different ranges of values or more values. It is a brute-force means of choosing hyperparameters. However, in a world where clusters with terabytes of memory and hundreds of cores are not uncommon, and with frameworks like Spark that can exploit parallelism and memory for speed, it becomes quite feasible.

It is not strictly required to understand what the hyperparameters mean, although it is helpful to know what normal ranges of values are in order to start the search over a parameter space that is neither too large nor too tiny.

This was a fairly manual way to loop over hyperparameters, build models, and evaluate them. In Chapter 4, after learning more about the Spark ML API, we'll find that there is a more automated way to compute this using `Pipelines` and `TrainVali dationSplit`.

Making Recommendations

Proceeding for the moment with the best set of hyperparameters, what does the new model recommend for user 2093760?

```
+-----------+
|       name|
+-----------+
|  [unknown]|
|The Beatles|
|     Eminem|
|         U2|
|  Green Day|
+-----------+
```

Anecdotally, this makes a bit more sense for this user, being dominated by pop rock instead of all hip-hop. [unknown] is plainly not an artist. Querying the original dataset reveals that it occurs 429,447 times, putting it nearly in the top 100! This is some default value for plays without an artist, maybe supplied by a certain scrobbling client. It is not useful information, and we should discard it from the input before starting again. It is an example of how the practice of data science is often iterative, with discoveries about the data occurring at every stage.

This model can be used to make recommendations for all users. This could be useful in a batch process that recomputes a model and recommendations for users every hour or even less, depending on the size of the data and speed of the cluster.

At the moment, however, Spark MLlib's ALS implementation does not support a method to recommend to all users. It is possible to recommend to one user at a time, as shown above, although each will launch a short-lived distributed job that takes a few seconds. This may be suitable for rapidly recomputing recommendations for small groups of users. Here, recommendations are made to 100 users taken from the data and printed:

```
some_users = all_data.select("user").distinct().limit(100) ❶
val someRecommendations =
```

```
someUsers.map(userID => (userID, makeRecommendations(model, userID, 5)))
someRecommendations.foreach { case (userID, recsDF) =>
  val recommendedArtists = recsDF.select("artist").as[Int].collect()
  println(s"$userID -> ${recommendedArtists.mkString(", ")}")
}

...
1000190 -> 6694932, 435, 1005820, 58, 1244362
1001043 -> 1854, 4267, 1006016, 4468, 1274
1001129 -> 234, 1411, 1307, 189, 121
...
```

❶ Subset of 100 distinct users

Here, the recommendations are just printed. They could just as easily be written to an external store like HBase (*https://oreil.ly/SQImy*), which provides fast lookup at runtime.

Where to Go from Here

Naturally, it's possible to spend more time tuning the model parameters and finding and fixing anomalies in the input, like the [unknown] artist. For example, a quick analysis of play counts reveals that user 2064012 played artist 4468 an astonishing 439,771 times! Artist 4468 is the implausibly successful alternate-metal band System of a Down, which turned up earlier in recommendations. Assuming an average song length of 4 minutes, this is over 33 years of playing hits like "Chop Suey!" and "B.Y.O.B." Because the band started making records in 1998, this would require playing four or five tracks at once for seven years. It must be spam or a data error, and another example of the types of real-world data problems that a production system would have to address.

ALS is not the only possible recommender algorithm, but at this time, it is the only one supported by Spark MLlib. However, MLlib also supports a variant of ALS for non-implicit data. Its use is identical, except that ALS is configured with setImplicit Prefs(false). This is appropriate when data is rating-like, rather than count-like. For example, it is appropriate when the dataset is user ratings of artists on a 1–5 scale. The resulting prediction column returned from ALSModel.transform recommendation methods then really is an estimated rating. In this case, the simple RMSE (root mean squared error) metric is appropriate for evaluating the recommender.

Later, other recommender algorithms may be available in Spark MLlib or other libraries.

In production, recommender engines often need to make recommendations in real time, because they are used in contexts like ecommerce sites where recommendations are requested frequently as customers browse product pages. Precomputing and storing recommendations is a reasonable way to make recommendations available at scale. One disadvantage of this approach is that it requires precomputing recommendations for all users who might need recommendations soon, which is potentially any of them. For example, if only 10,000 of 1 million users visit a site in a day, precomputing all million users' recommendations each day is 99% wasted effort.

It would be nicer to compute recommendations on the fly, as needed. While we can compute recommendations for one user using the `ALSModel`, this is necessarily a distributed operation that takes several seconds, because `ALSModel` is uniquely large and therefore actually a distributed dataset. This is not true of other models, which afford much faster scoring.

## CHAPTER 4

Making Predictions with Decision Trees and Decision Forests

Classification and regression are the oldest and most well-studied types of predictive analytics. Most algorithms you will likely encounter in analytics packages and libraries are classification or regression techniques, like support vector machines, logistic regression, neural networks, and deep learning. The common thread linking regression and classification is that both involve predicting one (or more) values given one (or more) other values. To do so, both require a body of inputs and outputs to learn from. They need to be fed both questions and known answers. For this reason, they are known as types of supervised learning.

PySpark MLlib offers implementations of a number of classification and regression algorithms. These include decision trees, naïve Bayes, logistic regression, and linear regression. The exciting thing about these algorithms is that they can help predict the future—or at least, predict the things we don't yet know for sure, like the likelihood you will buy a car based on your online behavior, whether an email is spam given the words it contains, or which acres of land are likely to grow the most crops given their location and soil chemistry.

In this chapter, we will focus on a popular and flexible type of algorithm for both classification and regression (decision trees) and the algorithm's extension (random decision forests). First, we will understand the basics of decision trees and forests and introduce the former's PySpark implementation. The PySpark implementation of decision trees supports binary and multiclass classification, and regression. The implementation partitions data by rows, allowing distributed training with millions or even billions of instances. This will be followed by preparation of our dataset and creating our first decision tree. Then we'll tune our decision tree model. We'll finish up by training a random forest model on our processed dataset and making predictions.

Although PySpark's decision tree implementation is easy to get started with, it is helpful to understand the fundamentals of decision tree and random forest algorithms. That is what we'll cover in the next section.

Decision Trees and Forests

Decision trees are a family of algorithms that can naturally handle both categorical and numeric features. Building a single tree can be done using parallel computing, and many trees can be built in parallel at once. They are robust to outliers in the data, meaning that a few extreme and possibly erroneous data points might not affect predictions at all. They can consume data of different types and on different scales without the need for preprocessing or normalization.

Decision tree–based algorithms have the advantage of being comparatively intuitive to understand and reason about. In fact, we all probably use the same reasoning embodied in decision trees, implicitly, in everyday life. For example, I sit down to have morning coffee with milk. Before I commit to that milk and add it to my brew, I want to predict: is the milk spoiled? I don't know for sure. I might check if the use-by date has passed. If not, I predict no, it's not spoiled. If the date has passed, but it was three or fewer days ago, I take my chances and predict no, it's not spoiled. Otherwise, I sniff the milk. If it smells funny, I predict yes, and otherwise no.

This series of yes/no decisions that leads to a prediction are what decision trees embody. Each decision leads to one of two results, which is either a prediction or another decision, as shown in Figure 4-1. In this sense, it is natural to think of the process as a tree of decisions, where each internal node in the tree is a decision, and each leaf node is a final answer.

That is a simplistic decision tree and was not built with any rigor. To elaborate, consider another example. A robot has taken a job in an exotic pet store. It wants to learn, before the shop opens, which animals in the shop would make a good pet for a child. The owner lists nine pets that would and wouldn't be suitable before hurrying off. The robot compiles the information found in Table 4-1 from examining the animals.

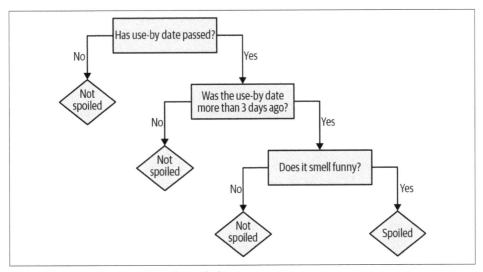

Figure 4-1. Decision tree: is milk spoiled?

Table 4-1. Exotic pet store "feature vectors"

Name	Weight (kg)	# Legs	Color	Good pet?
Fido	20.5	4	Brown	Yes
Mr. Slither	3.1	0	Green	No
Nemo	0.2	0	Tan	Yes
Dumbo	1390.8	4	Gray	No
Kitty	12.1	4	Gray	Yes
Jim	150.9	2	Tan	No
Millie	0.1	100	Brown	No
McPigeon	1.0	2	Gray	No
Spot	10.0	4	Brown	Yes

The robot can make a decision for the nine listed pets. There are many more pets available in the store. It still needs a methodology for deciding which animals among the rest will be suitable as pets for kids. We can assume that the characteristics of all animals are available. Using the decision data provided by the store owner and a decision tree, we can help the robot learn what a good pet for a kid looks like.

Although a name is given, it will not be included as a feature in our decision tree model. There is little reason to believe the name alone is predictive; "Felix" could name a cat or a poisonous tarantula, for all the robot knows. So, there are two numeric features (weight, number of legs) and one categorical feature (color) predicting a categorical target (is/is not a good pet for a child.

The way a decision tree works is by making one or more decisions in sequence based on provided features. To start off, the robot might try to fit a simple decision tree to this training data, consisting of a single decision based on weight, as shown in Figure 4-2.

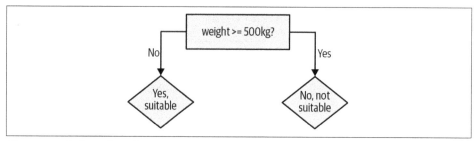

Figure 4-2. Robot's first decision tree

The logic of the decision tree is easy to read and make sense of: 500kg animals certainly sound unsuitable as pets. This rule predicts the correct value in five of nine cases. A quick glance suggests that we could improve the rule by lowering the weight threshold to 100kg. This gets six of nine examples correct. The heavy animals are now predicted correctly; the lighter animals are only partly correct.

So, a second decision can be constructed to further refine the prediction for examples with weights less than 100kg. It would be good to pick a feature that changes some of the incorrect Yes predictions to No. For example, there is one small green animal, sounding suspiciously like a snake, that will be classified by our current model as a suitable pet candidate. The robot could predict correctly by adding a decision based on color, as shown in Figure 4-3.

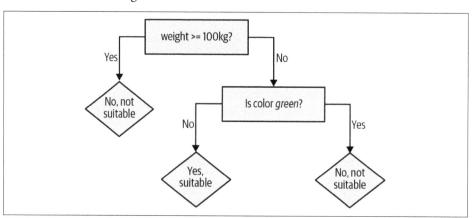

Figure 4-3. Robot's next decision tree

Now, seven of nine examples are correct. Of course, decision rules could be added until all nine were correctly predicted. The logic embodied in the resulting decision tree would probably sound implausible when translated into common speech: "If the animal's weight is less than 100kg, its color is brown instead of green, and it has fewer than 10 legs, then yes, it is a suitable pet." While perfectly fitting the given examples, a decision tree like this would fail to predict that a small, brown, four-legged wolverine is not a suitable pet. Some balance is needed to avoid this phenomenon, known as *overfitting*.

Decision trees generalize into a more powerful algorithm, called *random forests*. Random forests combine many decision trees to reduce the risk of overfitting and train the decision trees separately. The algorithm injects randomness into the training process so that each decision tree is a bit different. Combining the predictions reduces the variance of the predictions, makes the resulting model more generalizable, and improves performance on test data.

This is enough of an introduction to decision trees and random forests for us to begin using them with PySpark. In the next section, we will introduce the dataset that we'll work with and prepare it for use in PySpark.

Preparing the Data

The dataset used in this chapter is the well-known Covtype dataset, available online (*https://oreil.ly/spUWl*) as a compressed CSV-format data file, *covtype.data.gz*, and accompanying info file, *covtype.info*.

The dataset records the types of forest-covered parcels of land in Colorado, USA. It's only a coincidence that the dataset concerns real-world forests! Each data record contains several features describing each parcel of land—like its elevation, slope, distance to water, shade, and soil type—along with the known forest type covering the land. The forest cover type is to be predicted from the rest of the features, of which there are 54 in total.

This dataset has been used in research and even a Kaggle competition (*https://oreil.ly/LpjgW*). It is an interesting dataset to explore in this chapter because it contains both categorical and numeric features. There are 581,012 examples in the dataset, which does not exactly qualify as big data but is large enough to be manageable as an example and still highlight some issues of scale.

Thankfully, the data is already in a simple CSV format and does not require much cleansing or other preparation to be used with PySpark MLlib. The *covtype.data* file should be extracted and copied into your local or cloud storage (such as AWS S3).

Start `pyspark-shell`. You may find it helpful to give the shell a healthy amount of memory to work with, as building decision forests can be resource intensive. If you have the memory, specify `--driver-memory 8g` or similar.

CSV files contain fundamentally tabular data, organized into rows of columns. Sometimes these columns are given names in a header line, although that's not the case here. The column names are given in the companion file, *covtype.info*. Conceptually, each column of a CSV file has a type as well—a number, a string—but a CSV file doesn't specify this.

It's natural to parse this data as a dataframe because this is PySpark's abstraction for tabular data, with a defined column schema, including column names and types. PySpark has built-in support for reading CSV data. Let's read our dataset as a Data-Frame using the built-in CSV reader:

```
data_without_header = spark.read.option("inferSchema", True)\
                    .option("header", False).csv("data/covtype.data")
data_without_header.printSchema()
...
root
 |-- _c0: integer (nullable = true)
 |-- _c1: integer (nullable = true)
 |-- _c2: integer (nullable = true)
 |-- _c3: integer (nullable = true)
 |-- _c4: integer (nullable = true)
 |-- _c5: integer (nullable = true)
...
```

This code reads the input as CSV and does not attempt to parse the first line as a header of column names. It also requests that the type of each column be inferred by examining the data. It correctly infers that all of the columns are numbers, and, more specifically, integers. Unfortunately, it can name the columns only `_c0` and so on.

We can look at the *covtype.info* file for the column names.

```
$ cat data/covtype.info


...
[...]
7.      Attribute information:

Given is the attribute name, attribute type, the measurement unit and
a brief description.  The forest cover type is the classification
problem.  The order of this listing corresponds to the order of
numerals along the rows of the database.

Name                              Data Type
Elevation                         quantitative
Aspect                            quantitative
Slope                             quantitative
Horizontal_Distance_To_Hydrology  quantitative
```

```
Vertical_Distance_To_Hydrology          quantitative
Horizontal_Distance_To_Roadways         quantitative
Hillshade_9am                           quantitative
Hillshade_Noon                          quantitative
Hillshade_3pm                           quantitative
Horizontal_Distance_To_Fire_Points      quantitative
Wilderness_Area (4 binary columns)      qualitative
Soil_Type (40 binary columns)           qualitative
Cover_Type (7 types)                    integer

Measurement                     Description

meters                          Elevation in meters
azimuth                         Aspect in degrees azimuth
degrees                         Slope in degrees
meters                          Horz Dist to nearest surface water features
meters                          Vert Dist to nearest surface water features
meters                          Horz Dist to nearest roadway
0 to 255 index                  Hillshade index at 9am, summer solstice
0 to 255 index                  Hillshade index at noon, summer soltice
0 to 255 index                  Hillshade index at 3pm, summer solstice
meters                          Horz Dist to nearest wildfire ignition point
0 (absence) or 1 (presence)     Wilderness area designation
0 (absence) or 1 (presence)     Soil Type designation
1 to 7                          Forest Cover Type designation
...
```

Looking at the column information, it's clear that some features are indeed numeric. `Elevation` is an elevation in meters; `Slope` is measured in degrees. However, `Wilder ness_Area` is something different, because it is said to span four columns, each of which is a 0 or 1. In reality, `Wilderness_Area` is a categorical value, not a numeric one.

These four columns are actually a one-hot or 1-of-N encoding. When this form of encoding is performed on a categorical feature, one categorical feature that takes on N distinct values becomes N numeric features, each taking on the value 0 or 1. Exactly one of the N values has value 1, and the others are 0. For example, a categorical feature for weather that can be `cloudy`, `rainy`, or `clear` would become three numeric features, where `cloudy` is represented by `1,0,0`; `rainy` by `0,1,0`; and so on. These three numeric features might be thought of as `is_cloudy`, `is_rainy`, and `is_clear` features. Likewise, 40 of the columns are really one `Soil_Type` categorical feature.

This isn't the only possible way to encode a categorical feature as a number. Another possible encoding simply assigns a distinct numeric value to each possible value of the categorical feature. For example, `cloudy` may become 1.0, `rainy` 2.0, and so on. The target itself, `Cover_Type`, is a categorical value encoded as a value 1 to 7.

Be careful when encoding a categorical feature as a single numeric feature. The original categorical values have no ordering, but when encoded as a number, they appear to. Treating the encoded feature as numeric leads to meaningless results because the algorithm is effectively pretending that rainy is somehow greater than, and two times larger than, cloudy. It's OK as long as the encoding's numeric value is not used as a number.

We have seen both types of encodings of categorical features. It would have, perhaps, been simpler and more straightforward to not encode such features (and in two ways, no less) and to instead simply include their values directly, like "Rawah Wilderness Area." This may be an artifact of history; the dataset was released in 1998. For performance reasons or to match the format expected by libraries of the day, which were built more for regression problems, datasets often contain data encoded in these ways.

In any event, before proceeding, it is useful to add column names to this DataFrame to make it easier to work with:

```
from pyspark.sql.types import DoubleType
from pyspark.sql.functions import col

colnames = ["Elevation", "Aspect", "Slope", \
            "Horizontal_Distance_To_Hydrology", \
            "Vertical_Distance_To_Hydrology", "Horizontal_Distance_To_Roadways", \
            "Hillshade_9am", "Hillshade_Noon", "Hillshade_3pm", \
            "Horizontal_Distance_To_Fire_Points"] + \ ❶
[f"Wilderness_Area_{i}" for i in range(4)] + \
[f"Soil_Type_{i}" for i in range(40)] + \
["Cover_Type"]

data = data_without_header.toDF(*colnames).\
                    withColumn("Cover_Type",
                              col("Cover_Type").cast(DoubleType()))

data.head()
...
Row(Elevation=2596,Aspect=51,Slope=3,Horizontal_Distance_To_Hydrology=258,...)
```

❶ + concatenates collections.

The wilderness- and soil-related columns are named Wilderness_Area_0, Soil_Type_0, etc., and a bit of Python can generate these 44 names without having to type them all out. Finally, the target Cover_Type column is cast to a double value up front, because it will actually be necessary to consume it as a double rather than int in all PySpark MLlib APIs. This will become apparent later.

You can call data.show to see some rows of the dataset, but the display is so wide that it will be difficult to read it all. data.head displays it as a raw Row object, which will be more readable in this case.

Now that we're familiar with our dataset and have processed it, we can train a decision tree model.

Our First Decision Tree

In Chapter 3, we built a recommender model right away on all of the available data. This created a recommender that could be sense-checked by anyone with some knowledge of music: looking at a user's listening habits and recommendations, we got some sense that it was producing good results. Here, that is not possible. We would have no idea how to make up a 54-feature description of a new parcel of land in Colorado, or what kind of forest cover to expect from such a parcel.

Instead, we must jump straight to holding out some data for purposes of evaluating the resulting model. Before, the AUC metric was used to assess the agreement between held-out listening data and predictions from recommendations. AUC may be viewed as the probability that a randomly chosen good recommendation ranks above a randomly chosen bad recommendation. The principle is the same here, although the evaluation metric will be different: *accuracy*. The majority—90%—of the data will again be used for training, and, later, we'll see that a subset of this training set will be held out for cross-validation (the CV set). The other 10% held out here is actually a third subset, a proper test set.

```
(train_data, test_data) = data.randomSplit([0.9, 0.1])
train_data.cache()
test_data.cache()
```

The data needs a little more preparation to be used with a classifier in MLlib. The input DataFrame contains many columns, each holding one feature that could be used to predict the target column. MLlib requires all of the inputs to be collected into *one* column, whose value is a vector. PySpark's VectorAssembler class is an abstraction for vectors in the linear algebra sense and contains only numbers. For most intents and purposes, they work like a simple array of double values (floating-point numbers). Of course, some of the input features are conceptually categorical, even if they're all represented with numbers in the input.

Fortunately, the VectorAssembler class can do this work:

```
from pyspark.ml.feature import VectorAssembler

input_cols = colnames[:-1] ❶
vector_assembler = VectorAssembler(inputCols=input_cols,
                                   outputCol="featureVector")
```

```
assembled_train_data = vector_assembler.transform(train_data)

assembled_train_data.select("featureVector").show(truncate = False)
...
+---------------------------------------------------------------- ...
|featureVector                                                    ...
+---------------------------------------------------------------- ...
|(54,[0,1,2,5,6,7,8,9,13,18],[1874.0,18.0,14.0,90.0,208.0,209.0, ...
|(54,[0,1,2,3,4,5,6,7,8,9,13,18],[1879.0,28.0,19.0,30.0,12.0,95.0, ...
...
```

❶ Excludes the label, Cover_Type

The key parameters of VectorAssembler are the columns to combine into the feature vector, and the name of the new column containing the feature vector. Here, all columns—*except* the target, of course—are included as input features. The resulting DataFrame has a new featureVector column, as shown.

The output doesn't look exactly like a sequence of numbers, but that's because this shows a raw representation of the vector, represented as a SparseVector instance to save storage. Because most of the 54 values are 0, it stores only nonzero values and their indices. This detail won't matter in classification.

Feature Vector

Consider predicting tomorrow's high temperature given today's weather. There is nothing wrong with this idea, but "today's weather" is a casual concept that requires structuring before it can be fed into a learning algorithm. Really, it is certain *features* of today's weather that may predict tomorrow's temperature, such as high temperature, low temperature, average humidity, whether it's cloudy, rainy, or clear today, and the number of weather forecasters predicting a cold snap tomorrow.

These features are also sometimes called *dimensions*, *predictors*, or just *variables*. Each of these features can be quantified. For example, high and low temperatures are measured in degrees Celsius, humidity can be measured as a fraction between 0 and 1, and weather type can be labeled cloudy, rainy, or clear. The number of forecasters is, of course, an integer count. Today's weather might therefore be reduced to a list of values like 13.1,19.0,0.73,cloudy,1.

These five features together, in order, are known as a *feature vector* and can describe any day's weather. This usage bears some resemblance to use of the term *vector* in linear algebra, except that a vector in this sense can conceptually contain nonnumeric values, and even lack some values. These features are not all of the same type. The first two features are measured in degrees Celsius, but the third is unitless, a fraction. The fourth is not a number at all, and the fifth is a number that is always a nonnegative integer.

A learning algorithm needs to train on data in order to make predictions. Feature vectors provide an organized way to describe input to a learning algorithm (here: 12.5,15.5,0.10,clear,0). The output, or *target*, of the prediction can also be thought of as a feature. Here, it is a numeric feature: 17.2.

It's not uncommon to simply include the target as another feature in the feature vector. The entire training example might be thought of as 12.5,15.5,0.10,clear,0,17.2. The collection of all of these examples is known as the *training set*.

VectorAssembler is an example of Transformer within the current MLlib Pipelines API. It transforms the input DataFrame into another DataFrame based on some logic, and is composable with other transformations into a pipeline. Later in this chapter, these transformations will be connected into an actual Pipeline. Here, the transformation is just invoked directly, which is sufficient to build a first decision tree classifier model:

```
from pyspark.ml.classification import DecisionTreeClassifier

classifier = DecisionTreeClassifier(seed = 1234, labelCol="Cover_Type",
                                    featuresCol="featureVector",
                                    predictionCol="prediction")

model = classifier.fit(assembled_train_data)
print(model.toDebugString)
...
DecisionTreeClassificationModel: uid=DecisionTreeClassifier_da03f8ab5e28, ...
  If (feature 0 <= 3036.5)
   If (feature 0 <= 2546.5)
    If (feature 10 <= 0.5)
     If (feature 0 <= 2412.5)
      If (feature 3 <= 15.0)
       Predict: 4.0
      Else (feature 3 > 15.0)
       Predict: 3.0
     Else (feature 0 > 2412.5)
       ...
```

Again, the essential configuration for the classifier consists of column names: the column containing the input feature vectors and the column containing the target value to predict. Because the model will later be used to predict new values of the target, it is given the name of a column to store predictions.

Printing a representation of the model shows some of its tree structure. It consists of a series of nested decisions about features, comparing feature values to thresholds. (Here, for historical reasons, the features are referred to only by number, not name, unfortunately.)

Decision trees are able to assess the importance of input features as part of their building process. That is, they can estimate how much each input feature contributes to making correct predictions. This information is simple to access from the model:

```
import pandas as pd

pd.DataFrame(model.featureImportances.toArray(),
        index=input_cols, columns=['importance']).\
        sort_values(by="importance", ascending=False)
...
                                    importance
Elevation                           0.826854
Hillshade_Noon                      0.029087
Soil_Type_1                         0.028647
Soil_Type_3                         0.026447
Wilderness_Area_0                   0.024917
Horizontal_Distance_To_Hydrology    0.024862
Soil_Type_31                        0.018573
Wilderness_Area_2                   0.012458
Horizontal_Distance_To_Roadways     0.003608
Hillshade_9am                       0.002840
...
```

This pairs importance values (higher is better) with column names and prints them in order from most to least important. Elevation seems to dominate as the most important feature; most features are estimated to have virtually no importance when predicting the cover type!

The resulting `DecisionTreeClassificationModel` is itself a transformer because it can transform a dataframe containing feature vectors into a dataframe also containing predictions.

For example, it might be interesting to see what the model predicts on the training data and compare its prediction with the known correct cover type:

```
predictions = model.transform(assembled_train_data)
predictions.select("Cover_Type", "prediction", "probability").\
        show(10, truncate = False)

...
+----------+----------+--------------------------------------------------- ...
|Cover_Type|prediction|probability                                         ...
+----------+----------+--------------------------------------------------- ...
|6.0       |4.0       |[0.0,0.0,0.028372324539571926,0.2936784469885515, ...
|6.0       |3.0       |[0.0,0.0,0.024558587479935796,0.6454654895666132, ...
|6.0       |3.0       |[0.0,0.0,0.024558587479935796,0.6454654895666132, ...
|6.0       |3.0       |[0.0,0.0,0.024558587479935796,0.6454654895666132, ...
...
```

Interestingly, the output also contains a `probability` column that gives the model's estimate of how likely it is that each possible outcome is correct. This shows that in these instances, it's fairly sure the answer is 3 in several cases and quite sure the answer isn't 1.

Eagle-eyed readers might note that the probability vectors actually have eight values even though there are only seven possible outcomes. The vector's values at indices 1 to 7 do contain the probability of outcomes 1 to 7. However, there is also a value at index 0, which always shows as probability 0.0. This can be ignored, as 0 isn't even a valid outcome, as this says. It's a quirk of representing this information as a vector that's worth being aware of.

Based on the above snippet, it looks like the model could use some work. Its predictions look like they are often wrong. As with the ALS implementation in Chapter 3, the DecisionTreeClassifier implementation has several hyperparameters for which a value must be chosen, and they've all been left to defaults here. Here, the test set can be used to produce an unbiased evaluation of the expected accuracy of a model built with these default hyperparameters.

We will now use MulticlassClassificationEvaluator to compute accuracy and other metrics that evaluate the quality of the model's predictions. It's an example of an evaluator in MLlib, which is responsible for assessing the quality of an output DataFrame in some way:

```
from pyspark.ml.evaluation import MulticlassClassificationEvaluator

evaluator = MulticlassClassificationEvaluator(labelCol="Cover_Type",
                                    predictionCol="prediction")

evaluator.setMetricName("accuracy").evaluate(predictions)
evaluator.setMetricName("f1").evaluate(predictions)


...
0.6989423087953562
0.6821216079701136
```

After being given the column containing the "label" (target, or known correct output value) and the name of the column containing the prediction, it finds that the two match about 70% of the time. This is the accuracy of this classifier. It can compute other related measures, like the F1 score. For our purposes here, accuracy will be used to evaluate classifiers.

This single number gives a good summary of the quality of the classifier's output. Sometimes, however, it can be useful to look at the *confusion matrix*. This is a table with a row and a column for every possible value of the target. Because there are seven target category values, this is a 7×7 matrix, where each row corresponds to an actual correct value, and each column to a predicted value, in order. The entry at row i and column j counts the number of times an example with true category i was predicted as category *j*. So, the correct predictions are the counts along the diagonal, and the predictions are everything else.

It's possible to calculate a confusion matrix directly with the DataFrame API, using its more general operators.

```
confusion_matrix = predictions.groupBy("Cover_Type").\
  pivot("prediction", range(1,8)).count().\
  na.fill(0.0).\ ❶
  orderBy("Cover_Type")

confusion_matrix.show()

...
```

```
+----------+------+------+-----+---+---+---+-----+
|Cover_Type|     1|     2|    3|  4|  5|  6|    7|
+----------+------+------+-----+---+---+---+-----+
|       1.0|133792| 51547|  109|  0|  0|  0| 5223|
|       2.0| 57026|192260| 4888| 57|  0|  0|  750|
|       3.0|     0|  3368|28238|590|  0|  0|    0|
|       4.0|     0|     0| 1493|956|  0|  0|    0|
|       5.0|     0|  8282|  283|  0|  0|  0|    0|
|       6.0|     0|  3371|11872|406|  0|  0|    0|
|       7.0|  8122|    74|    0|  0|  0|  0|10319|
+----------+------+------+-----+---+---+---+-----+
```

❶ Replace null with 0.

Spreadsheet users may have recognized the problem as just like that of computing a pivot table. A pivot table groups values by two dimensions, whose values become rows and columns of the output, and computes some aggregation within those groupings, like a count here. This is also available as a PIVOT function in several databases and is supported by Spark SQL. It's arguably more elegant and powerful to compute it this way.

Although 70% accuracy sounds decent, it's not immediately clear whether it is outstanding or poor. How well would a simplistic approach do to establish a baseline? Just as a broken clock is correct twice a day, randomly guessing a classification for each example would also occasionally produce the correct answer.

We could construct such a random "classifier" by picking a class at random in proportion to its prevalence in the training set. For example, if 30% of the training set were cover type 1, then the random classifier would guess "1" 30% of the time. Each classification would be correct in proportion to its prevalence in the test set. If 40% of the test set were cover type 1, then guessing "1" would be correct 40% of the time. Cover type 1 would then be guessed correctly 30% x 40% = 12% of the time and contribute 12% to overall accuracy. Therefore, we can evaluate the accuracy by summing these products of probabilities:

```
from pyspark.sql import DataFrame

def class_probabilities(data):
    total = data.count()
    return data.groupBy("Cover_Type").count().\ ❶
        orderBy("Cover_Type").\ ❷
        select(col("count").cast(DoubleType())).\
        withColumn("count_proportion", col("count")/total).\
        select("count_proportion").collect()


train_prior_probabilities = class_probabilities(train_data)
test_prior_probabilities = class_probabilities(test_data)

train_prior_probabilities
...

[Row(count_proportion=0.36455357859838705),
 Row(count_proportion=0.4875111371136425),
 Row(count_proportion=0.06155716924206445),
 Row(count_proportion=0.00468236760696409),
 Row(count_proportion=0.016375858943914835),
 Row(count_proportion=0.029920118693908142),
 Row(count_proportion=0.03539976980111887)]


...

train_prior_probabilities = [p[0] for p in train_prior_probabilities]
test_prior_probabilities = [p[0] for p in test_prior_probabilities]

sum([train_p * cv_p for train_p, cv_p in zip(train_prior_probabilities,
                                    test_prior_probabilities)]) ❸
...

0.37735294664034547
```

❶ Count by category

❷ Order counts by category

❸ Sum products of pairs in training and test sets

Random guessing achieves 37% accuracy then, which makes 70% seem like a good result after all. But the latter result was achieved with default hyperparameters. We can do even better by exploring what the hyperparameters actually mean for the tree-building process. That is what we will do in the next section.

Decision Tree Hyperparameters

In Chapter 3, the ALS algorithm exposed several hyperparameters whose values we had to choose by building models with various combinations of values and then assessing the quality of each result using some metric. The process is the same here, although the metric is now multiclass accuracy instead of AUC. The hyperparameters controlling how the tree's decisions are chosen will be quite different as well: maximum depth, maximum bins, impurity measure, and minimum information gain.

Maximum depth simply limits the number of levels in the decision tree. It is the maximum number of chained decisions that the classifier will make to classify an example. It is useful to limit this to avoid overfitting the training data, as illustrated previously in the pet store example.

The decision tree algorithm is responsible for coming up with potential decision rules to try at each level, like the `weight >= 100` or `weight >= 500` decisions in the pet store example. Decisions are always of the same form: for numeric features, decisions are of the form `feature >= value`; and for categorical features, they are of the form `feature in (value1, value2, …)`. So, the set of decision rules to try is really a set of values to plug in to the decision rule. These are referred to as *bins* in the PySpark MLlib implementation. A larger number of bins requires more processing time but might lead to finding a more optimal decision rule.

What makes a decision rule good? Intuitively, a good rule would meaningfully distinguish examples by target category value. For example, a rule that divides the Covtype dataset into examples with only categories 1–3 on the one hand and 4–7 on the other would be excellent because it clearly separates some categories from others. A rule that resulted in about the same mix of all categories as are found in the whole dataset doesn't seem helpful. Following either branch of such a decision leads to about the same distribution of possible target values and so doesn't really make progress toward a confident classification.

Put another way, good rules divide the training data's target values into relatively homogeneous, or "pure," subsets. Picking a best rule means minimizing the impurity of the two subsets it induces. There are two commonly used measures of impurity: Gini impurity and entropy.

Gini impurity is directly related to the accuracy of the random guess classifier. Within a subset, it is the probability that a randomly chosen classification of a randomly chosen example (both according to the distribution of classes in the subset) is *incorrect*. To calculate this value, we first multiply each class with its respective proportion among all classes. Then we subtract the sum of all the values from 1. If a subset has N classes and p_i is the proportion of examples of class i, then its Gini impurity is given in the Gini impurity equation:

$$I_G(p) = 1 - \sum_{i=1}^{N} p_i^2$$

If the subset contains only one class, this value is 0 because it is completely "pure." When there are N classes in the subset, this value is larger than 0 and is largest when the classes occur the same number of times—maximally impure.

Entropy is another measure of impurity, borrowed from information theory. Its nature is more difficult to explain, but it captures how much uncertainty the collection of target values in the subset implies about predictions for data that falls in that subset. A subset containing one class suggests that the outcome for the subset is completely certain and has 0 entropy—no uncertainty. A subset containing one of each possible class, on the other hand, suggests a lot of uncertainty about predictions for that subset because data has been observed with all kinds of target values. This has high entropy. Hence, low entropy, like low Gini impurity, is a good thing. Entropy is defined by the entropy equation:

$$I_E(p) = \sum_{i=1}^{N} p_i \log \left(\frac{1}{p_i}\right) = - \sum_{i=1}^{N} p_i \log (p_i)$$

Interestingly, uncertainty has units. Because the logarithm is the natural log (base e), the units are *nats*, the base e counterpart to more familiar *bits* (which we can obtain by using log base 2 instead). It really is measuring information, so it's also common to talk about the *information gain* of a decision rule when using entropy with decision trees.

One or the other measure may be a better metric for picking decision rules in a given dataset. They are, in a way, similar. Both involve a weighted average: a sum over values weighted by p_i. The default in PySpark's implementation is Gini impurity.

Finally, *minimum information gain* is a hyperparameter that imposes a minimum information gain, or decrease in impurity, for candidate decision rules. Rules that do not improve the subsets' impurity enough are rejected. Like a lower maximum depth, this can help the model resist overfitting because decisions that barely help divide the training input may in fact not helpfully divide future data at all.

Now that we understand the relevant hyperparameters of a decision tree algorithm, we will tune our model in the next section to improve its performance.

Tuning Decision Trees

It's not obvious from looking at the data which impurity measure leads to better accuracy or what maximum depth or number of bins is enough without being excessive. Fortunately, as in Chapter 3, it's simple to let PySpark try a number of combinations of these values and report the results.

First, it's necessary to set up a pipeline encapsulating the two steps we performed in previous sections—creating a feature vector and using it to create a decision tree model. Creating the `VectorAssembler` and `DecisionTreeClassifier` and chaining these two `Transformers` together results in a single `Pipeline` object that represents these two operations together as one operation:

```
from pyspark.ml import Pipeline

assembler = VectorAssembler(inputCols=input_cols, outputCol="featureVector")
classifier = DecisionTreeClassifier(seed=1234, labelCol="Cover_Type",
                                    featuresCol="featureVector",
                                    predictionCol="prediction")

pipeline = Pipeline(stages=[assembler, classifier])
```

Naturally, pipelines can be much longer and more complex. This is about as simple as it gets. Now we can also define the combinations of hyperparameters that should be tested using the PySpark ML API's built-in support, `ParamGridBuilder`. It's also time to define the evaluation metric that will be used to pick the "best" hyperparameters, and that is again `MulticlassClassificationEvaluator`:

```
from pyspark.ml.tuning import ParamGridBuilder

paramGrid = ParamGridBuilder(). \
  addGrid(classifier.impurity, ["gini", "entropy"]). \
  addGrid(classifier.maxDepth, [1, 20]). \
  addGrid(classifier.maxBins, [40, 300]). \
  addGrid(classifier.minInfoGain, [0.0, 0.05]). \
  build()

multiclassEval = MulticlassClassificationEvaluator(). \
  setLabelCol("Cover_Type"). \
  setPredictionCol("prediction"). \
  setMetricName("accuracy")
```

This means that a model will be built and evaluated for two values of four hyperparameters. That's 16 models. They'll be evaluated by multiclass accuracy. Finally, `TrainValidationSplit` brings these components together—the pipeline that makes models, model evaluation metrics, and hyperparameters to try—and can run the evaluation on the training data. It's worth noting that `CrossValidator` could be used here as well to perform full k-fold cross-validation, but it is *k* times more expensive and doesn't add as much value in the presence of big data. So, `TrainValidationSplit` is used here:

```
from pyspark.ml.tuning import TrainValidationSplit

validator = TrainValidationSplit(seed=1234,
    estimator=pipeline,
    evaluator=multiclassEval,
    estimatorParamMaps=paramGrid,
    trainRatio=0.9)

validator_model = validator.fit(train_data)
```

This will take several minutes or more, depending on your hardware, because it's building and evaluating many models. Note the train ratio parameter is set to 0.9. This means that the training data is actually further subdivided by `TrainValidationS` `plit` into 90%/10% subsets. The former is used for training each model. The remaining 10% of the input is held out as a cross-validation set to evaluate the model. If it's already holding out some data for evaluation, then why did we hold out 10% of the original data as a test set?

If the purpose of the CV set was to evaluate *parameters* that fit to the *training* set, then the purpose of the test set is to evaluate *hyperparameters* that were "fit" to the CV set. That is, the test set ensures an unbiased estimate of the accuracy of the final, chosen model and its hyperparameters.

Say that the best model chosen by this process exhibits 90% accuracy on the CV set. It seems reasonable to expect it will exhibit 90% accuracy on future data. However, there's an element of randomness in how these models are built. By chance, this model and evaluation could have turned out unusually well. The top model and evaluation result could have benefited from a bit of luck, so its accuracy estimate is likely to be slightly optimistic. Put another way, hyperparameters can overfit too.

To really assess how well this best model is likely to perform on future examples, we need to evaluate it on examples that were not used to train it. But we also need to avoid examples in the CV set that were used to evaluate it. That is why a third subset, the test set, was held out.

The result of the validator contains the best model it found. This itself is a representation of the best overall *pipeline* it found, because we provided an instance of a pipeline to run. To query the parameters chosen by `DecisionTreeClassifier`, it's necessary to manually extract `DecisionTreeClassificationModel` from the resulting `PipelineModel`, which is the final stage in the pipeline:

```
from pprint import pprint

best_model = validator_model.bestModel
pprint(best_model.stages[1].extractParamMap())
```

```
...
{Param(...name='predictionCol', doc='prediction column name.'): 'prediction',
 Param(...name='probabilityCol', doc='...'): 'probability',
 [...]
 Param(...name='impurity', doc='...'): 'entropy',
 Param(...name='maxDepth', doc='...'): 20,
 Param(...name='minInfoGain', doc='...'): 0.0,
 [...]
 Param(...name='featuresCol', doc='features column name.'): 'featureVector',
 Param(...name='maxBins', doc='...'): 40,
 [...]
 Param(...name='labelCol', doc='label column name.'): 'Cover_Type'}
 ...
}
```

This output contains a lot of information about the fitted model, but it also tells us that entropy apparently worked best as the impurity measure and that a max depth of 20 was not surprisingly better than 1. It might be surprising that the best model was fit with just 40 bins, but this is probably a sign that 40 was "plenty" rather than "better" than 300. Lastly, no minimum information gain was better than a small minimum, which could imply that the model is more prone to underfit than overfit.

You may wonder if it is possible to see the accuracy that each of the models achieved for each combination of hyperparameters. The hyperparameters and the evaluations are exposed by `getEstimatorParamMaps` and `validationMetrics`, respectively. They can be combined to display all of the parameter combinations sorted by metric value:

```
validator_model = validator.fit(train_data)

metrics = validator_model.validationMetrics
params = validator_model.getEstimatorParamMaps()
metrics_and_params = list(zip(metrics, params))

metrics_and_params.sort(key=lambda x: x[0], reverse=True)
metrics_and_params

...
[(0.9130409881445563,
  {Param(...name='minInfoGain' ...): 0.0,
   Param(...name='maxDepth'...): 20,
   Param(...name='maxBins' ...): 40,
   Param(...name='impurity'...): 'entropy'}),
 (0.9112655352131498,
  {Param(...name='minInfoGain',...): 0.0,
   Param(...name='maxDepth' ...): 20,
   Param(...name='maxBins'...): 300,
   Param(...name='impurity'...: 'entropy'}),
 ...
```

What was the accuracy that this model achieved on the CV set? And, finally, what accuracy does the model achieve on the test set?

```
metrics.sort(reverse=True)
print(metrics[0])
...

0.9130409881445563
...

multiclassEval.evaluate(best_model.transform(test_data)) ❶


...
0.9138921373048084
```

❶ best_Model is a complete pipeline.

The results are both about 91%. It happens that the estimate from the CV set was pretty fine to begin with. In fact, it is not usual for the test set to show a very different result.

This is an interesting point at which to revisit the issue of overfitting. As discussed previously, it's possible to build a decision tree so deep and elaborate that it fits the given training examples very well or perfectly but fails to generalize to other examples because it has fit the idiosyncrasies and noise of the training data too closely. This is a problem common to most machine learning algorithms, not just decision trees.

When a decision tree has overfit, it will exhibit high accuracy when run on the same training data that it fit the model to, but low accuracy on other examples. Here, the final model's accuracy was about 91% on other, new examples. Accuracy can just as easily be evaluated over the same data that the model was trained on, trainData. This gives an accuracy of about 95%. The difference is not large but suggests that the decision tree has overfit the training data to some extent. A lower maximum depth might be a better choice.

So far, we've implicitly treated all input features, including categoricals, as if they're numeric. Can we improve our model's performance further by treating categorical features as exactly that? We will explore this next.

Categorical Features Revisited

The categorical features in our dataset are one-hot encoded as several binary 0/1 values. Treating these individual features as numeric turns out to be fine, because any decision rule on the "numeric" features will choose thresholds between 0 and 1, and all are equivalent since all values are 0 or 1.

Of course, this encoding forces the decision tree algorithm to consider the values of the underlying categorical features individually. Because features like soil type are broken down into many features and because decision trees treat features individually, it is harder to relate information about related soil types.

For example, nine different soil types are actually part of the Leighton family, and they may be related in ways that the decision tree can exploit. If soil type were encoded as a single categorical feature with 40 soil values, then the tree could express rules like "if the soil type is one of the nine Leighton family types" directly. However, when encoded as 40 features, the tree would have to learn a sequence of nine decisions on soil type to do the same, this expressiveness may lead to better decisions and more efficient trees.

However, having 40 numeric features represent one 40-valued categorical feature increases memory usage and slows things down.

What about undoing the one-hot encoding? This would replace, for example, the four columns encoding wilderness type with one column that encodes the wilderness type as a number between 0 and 3, like Cover_Type:

```
def unencode_one_hot(data):
    wilderness_cols = ['Wilderness_Area_' + str(i) for i in range(4)]
    wilderness_assembler = VectorAssembler().\
                                setInputCols(wilderness_cols).\
                                setOutputCol("wilderness")

    unhot_udf = udf(lambda v: v.toArray().tolist().index(1))  ❶

    with_wilderness = wilderness_assembler.transform(data).\
      drop(*wilderness_cols).\  ❷
      withColumn("wilderness", unhot_udf(col("wilderness")))

    soil_cols = ['Soil_Type_' + str(i) for i in range(40)]
    soil_assembler = VectorAssembler().\
                    setInputCols(soil_cols).\
                    setOutputCol("soil")
    with_soil = soil_assembler.\
                transform(with_wilderness).\
                drop(*soil_cols).\
                withColumn("soil", unhot_udf(col("soil")))

    return with_soil
```

❶ Note UDF definition

❷ Drop one-hot columns; no longer needed

Here VectorAssembler is deployed to combine the 4 and 40 wilderness and soil type columns into two Vector columns. The values in these Vectors are all 0, except for one location that has a 1. There's no simple DataFrame function for this, so we have to define our own UDF that can be used to operate on columns. This turns these two new columns into numbers of just the type we need.

We can now transform our dataset by removing one-hot encoding using our function defined above:

```
unenc_train_data = unencode_one_hot(train_data)
unenc_train_data.printSchema()
...
root
 |-- Elevation: integer (nullable = true)
 |-- Aspect: integer (nullable = true)
 |-- Slope: integer (nullable = true)
 |-- Horizontal_Distance_To_Hydrology: integer (nullable = true)
 |-- Vertical_Distance_To_Hydrology: integer (nullable = true)
 |-- Horizontal_Distance_To_Roadways: integer (nullable = true)
 |-- Hillshade_9am: integer (nullable = true)
 |-- Hillshade_Noon: integer (nullable = true)
 |-- Hillshade_3pm: integer (nullable = true)
 |-- Horizontal_Distance_To_Fire_Points: integer (nullable = true)
 |-- Cover_Type: double (nullable = true)
 |-- wilderness: string (nullable = true)
 |-- soil: string (nullable = true)
...

unenc_train_data.groupBy('wilderness').count().show()
...

+----------+------+
|wilderness| count|
+----------+------+
|         3| 33271|
|         0|234532|
|         1| 26917|
|         2|228144|
+----------+------+
```

From here, nearly the same process as above can be used to tune the hyperparameters of a decision tree model built on this data and to choose and evaluate a best model. There's one important difference, however. The two new numeric columns have nothing about them that indicates they're actually an encoding of categorical values. To treat them as numbers is not correct, as their ordering is meaningless. The model will still get built but because of some information in these features not being available, the accuracy may suffer.

Internally MLlib can store additional metadata about each column. The details of this data are generally hidden from the caller but include information such as whether the column encodes a categorical value and how many distinct values it takes on. To add this metadata, it's necessary to put the data through VectorIndexer. Its job is to turn input into properly labeled categorical feature columns. Although we did much of the work already to turn the categorical features into 0-indexed values, `VectorIndexer` will take care of the metadata.

We need to add this stage to the `Pipeline`:

```python
from pyspark.ml.feature import VectorIndexer

cols = unenc_train_data.columns
inputCols = [c for c in cols if c!='Cover_Type']

assembler = VectorAssembler().setInputCols(inputCols).setOutputCol("featureVector")

indexer = VectorIndexer().\
  setMaxCategories(40).\ ❶
  setInputCol("featureVector").setOutputCol("indexedVector")

classifier = DecisionTreeClassifier().setLabelCol("Cover_Type").\
                                       setFeaturesCol("indexedVector").\
                                       setPredictionCol("prediction")

pipeline = Pipeline().setStages([assembler, indexer, classifier])
```

❶ >= 40 because soil has 40 values

The approach assumes that the training set contains all possible values of each of the categorical features at least once. That is, it works correctly only if all 4 soil values and all 40 wilderness values appear in the training set so that all possible values get a mapping. Here, that happens to be true, but may not be for small training sets of data in which some labels appear very infrequently. In those cases, it could be necessary to manually create and add a `VectorIndexerModel` with the complete value mapping supplied manually.

Aside from that, the process is the same as before. You should find that it chose a similar best model but that accuracy on the test set is about 93%. By treating categorical features as actual categorical features in the previous sections, the classifier improved its accuracy by almost 2%.

We have trained and tuned a decision tree. Now, we will move on to random forests, a more powerful algorithm. As we will see in the next section, implementing them using PySpark will be surprisingly straightforward at this point.

Random Forests

If you have been following along with the code examples, you may have noticed that your results differ slightly from those presented in the code listings in the book. That is because there is an element of randomness in building decision trees, and the randomness comes into play when you're deciding what data to use and what decision rules to explore.

The algorithm does not consider every possible decision rule at every level. To do so would take an incredible amount of time. For a categorical feature over N values, there are 2^N-2 possible decision rules (every subset except the empty set and entire set). For an even moderately large N, this would create billions of candidate decision rules.

Instead, decision trees use several heuristics to determine which few rules to actually consider. The process of picking rules also involves some randomness; only a few features picked at random are looked at each time, and only values from a random subset of the training data. This trades a bit of accuracy for a lot of speed, but it also means that the decision tree algorithm won't build the same tree every time. This is a good thing.

It's good for the same reason that the "wisdom of the crowds" usually beats individual predictions. To illustrate, take this quick quiz: how many black taxis operate in London?

Don't peek at the answer; guess first.

I guessed 10,000, which is well off the correct answer of about 19,000. Because I guessed low, you're a bit more likely to have guessed higher than I did, and so the average of our answers will tend to be more accurate. There's that regression to the mean again. The average guess from an informal poll of 13 people in the office was indeed closer: 11,170.

A key to this effect is that the guesses were independent and didn't influence one another. (You didn't peek, did you?) The exercise would be useless if we had all agreed on and used the same methodology to make a guess, because the guesses would have been the same answer—the same potentially quite wrong answer. It would even have been different and worse if I'd merely influenced you by stating my guess up front.

It would be great to have not one tree but many trees, each producing reasonable but different and independent estimations of the right target value. Their collective average prediction should fall close to the true answer, more than any individual tree's does. It's the *randomness* in the process of building that helps create this independence. This is the key to *random forests*.

Randomness is injected by building many trees, each of which sees a different random subset of data—and even of features. This makes the forest as a whole less prone to overfitting. If a particular feature contains noisy data or is deceptively predictive only in the *training* set, then most trees will not consider this problem feature most of the time. Most trees will not fit the noise and will tend to "outvote" the trees that have fit the noise in the forest.

The prediction of a random forest is simply a weighted average of the trees' predictions. For a categorical target, this can be a majority vote or the most probable value based on the average of probabilities produced by the trees. Random forests, like decision trees, also support regression, and the forest's prediction in this case is the average of the number predicted by each tree.

While random forests are a more powerful and complex classification technique, the good news is that it's virtually no different to use it in the pipeline that has been developed in this chapter. Simply drop in a `RandomForestClassifier` in place of `DecisionTreeClassifier` and proceed as before. There's really no more code or API to understand in order to use it:

```
from pyspark.ml.classification import RandomForestClassifier

classifier = RandomForestClassifier(seed=1234, labelCol="Cover_Type",
                                    featuresCol="indexedVector",
                                    predictionCol="prediction")
```

Note that this classifier has another hyperparameter: the number of trees to build. Like the max bins hyperparameter, higher values should give better results up to a point. The cost, however, is that building many trees of course takes many times longer than building one.

The accuracy of the best random forest model produced from a similar tuning process is 95% off the bat—about 2% better already, although viewed another way, that's a 28% reduction in the error rate over the best decision tree built previously, from 7% down to 5%. You may do better with further tuning.

Incidentally, at this point we have a more reliable picture of feature importance:

```
forest_model = best_model.stages[1]

feature_importance_list = list(zip(input_cols,
                                   forest_model.featureImportances.toArray()))
feature_importance_list.sort(key=lambda x: x[1], reverse=True)

pprint(feature_importance_list)
...
(0.28877055118903183,Elevation)
(0.17288279582959612,soil)
(0.12105056811661499,Horizontal_Distance_To_Roadways)
(0.1121550648692802,Horizontal_Distance_To_Fire_Points)
(0.08805270405239551,wilderness)
(0.04467393191338021,Vertical_Distance_To_Hydrology)
(0.04293099150373547,Horizontal_Distance_To_Hydrology)
(0.03149644050848614,Hillshade_Noon)
(0.028408483578137605,Hillshade_9am)
(0.027185325937200706,Aspect)
(0.027075578474331806,Hillshade_3pm)
(0.015317564027809389,Slope)
```

Random forests are appealing in the context of big data because trees are supposed to be built independently, and big data technologies like Spark and MapReduce inherently need *data-parallel* problems, where parts of the overall solution can be computed independently on parts of the data. The fact that trees can, and should, train on only a subset of features or input data makes it trivial to parallelize building the trees.

Making Predictions

Building a classifier, while an interesting and nuanced process, is not the end goal. The goal is to make predictions. This is the payoff, and it is comparatively quite easy.

The resulting "best model" is actually a whole pipeline of operations. It encapsulates how input is transformed for use with the model and includes the model itself, which can make predictions. It can operate on a dataframe of new input. The only difference from the `data` DataFrame we started with is that it lacks the `Cover_Type` column. When we're making predictions—especially about the future, says Mr. Bohr—the output is of course not known.

To prove it, try dropping the `Cover_Type` from the test data input and obtaining a prediction:

```
unenc_test_data = unencode_one_hot(test_data)
bestModel.transform(unenc_test_data.drop("Cover_Type")).\
                    select("prediction").show()


...
+----------+
|prediction|
+----------+
|       6.0|
+----------+
```

The result should be 6.0, which corresponds to class 7 (the original feature was 1-indexed) in the original Covtype dataset. The predicted cover type for the land described in this example is Krummholz.

Where to Go from Here

This chapter introduced two related and important types of machine learning, classification and regression, along with some foundational concepts in building and tuning models: features, vectors, training, and cross-validation. It demonstrated how to predict a type of forest cover from things like location and soil type using the Covtype dataset, with decision trees and forests implemented in PySpark.

As with recommenders in Chapter 3, it could be useful to continue exploring the effect of hyperparameters on accuracy. Most decision tree hyperparameters trade time for accuracy: more bins and trees generally produce better accuracy but hit a point of diminishing returns.

The classifier here turned out to be very accurate. It's unusual to achieve more than 95% accuracy. In general, you will achieve further improvements in accuracy by including more features or transforming existing features into a more predictive form. This is a common, repeated step in iteratively improving a classifier model. For example, for this dataset, the two features encoding horizontal and vertical distance-to-surface-water features could produce a third feature: straight-line distance-to-surface-water features. This might turn out to be more useful than either original feature. Or, if it were possible to collect more data, we might try adding new information like soil moisture to improve classification.

Of course, not all prediction problems in the real world are exactly like the Covtype dataset. For example, some problems require predicting a continuous numeric value, not a categorical value. Much of the same analysis and code applies to this type of *regression* problem; the RandomForestRegressor class will be of use in this case.

Furthermore, decision trees and forests are not the only classification or regression algorithms, and not the only ones implemented in PySpark. Each algorithm operates quite differently from decision trees and forests. However, many elements are the same: they plug into a Pipeline and operate on columns in a dataframe, and have hyperparameters that you must select using training, cross-validation, and test subsets of the input data. The same general principles, with these other algorithms, can also be deployed to model classification and regression problems.

These have been examples of supervised learning. What happens when some, or all, of the target values are unknown? The following chapter will explore what can be done in this situation.

## CHAPTER 5

Anomaly Detection
with K-means Clustering

Classification and regression are powerful, well-studied techniques in machine learning. Chapter 4 demonstrated using a classifier as a predictor of unknown values. But there was a catch: to predict unknown values for new data, we had to know the target values for many previously seen examples. Classifiers can help only if we, the data scientists, know what we are looking for and can provide plenty of examples where input produced a known output. These were collectively known as *supervised learning* techniques, because their learning process receives the correct output value for each example in the input.

However, sometimes the correct output is unknown for some or all examples. Consider the problem of dividing up an ecommerce site's customers by their shopping habits and tastes. The input features are their purchases, clicks, demographic information, and more. The output should be groupings of customers: perhaps one group will represent fashion-conscious buyers, another will turn out to correspond to price-sensitive bargain hunters, and so on.

If you were asked to determine this target label for each new customer, you would quickly run into a problem in applying a supervised learning technique like a classifier: you don't know a priori who should be considered fashion-conscious, for example. In fact, you're not even sure if "fashion-conscious" is a meaningful grouping of the site's customers to begin with!

Fortunately, *unsupervised learning* techniques can help. These techniques do not learn to predict a target value, because none is available. They can, however, learn structure in data and find groupings of similar inputs, or learn what types of input are likely to occur and what types are not. This chapter will introduce unsupervised learning using clustering implementations in MLlib. Specifically, we will use the K-means clustering algorithm for identifying anomalies in network traffic data. Anomaly detection is often used to find fraud, detect network attacks, or discover problems in servers or other sensor-equipped machinery. In these cases, it's important to be able to find new types of anomalies that have never been seen before—new forms of fraud, intrusions, and failure modes for servers. Unsupervised learning techniques are useful in these cases because they can learn what input data normally looks like and therefore detect when new data is unlike past data. Such new data is not necessarily attacks or fraud; it is simply unusual and therefore worth further investigation.

We will start with the basics of the K-means clustering algorithm. This will be followed by an introduction to the KDD Cup 1999 dataset. We'll then create our first K-means model using PySpark. Then we'll go over methods for determining a good value of k—number of clusters—when implementing the K-means algorithm. Next, we'll improve our model by normalizing the input features and using previously discarded categorical features by implementing the one-hot encoding method. We will wrap up by going over the entropy metric and exploring some results from our model.

K-means Clustering

The inherent problem of anomaly detection is, as its name implies, that of finding unusual things. If we already knew what "anomalous" meant for a dataset, we could easily detect anomalies in the data with supervised learning. An algorithm would receive inputs labeled "normal" and "anomaly" and learn to distinguish the two. However, the nature of anomalies is that they are unknown unknowns. Put another way, an anomaly that has been observed and understood is no longer an anomaly.

Clustering is the best-known type of unsupervised learning. Clustering algorithms try to find natural groupings in data. Data points that are like one another but unlike others are likely to represent a meaningful grouping, so clustering algorithms try to put such data into the same cluster.

K-means clustering may be the most widely used clustering algorithm. It attempts to detect k clusters in a dataset, where k is given by the data scientist. k is a hyperparameter of the model, and the right value will depend on the dataset. In fact, choosing a good value for k will be a central plot point in this chapter.

What does "like" mean when the dataset contains information such as customer activity? Or transactions? K-means requires a notion of distance between data points. It is common to use simple Euclidean distance to measure distance between data points with K-means, and as it happens, this is one of two distance functions supported by Spark MLlib as of this writing, the other one being Cosine. The Euclidean distance is defined for data points whose features are all numeric. "Like" points are those whose intervening distance is small.

To K-means, a cluster is simply a point: the center of all the points that make up the cluster. These are, in fact, just feature vectors containing all numeric features and can be called vectors. However, it may be more intuitive to think of them as points here, because they are treated as points in a Euclidean space.

This center is called the cluster *centroid* and is the arithmetic mean of the points—hence the name K-*means*. To start, the algorithm picks some data points as the initial cluster centroids. Then each data point is assigned to the nearest centroid. Then for each cluster, a new cluster centroid is computed as the mean of the data points just assigned to that cluster. This process is repeated.

We will now look at a use case that depicts how K-means clustering can help us identify potentially anomalous activity in a network.

Identifying Anomalous Network Traffic

Cyberattacks are increasingly visible in the news. Some attacks attempt to flood a computer with network traffic to crowd out legitimate traffic. But in other cases, attacks attempt to exploit flaws in networking software to gain unauthorized access to a computer. While it's quite obvious when a computer is being bombarded with traffic, detecting an exploit can be like searching for a needle in an incredibly large haystack of network requests.

Some exploit behaviors follow known patterns. For example, accessing every port on a machine in rapid succession is not something any normal software program should ever need to do. However, it is a typical first step for an attacker looking for services running on the computer that may be exploitable.

If you were to count the number of distinct ports accessed by a remote host in a short time, you would have a feature that probably predicts a port-scanning attack quite well. A handful is probably normal; hundreds indicate an attack. The same goes for detecting other types of attacks from other features of network connections—number of bytes sent and received, TCP errors, and so forth.

But what about those unknown unknowns? The biggest threat may be the one that has never yet been detected and classified. Part of detecting potential network intrusions is detecting anomalies. These are connections that aren't known to be attacks but do not resemble connections that have been observed in the past.

Here, unsupervised learning techniques like K-means can be used to detect anomalous network connections. K-means can cluster connections based on statistics about each of them. The resulting clusters themselves aren't interesting per se, but they collectively define types of connections that are like past connections. Anything not close to a cluster could be anomalous. Clusters are interesting insofar as they define regions of normal connections; everything else is unusual and potentially anomalous.

KDD Cup 1999 Dataset

The KDD Cup (*https://oreil.ly/UtYd9*) was an annual data mining competition organized by a special interest group of the Association for Computing Machinery (ACM). Each year, a machine learning problem was posed, along with a dataset, and researchers were invited to submit a paper detailing their best solution to the problem. In 1999, the topic was network intrusion, and the dataset is still available (*https://oreil.ly/ezBDa*) at the KDD website. We will need to download the *kddcupdata.data.gz* and *kddcup.info* files from the website. The remainder of this chapter will walk through building a system to detect anomalous network traffic using Spark, by learning from this data.

 Don't use this dataset to build a real network intrusion system! The data did not necessarily reflect real network traffic at the time—even if it did, it reflects traffic patterns from more than 20 years ago.

Fortunately, the organizers had already processed raw network packet data into summary information about individual network connections. The dataset is about 708 MB in size and contains about 4.9 million connections. This is large, if not massive, and is certainly sufficient for our purposes here. For each connection, the dataset contains information such as the number of bytes sent, login attempts, TCP errors, and so on. Each connection is one line of CSV-formatted data, containing 38 features. Feature information and ordering can be found in the *kddcup.info* file.

Unzip the *kddcup.data.gz* data file and copy it into your storage. This example, like others, will assume the file is available at *data/kddcup.data*. Let's see the data in its raw form:

```
head -n 1 data/kddcup.data

...

0,tcp,http,SF,215,45076,0,0,0,0,0,1,0,0,0,0,0,0,0,0,0,0,1,1,...
```

This connection, for example, was a TCP connection to an HTTP service—215 bytes were sent, and 45,706 bytes were received. The user was logged in, and so on.

Many features are counts, like num_file_creations in the 17th column, as listed in the *kddcup.info* file. Many features take on the value 0 or 1, indicating the presence or absence of a behavior, like su_attempted in the 15th column. They look like the one-hot encoded categorical features from Chapter 4, but are not grouped and related in the same way. Each is like a yes/no feature, and is therefore arguably a categorical feature. It is not always valid to translate categorical features as numbers and treat them as if they had an ordering. However, in the special case of a binary categorical feature, in most machine learning algorithms, mapping these to a numeric feature taking on values 0 and 1 will work well.

The rest are ratios like dst_host_srv_rerror_rate in the next-to-last column and take on values from 0.0 to 1.0, inclusive.

Interestingly, a label is given in the last field. Most connections are labeled normal., but some have been identified as examples of various types of network attacks. These would be useful in learning to distinguish a known attack from a normal connection, but the problem here is anomaly detection and finding potentially new and unknown attacks. This label will be mostly set aside for our purposes.

A First Take on Clustering

Open the pyspark-shell, and load the CSV data as a dataframe. It's a CSV file again, but without header information. It's necessary to supply column names as given in the accompanying *kddcup.info* file.

```
data_without_header = spark.read.option("inferSchema", True).\
                            option("header", False).\
                            csv("data/kddcup.data")

column_names = [  "duration", "protocol_type", "service", "flag",
  "src_bytes", "dst_bytes", "land", "wrong_fragment", "urgent",
  "hot", "num_failed_logins", "logged_in", "num_compromised",
  "root_shell", "su_attempted", "num_root", "num_file_creations",
  "num_shells", "num_access_files", "num_outbound_cmds",
  "is_host_login", "is_guest_login", "count", "srv_count",
  "serror_rate", "srv_serror_rate", "rerror_rate", "srv_rerror_rate",
  "same_srv_rate", "diff_srv_rate", "srv_diff_host_rate",
  "dst_host_count", "dst_host_srv_count",
  "dst_host_same_srv_rate", "dst_host_diff_srv_rate",
  "dst_host_same_src_port_rate", "dst_host_srv_diff_host_rate",
  "dst_host_serror_rate", "dst_host_srv_serror_rate",
  "dst_host_rerror_rate", "dst_host_srv_rerror_rate",
  "label"]

data = data_without_header.toDF(*column_names)
```

Begin by exploring the dataset. What labels are present in the data, and how many are there of each? The following code simply counts by label and prints the results in descending order by count:

```
from pyspark.sql.functions import col
data.select("label").groupBy("label").count().\
    orderBy(col("count").desc()).show(25)

...
+----------------+-------+
|           label|  count|
```

```
+-----------------+-------+
|          smurf.|2807886|
|        neptune.|1072017|
|         normal.| 972781|
|          satan.|  15892|
...
|            phf.|      4|
|           perl.|      3|
|            spy.|      2|
+-----------------+-------+
```

There are 23 distinct labels, and the most frequent are smurf. and neptune. attacks.

Note that the data contains nonnumeric features. For example, the second column may be tcp, udp, or icmp, but K-means clustering requires numeric features. The final label column is also nonnumeric. To begin, these will simply be ignored.

Aside from this, creating a K-means clustering of the data follows the same pattern as was seen in Chapter 4. A VectorAssembler creates a feature vector, a KMeans implementation creates a model from the feature vectors, and a Pipeline stitches it all together. From the resulting model, it's possible to extract and examine the cluster centers.

```python
from pyspark.ml.feature import VectorAssembler
from pyspark.ml.clustering import KMeans, KMeansModel
from pyspark.ml import Pipeline

numeric_only = data.drop("protocol_type", "service", "flag").cache()

assembler = VectorAssembler().setInputCols(numeric_only.columns[:-1]).\
                              setOutputCol("featureVector")

kmeans = KMeans().setPredictionCol("cluster").setFeaturesCol("featureVector")

pipeline = Pipeline().setStages([assembler, kmeans])
pipeline_model = pipeline.fit(numeric_only)
kmeans_model = pipeline_model.stages[1]

from pprint import pprint
pprint(kmeans_model.clusterCenters())

...
[array([4.83401949e+01, 1.83462155e+03, 8.26203190e+02, 5.71611720e-06,
        6.48779303e-04, 7.96173468e-06...]),
 array([1.0999000e+04, 0.0000000e+00, 1.3099374e+09, 0.0000000e+00,
        0.0000000e+00, 0.0000000e+00,...])]
```

It's not easy to interpret the numbers intuitively, but each of these represents the center (also known as centroid) of one of the clusters that the model produced. The values are the coordinates of the centroid in terms of each of the numeric input features.

Two vectors are printed, meaning K-means was fitting $k=2$ clusters to the data. For a complex dataset that is known to exhibit at least 23 distinct types of connections, this is almost certainly not enough to accurately model the distinct groupings within the data.

This is a good opportunity to use the given labels to get an intuitive sense of what went into these two clusters by counting the labels within each cluster.

```
with_cluster = pipeline_model.transform(numeric_only)

with_cluster.select("cluster", "label").groupBy("cluster", "label").count().\
        orderBy(col("cluster"), col("count").desc()).show(25)
```

```
...
+-------+----------------+-------+
|cluster|           label|  count|
+-------+----------------+-------+
|      0|          smurf.|2807886|
|      0|        neptune.|1072017|
|      0|         normal.| 972781|
|      0|          satan.|  15892|
|      0|         ipsweep.|  12481|
...
|      0|            phf.|      4|
|      0|           perl.|      3|
|      0|            spy.|      2|
|      1|      portsweep.|      1|
+-------+----------------+-------+
```

The result shows that the clustering was not at all helpful. Only one data point ended up in cluster 1!

Choosing k

Two clusters are plainly insufficient. How many clusters are appropriate for this dataset? It's clear that there are 23 distinct patterns in the data, so it seems that k could be at least 23, or likely even more. Typically, many values of k are tried to find the best one. But what is "best"?

A clustering could be considered good if each data point were near its closest centroid, where "near" is defined by the Euclidean distance. This is a simple, common way to evaluate the quality of a clustering, by the mean of these distances over all points, or sometimes, the mean of the distances squared. In fact, KMeansModel offers a ClusteringEvaluator method that computes the sum of squared distances and can easily be used to compute the mean squared distance.

It's simple enough to manually evaluate the clustering cost for several values of *k*. Note that this code could take 10 minutes or more to run:

```python
from pyspark.sql import DataFrame
from pyspark.ml.evaluation import ClusteringEvaluator

from random import randint

def clustering_score(input_data, k):
    input_numeric_only = input_data.drop("protocol_type", "service", "flag")
    assembler = VectorAssembler().setInputCols(input_numeric_only.columns[:-1]).\
                            setOutputCol("featureVector")
    kmeans = KMeans().setSeed(randint(100,100000)).setK(k).\
                    setPredictionCol("cluster").\
                    setFeaturesCol("featureVector")
    pipeline = Pipeline().setStages([assembler, kmeans])
    pipeline_model = pipeline.fit(input_numeric_only)

    evaluator = ClusteringEvaluator(predictionCol='cluster',
                                featuresCol="featureVector")
    predictions = pipeline_model.transform(numeric_only)
    score = evaluator.evaluate(predictions)
    return score

for k in list(range(20,100, 20)):
    print(clustering_score(numeric_only, k)) ❶

...
(20,6.649218115128446E7)
(40,2.5031424366033625E7)
(60,1.027261913057096E7)
(80,1.2514131711109027E7)
(100,7235531.565096531)
```

❶ Scores will be shown here using scientific notation.

The printed result shows that the score decreases as *k* increases. Note that scores are shown in scientific notation; the first value is over 10^7, not just a bit over 6.

> Again, your values will be somewhat different. The clustering depends on a randomly chosen initial set of centroids.

However, this much is obvious. As more clusters are added, it should always be possible to put data points closer to the nearest centroid. In fact, if *k* is chosen to equal the number of data points, the average distance will be 0 because every point will be its own cluster of one!

Worse, in the preceding results, the distance for $k=80$ is higher than for $k=60$. This shouldn't happen because a higher k always permits at least as good a clustering as a lower k. The problem is that K-means is not necessarily able to find the optimal clustering for a given k. Its iterative process can converge from a random starting point to a local minimum, which may be good but is not optimal.

This is still true even when more intelligent methods are used to choose initial centroids. K-means++ and K-means|| (*https://oreil.ly/zes8d*) are variants of selection algorithms that are more likely to choose diverse, separated centroids and lead more reliably to good clustering. Spark MLlib, in fact, implements K-means||. However, all still have an element of randomness in selection and can't guarantee an optimal clustering.

The random starting set of clusters chosen for $k=80$ perhaps led to a particularly suboptimal clustering, or it may have stopped early before it reached its local optimum.

We can improve it by running the iteration longer. The algorithm has a threshold via setTol that controls the minimum amount of cluster centroid movement considered significant; lower values mean the K-means algorithm will let the centroids continue to move longer. Increasing the maximum number of iterations with setMaxIter also prevents it from potentially stopping too early at the cost of possibly more computation.

```
def clustering_score_1(input_data, k):
    input_numeric_only = input_data.drop("protocol_type", "service", "flag")
    assembler = VectorAssembler().\
                setInputCols(input_numeric_only.columns[:-1]).\
                setOutputCol("featureVector")
    kmeans = KMeans().setSeed(randint(100,100000)).setK(k).setMaxIter(40).\ ❶
        setTol(1.0e-5).\ ❷
        setPredictionCol("cluster").setFeaturesCol("featureVector")
    pipeline = Pipeline().setStages([assembler, kmeans])
    pipeline_model = pipeline.fit(input_numeric_only)
    #
    evaluator = ClusteringEvaluator(predictionCol='cluster',
                                    featuresCol="featureVector")
    predictions = pipeline_model.transform(numeric_only)
    score = evaluator.evaluate(predictions)
    #
    return score


for k in list(range(20,101, 20)):
    print(k, clustering_score_1(numeric_only, k))
```

❶ Increase from default 20.

❷ Decrease from default 1.0e-4.

This time, at least the scores decrease consistently:

```
(20,1.8041795813813403E8)
(40,6.33056876207124E7)
(60,9474961.544965891)
(80,9388117.93747141)
(100,8783628.926311461)
```

We want to find a point past which increasing k stops reducing the score much—or an "elbow" in a graph of k versus score, which is generally decreasing but eventually flattens out. Here, it seems to be decreasing notably past 100. The right value of k may be past 100.

Visualization with SparkR

At this point, it could be useful to step back and understand more about the data before clustering again. In particular, looking at a plot of the data points could be helpful.

Spark itself has no tools for visualization, but the popular open source statistical environment R (*https://www.r-project.org*) has libraries for both data exploration and data visualization. Furthermore, Spark also provides some basic integration with R via SparkR (*https://oreil.ly/XX0Q9*). This brief section will demonstrate using R and SparkR to cluster the data and explore the clustering.

SparkR is a variant of the `spark-shell` used throughout this book and is invoked with the command `sparkR`. It runs a local R interpreter, like `spark-shell` runs a variant of the Scala shell as a local process. The machine that runs `sparkR` needs a local installation of R, which is not included with Spark. This can be installed, for example, with `sudo apt-get install r-base` on Linux distributions like Ubuntu, or `brew install R` with Homebrew (*http://brew.sh*) on macOS.

SparkR is a command-line shell environment, like R. To view visualizations, it's necessary to run these commands within an IDE-like environment that can display images. RStudio (*https://www.rstudio.com*) is an IDE for R (and works with SparkR); it runs on a desktop operating system so it will be usable here only if you are experimenting with Spark locally rather than on a cluster.

If you are running Spark locally, download (*https://oreil.ly/JZGQm*) the free version of RStudio and install it. If not, then most of the rest of this example can still be run with `sparkR` on a command line—for example, on a cluster—though it won't be possible to display visualizations this way.

If you're running via RStudio, launch the IDE and configure `SPARK_HOME` and `JAVA_HOME`, if your local environment does not already set them, to point to the Spark and JDK installation directories, respectively:

```
Sys.setenv(SPARK_HOME = "/path/to/spark") ❶
Sys.setenv(JAVA_HOME = "/path/to/java")
library(SparkR, lib.loc = c(file.path(Sys.getenv("SPARK_HOME"), "R", "lib")))
sparkR.session(master = "local[*]",
  sparkConfig = list(spark.driver.memory = "4g"))
```

❶   Replace with actual paths, of course.

Note that these steps aren't needed if you are running sparkR on the command line. Instead, it accepts command-line configuration parameters such as `--driver-memory`, just like `spark-shell`.

SparkR is an R-language wrapper around the same DataFrame and MLlib APIs that have been demonstrated in this chapter. It's therefore possible to re-create a K-means simple clustering of the data:

```
clusters_data <- read.df("/path/to/kddcup.data", "csv", ❶
                         inferSchema = "true", header = "false")
colnames(clusters_data) <- c( ❷
  "duration", "protocol_type", "service", "flag",
  "src_bytes", "dst_bytes", "land", "wrong_fragment", "urgent",
  "hot", "num_failed_logins", "logged_in", "num_compromised",
  "root_shell", "su_attempted", "num_root", "num_file_creations",
  "num_shells", "num_access_files", "num_outbound_cmds",
  "is_host_login", "is_guest_login", "count", "srv_count",
  "serror_rate", "srv_serror_rate", "rerror_rate", "srv_rerror_rate",
  "same_srv_rate", "diff_srv_rate", "srv_diff_host_rate",
  "dst_host_count", "dst_host_srv_count",
  "dst_host_same_srv_rate", "dst_host_diff_srv_rate",
  "dst_host_same_src_port_rate", "dst_host_srv_diff_host_rate",
  "dst_host_serror_rate", "dst_host_srv_serror_rate",
  "dst_host_rerror_rate", "dst_host_srv_rerror_rate",
  "label")

numeric_only <- cache(drop(clusters_data, ❸
                      c("protocol_type", "service", "flag", "label")))

kmeans_model <- spark.kmeans(numeric_only, ~ ., ❹
                             k = 100, maxIter = 40, initMode = "k-means||")
```

❶   Replace with path to *kddcup.data*.

❷   Name columns.

❸   Drop nonnumeric columns again.

❹   ~ . means all columns.

From here, it's straightforward to assign a cluster to each data point. The operations above show usage of the SparkR APIs which naturally correspond to core Spark APIs, but are expressed as R libraries in R-like syntax. The actual clustering is executed using the same JVM-based, Scala language implementation in MLlib. These operations are effectively a *handle*, or remote control, to distributed operations that are not executing in R.

R has its own rich set of libraries for analysis and its own similar concept of a dataframe. It is sometimes useful, therefore, to pull some data down into the R interpreter to be able to use these native R libraries, which are unrelated to Spark.

Of course, R and its libraries are not distributed, and so it's not feasible to pull the whole dataset of 4,898,431 data points into R. However, it's easy to pull only a sample:

```
clustering <- predict(kmeans_model, numeric_only)
clustering_sample <- collect(sample(clustering, FALSE, 0.01))  ❶

str(clustering_sample)

...
'data.frame': 48984 obs. of  39 variables:
 $ duration        : int  0 0 0 0 0 0 0 0 0 ...
 $ src_bytes       : int  181 185 162 254 282 310 212 214 181 ...
 $ dst_bytes       : int  5450 9020 4528 849 424 1981 2917 3404 ...
 $ land            : int  0 0 0 0 0 0 0 0 0 ...
...
 $ prediction      : int  33 33 33 0 0 0 0 0 33 33 ...
```

❶ 1% sample without replacement

`clustering_sample` is actually a local R dataframe, not a Spark DataFrame, so it can be manipulated like any other data in R. Above, `str` shows the structure of the dataframe.

For example, it's possible to extract the cluster assignment and then show statistics about the distribution of assignments:

```
clusters <- clustering_sample["prediction"]  ❶
data <- data.matrix(within(clustering_sample, rm("prediction")))  ❷

table(clusters)

...
clusters
    0    11    14    18    23    25    28    30    31    33    36  ...
47294     3     1     2     2   308   105     1    27  1219    15  ...
```

❶ Only the clustering assignment column

❷ Everything but the clustering assignment

For example, this shows that most points fell into cluster 0. Although much more could be done with this data in R, further coverage of this is beyond the scope of this book.

To visualize the data, a library called `rgl` is required. It will be functional only if running this example in RStudio. First, install (once) and load the library:

```
install.packages("rgl")
library(rgl)
```

Note that R may prompt you to download other packages or compiler tools to complete installation, because installing the package means compiling its source code.

This dataset is 38-dimensional. It will have to be projected down into at most three dimensions to visualize it with a *random projection*:

```
random_projection <- matrix(data = rnorm(3*ncol(data)), ncol = 3) ❶
random_projection_norm <-
  random_projection / sqrt(rowSums(random_projection*random_projection))

projected_data <- data.frame(data %*% random_projection_norm) ❷
```

❶ Make a random 3-D projection and normalize.

❷ Project and make a new dataframe.

This creates a 3-D dataset out of a 38-D dataset by choosing three random unit vectors and projecting the data onto them. This is a simplistic, rough-and-ready form of dimension reduction. Of course, there are more sophisticated dimension reduction algorithms, like principal component analysis or the singular value decomposition. These are available in R but take much longer to run. For purposes of visualization in this example, a random projection achieves much the same result, faster.

Finally, the clustered points can be plotted in an interactive 3-D visualization:

```
num_clusters <- max(clusters)
palette <- rainbow(num_clusters)
colors = sapply(clusters, function(c) palette[c])
plot3d(projected_data, col = colors, size = 10)
```

Note that this will require running RStudio in an environment that supports the `rgl` library and graphics.

The resulting visualization in Figure 5-1 shows data points in 3-D space. Many points fall on top of one another, and the result is sparse and hard to interpret. However, the dominant feature of the visualization is its L shape. The points seem to vary along two distinct dimensions, and little in other dimensions.

This makes sense because the dataset has two features that are on a much larger scale than the others. Whereas most features have values between 0 and 1, the bytes-sent and bytes-received features vary from 0 to tens of thousands. The Euclidean distance between points is therefore almost completely determined by these two features. It's almost as if the other features don't exist! So it's important to normalize away these differences in scale to put features on near-equal footing.

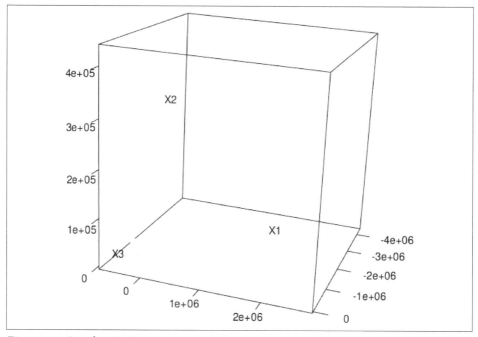

Figure 5-1. Random 3-D projection

Feature Normalization

We can normalize each feature by converting it to a standard score. This means subtracting the mean of the feature's values from each value and dividing by the standard deviation, as shown in the standard score equation:

$$normalized_i = \frac{feature_i - \mu_i}{\sigma_i}$$

In fact, subtracting means has no effect on the clustering because the subtraction effectively shifts all the data points by the same amount in the same direction. This does not affect interpoint Euclidean distances.

MLlib provides StandardScaler, a component that can perform this kind of standardization and be easily added to the clustering pipeline.

We can run the same test with normalized data on a higher range of k:

```
from pyspark.ml.feature import StandardScaler

def clustering_score_2(input_data, k):
    input_numeric_only = input_data.drop("protocol_type", "service", "flag")
    assembler = VectorAssembler().\
                setInputCols(input_numeric_only.columns[:-1]).\
                setOutputCol("featureVector")
    scaler = StandardScaler().setInputCol("featureVector").\
                setOutputCol("scaledFeatureVector").\
                setWithStd(True).setWithMean(False)
    kmeans = KMeans().setSeed(randint(100,100000)).\
                setK(k).setMaxIter(40).\
                setTol(1.0e-5).setPredictionCol("cluster").\
                setFeaturesCol("scaledFeatureVector")
    pipeline = Pipeline().setStages([assembler, scaler, kmeans])
    pipeline_model = pipeline.fit(input_numeric_only)
    #
    evaluator = ClusteringEvaluator(predictionCol='cluster',
                                featuresCol="scaledFeatureVector")
    predictions = pipeline_model.transform(numeric_only)
    score = evaluator.evaluate(predictions)
    #
    return score

for k in list(range(60, 271, 30)):
    print(k, clustering_score_2(numeric_only, k))
...
(60,1.2454250178069293)
(90,0.7767730051608682)
(120,0.5070473497003614)
(150,0.4077081720067704)
(180,0.3344486714980788)
(210,0.276237617334138)
(240,0.24571877339169032)
(270,0.21818167354866858)
```

This has helped put dimensions on more equal footing, and the absolute distances between points (and thus the cost) is much smaller in absolute terms. However, the above output doesn't yet provide an obvious value of k beyond which increasing it does little to improve the cost.

Another 3-D visualization of the normalized data points reveals a richer structure, as expected. Some points are spaced in regular, discrete intervals in one direction; these are likely projections of discrete dimensions in the data, like counts. With 100 clusters, it's hard to make out which points come from which clusters. One large cluster seems to dominate, and many clusters correspond to small, compact subregions (some of which are omitted from this zoomed detail of the entire 3-D visualization). The result, shown in Figure 5-2, does not necessarily advance the analysis but is an interesting sanity check.

Figure 5-2. Random 3-D projection, normalized

Categorical Variables

Normalization was a valuable step forward, but more can be done to improve the clustering. In particular, several features have been left out entirely because they aren't numeric. This is throwing away valuable information. Adding them back, in some form, should produce a better-informed clustering.

Earlier, three categorical features were excluded because nonnumeric features can't be used with the Euclidean distance function that K-means uses in MLlib. This is the reverse of the issue noted in "Random Forests" on page 82, where numeric features were used to represent categorical values but a categorical feature was desired.

The categorical features can be translated into several binary indicator features using one-hot encoding, which can be viewed as numeric dimensions. For example, the second column contains the protocol type: tcp, udp, or icmp. This feature could be thought of as *three* features, as if features "is TCP," "is UDP," and "is ICMP" were in the dataset. The single feature value `tcp` might become 1,0,0; udp might be 0,1,0; and so on.

Here again, MLlib provides components that implement this transformation. In fact, one-hot encoding string-valued features like `protocol_type` are actually a two-step process. First, the string values are converted to integer indices like 0, 1, 2, and so on using `StringIndexer`. Then, these integer indices are encoded into a vector with `OneHotEncoder`. These two steps can be thought of as a small `Pipeline` in themselves.

```python
from pyspark.ml.feature import OneHotEncoder, StringIndexer

def one_hot_pipeline(input_col):
    indexer = StringIndexer().setInputCol(input_col).\
                                setOutputCol(input_col + "-_indexed")
    encoder = OneHotEncoder().setInputCol(input_col + "indexed").\
                                setOutputCol(input_col + "_vec")
    pipeline = Pipeline().setStages([indexer, encoder])
    return pipeline, input_col + "_vec"  ❶
```

❶ Return pipeline and name of output vector column

This method produces a `Pipeline` that can be added as a component in the overall clustering pipeline; pipelines can be composed. All that is left is to make sure to add the new vector output columns into `VectorAssembler`'s output and proceed as before with scaling, clustering, and evaluation. The source code is omitted for brevity here, but can be found in the repository accompanying this chapter.

```
(60,39.739250062068685)
(90,15.814341529964691)
(120,3.5008631362395413)
(150,2.2151974068685547)
(180,1.587330730808905)
(210,1.3626704802348888)
(240,1.1202477806210747)
(270,0.9263659836264369)
```

These sample results suggest, possibly, $k=180$ as a value where the score flattens out a bit. At least the clustering is now using all input features.

Using Labels with Entropy

Earlier, we used the given label for each data point to create a quick sanity check of the quality of the clustering. This notion can be formalized further and used as an alternative means of evaluating clustering quality and, therefore, of choosing k.

The labels tell us something about the true nature of each data point. A good clustering, it seems, should agree with these human-applied labels. It should put together points that share a label frequently and not lump together points of many different labels. It should produce clusters with relatively homogeneous labels.

You may recall from "Random Forests" on page 82 that we have metrics for homogeneity: Gini impurity and entropy. These are functions of the proportions of labels in each cluster and produce a number that is low when the proportions are skewed toward few, or one, label. Entropy will be used here for illustration:

```python
from math import log

def entropy(counts):
    values = [c for c in counts if (c > 0)]
    n = sum(values)
    p = [v/n for v in values]
    return sum([-1*(p_v) * log(p_v) for p_v in p])
```

A good clustering would have clusters whose collections of labels are homogeneous and so have low entropy. A weighted average of entropy can therefore be used as a cluster score:

```python
from pyspark.sql import functions as fun
from pyspark.sql import Window

cluster_label = pipeline_model.\
                    transform(data).\
                    select("cluster", "label") ❶

df = cluster_label.\
        groupBy("cluster", "label").\
        count().orderBy("cluster") ❷

w = Window.partitionBy("cluster")

p_col = df['count'] / fun.sum(df['count']).over(w)
with_p_col = df.withColumn("p_col", p_col)

result = with_p_col.groupBy("cluster").\
            agg(-fun.sum(col("p_col") * fun.log2(col("p_col"))))\
                .alias("entropy"),
                fun.sum(col("count"))\
                .alias("cluster_size"))

result = result.withColumn('weightedClusterEntropy',
                    col('entropy') * col('cluster_size')) ❸

weighted_cluster_entropy_avg = result.\
                        agg(fun.sum(
                            col('weightedClusterEntropy'))).\
                        collect()
weighted_cluster_entropy_avg[0][0]/data.count()
```

❶ Predict cluster for each datum.

❷ Count labels, per cluster

❸ Average entropy weighted by cluster size.

As before, this analysis can be used to obtain some idea of a suitable value of *k*. Entropy will not necessarily decrease as *k* increases, so it is possible to look for a local minimum value. Here again, results suggest *k*=180 is a reasonable choice because its score is actually lower than 150 and 210:

```
(60,0.03475331900669869)
(90,0.051512668026335535)
(120,0.02020028911919293)
(150,0.019962563512905682)
(180,0.01110240886325257)
(210,0.01259738444250231)
(240,0.01357435960663116)
(270,0.010119881917660544)
```

Clustering in Action

Finally, with confidence, we can cluster the full, normalized dataset with *k*=180. Again, we can print the labels for each cluster to get some sense of the resulting clustering. Clusters do seem to be dominated by one type of attack each and contain only a few types:

```
pipeline_model = fit_pipeline_4(data, 180) ❶
count_by_cluster_label = pipeline_model.transform(data).\
                                select("cluster", "label").\
                                groupBy("cluster", "label").\
                                count().orderBy("cluster", "label")
count_by_cluster_label.show()

...
+-------+----------+------+
|cluster|     label| count|
+-------+----------+------+
|      0|     back.|   324|
|      0|   normal.| 42921|
|      1|  neptune.|  1039|
|      1|portsweep.|     9|
|      1|    satan.|     2|
|      2|  neptune.|365375|
|      2|portsweep.|   141|
|      3|portsweep.|     2|
|      3|    satan.| 10627|
|      4|  neptune.|  1033|
|      4|portsweep.|     6|
|      4|    satan.|     1|
...
```

❶ See accompanying source code for `fit_pipeline_4` definition.

Now we can make an actual anomaly detector. Anomaly detection amounts to measuring a new data point's distance to its nearest centroid. If this distance exceeds some threshold, it is anomalous. This threshold might be chosen to be the distance of, say, the 100th-farthest data point from among known data:

```python
import numpy as np

from pyspark.spark.ml.linalg import Vector, Vectors
from pyspark.sql.functions import udf

k_means_model = pipeline_model.stages[-1]
centroids = k_means_model.clusterCenters

clustered = pipeline_model.transform(data)

def dist_func(cluster, vec):
    return float(np.linalg.norm(centroids[cluster] - vec))
dist = udf(dist_func)

threshold = clustered.select("cluster", "scaledFeatureVector").\
    withColumn("dist_value",
        dist(col("cluster"), col("scaledFeatureVector"))).\
    orderBy(col("dist_value").desc()).take(100)
```

The final step can be to apply this threshold to all new data points as they arrive. For example, Spark Streaming can be used to apply this function to small batches of input data arriving from sources like Kafka or files in cloud storage. Data points exceeding the threshold might trigger an alert that sends an email or updates a database.

Where to Go from Here

The KMeansModel is, by itself, the essence of an anomaly detection system. The preceding code demonstrated how to apply it to data to detect anomalies. This same code could be used within Spark Streaming (*https://oreil.ly/UHHBR*) to score new data as it arrives in near real time, and perhaps trigger an alert or review.

MLlib also includes a variation called StreamingKMeans, which can update a clustering incrementally as new data arrives in a StreamingKMeansModel. We could use this to continue to learn, approximately, how new data affects the clustering, and not just to assess new data against existing clusters. It can be integrated with Spark Streaming as well. However, it has not been updated for the new DataFrame-based APIs.

This model is only a simplistic one. For example, Euclidean distance is used in this example because it is the only distance function supported by Spark MLlib at this time. In the future, it may be possible to use distance functions that can better account for the distributions of and correlations between features, such as the Mahalanobis distance (*https://oreil.ly/PKG7A*).

There are also more sophisticated cluster-quality evaluation metrics (*https://oreil.ly/9yE9P*) that could be applied (even without labels) to pick k, such as the Silhouette coefficient (*https://oreil.ly/LMN1h*). These tend to evaluate not just closeness of points within one cluster, but closeness of points to other clusters. Finally, different models could be applied instead of simple K-means clustering; for example, a Gaussian mixture model (*https://oreil.ly/KTgD6*) or DBSCAN (*https://oreil.ly/xlshs*) could capture more subtle relationships between data points and the cluster centers. Spark MLlib already implements Gaussian mixture models (*https://oreil.ly/LG84u*); implementations of others may become available in Spark MLlib or other Spark-based libraries in the future.

Of course, clustering isn't just for anomaly detection. In fact, it's more often associated with use cases where the actual clusters matter! For example, clustering can also be used to group customers according to their behaviors, preferences, and attributes. Each cluster, by itself, might represent a usefully distinguishable type of customer. This is a more data-driven way to segment customers rather than leaning on arbitrary, generic divisions like "age 20–34" and "female."

## CHAPTER 6

Understanding Wikipedia with LDA and Spark NLP

With the growing amount of unstructured text data in recent years, it has become difficult to obtain the relevant and desired information. Language technology provides powerful methods that can be used to mine through text data and fetch the information that we are looking for. In this chapter, we will use PySpark and the Spark NLP (natural language processing) library to use one such technique—topic modeling. Specifically, we will use the latent Dirichlet algorithm (LDA) to understand a dataset of Wikipedia documents.

Topic modeling, one of the most common tasks in natural language processing, is a statistical approach for data modeling that helps in discovering underlying topics that are present in a collection of documents. Extracting topic distribution from millions of documents can be useful in many ways—for example, identifying the reasons for complaints about a particular product or all products, or identifying topics in news articles. The most popular algorithm for topic modeling is LDA. It is a generative model that assumes that documents are represented by a distribution of topics. Topics, in turn, are represented by a distribution of words. PySpark MLlib offers an optimized version of LDA that is specifically designed to work in a distributed environment. We will build a simple topic modeling pipeline using Spark NLP for preprocessing the data and Spark MLlib's LDA to extract topics from the data.

In this chapter, we'll embark upon the modest task of distilling the human knowledge based on latent (hidden) topics and relationships. We'll apply LDA to a corpus consisting of the articles contained in Wikipedia. We will start by understanding the basics of LDA and go over its implementation in PySpark. Then we'll download the dataset and set up our programming environment by installing Spark NLP. This will be followed by data preprocessing. You will witness the power of Spark NLP library's out-of-the-box methods, which make NLP tasks significantly easier.

Then we will score the terms in our documents using the TF-IDF (term frequency-inverse document frequency) technique and feed the resulting output into our LDA model. To finish up, we'll go through the topics assigned by our model to the input documents. We should be able to understand which bucket an entry belongs in without the need to read it. Let's begin by going over the fundamentals of LDA.

Latent Dirichlet Allocation

The idea behind latent Dirichlet allocation is that documents are generated based on a set of topics. In this process, we assume that each document is distributed over the topics, and each topic is distributed over a set of terms. Each document and each word are generated from sampling these distributions. The LDA learner works backward and tries to identify the distributions where the observed is most probable.

It attempts to distill the corpus into a set of relevant *topics*. Each topic captures a thread of variation in the data and often corresponds to one of the ideas that the corpus discusses. A document can be a part of multiple topics. You can think of LDA as providing a way to *soft cluster* the documents, too. Without delving into the mathematics, an LDA topic model describes two primary attributes: a chance of selecting a topic when sampling a particular document, and a chance of selecting a particular term when selecting a topic. For example, LDA might discover a topic with strong association with the terms "Asimov" and "robot," and with the documents "foundation series" and "science fiction." By selecting only the most important concepts, LDA can throw away some irrelevant noise and merge co-occurring strands to come up with a simpler representation of the data.

We can employ this technique in a variety of tasks. For example, it can help us recommend similar Wikipedia entries when provided with an input entry. By encapsulating the patterns of variance in the corpus, it can base scores on a deeper understanding than simply on counting occurrences and co-occurrences of words. Up next, let's have a look at PySpark's LDA implementation.

LDA in PySpark

PySpark MLlib offers an LDA implementation as one of its clustering algorithms. Here's some example code:

```
from pyspark.ml.linalg import Vectors
from pyspark.ml.clustering import LDA

df = spark.createDataFrame([[1, Vectors.dense([0.0, 1.0])],
    [2, Vectors.dense([2.0, 3.0])],],
    ["id", "features"])
```

```
lda = LDA(k=2, seed=1) ❶
lda.setMaxIter(10)

model = lda.fit(df)

model.vocabSize()
2

model.describeTopics().show() ❷
+-----+-----------+--------------------+
|topic|termIndices|         termWeights|
+-----+-----------+--------------------+
|    0|     [0, 1]|[0.53331100994293...|
|    1|     [1, 0]|[0.50230220117597...|
+-----+-----------+--------------------+
```

❶ We apply LDA to our dataframe with the number of topics (k) set to 2.

❷ Dataframe describing the probability weight associated with each term in our topics.

We will explore PySpark's LDA implementation and associated parameters when applying it to the Wikipedia dataset. First, though, we need to download the relevant dataset. That's what we will do next.

Getting the Data

Wikipedia makes dumps of all its articles available. The full dump comes in a single, large XML file. These can be downloaded (*https://oreil.ly/DhGlJ*) and then placed on a cloud storage solution (such as AWS S3 or GCS, Google Cloud Storage) or HDFS. For example:

```
$ curl -s -L https://dumps.wikimedia.org/enwiki/latest/\
$ enwiki-latest-pages-articles-multistream.xml.bz2 \
$   | bzip2 -cd \
$   | hadoop fs -put - wikidump.xml
```

This can take a little while.

Chugging through this volume of data makes the most sense with a cluster of a few nodes to work with. To run this chapter's code on a local machine, a better option is to generate a smaller dump using Wikipedia's export pages (*https://oreil.ly/Rrpmr*). Try getting all the pages from multiple categories that have many pages and few subcategories, such as biology, health, and geometry. For the following code to work, download the dump into the *ch06-LDA/* directory and rename it to *wikidump.xml*.

We need to convert the Wikipedia XML dump into a format that we can easily work with in PySpark. When working on our local machine, we can use the convenient

WikiExtractor tool (*https://oreil.ly/pfwrE*) for this. It extracts and cleans text from Wikipedia database dumps such as what we have.

Install it using pip:

```
$ pip3 install wikiextractor
```

Then it's as simple as running the following command in the directory containing the downloaded file:

```
$ wikiextractor wikidump.xml
```

The output is stored in a single or several files of similar size in a given directory named text. Each file will contains several documents in the following format:

```
$ mv text wikidump ❶
$ tree wikidump
...
wikidump
└── AA
    └── wiki_00

...
$ head -n 5 wikidump/AA/wiki_00
...

<doc id="18831" url="?curid=18831" title="Mathematics">
Mathematics

Mathematics (from Greek: ) includes the study of such topics as numbers ...
...
```

❶ Rename text directory to wikidump

Next, let's get familiar with the Spark NLP library before we start working on the data.

Spark NLP

The Spark NLP library was originally designed by John Snow Labs (*https://oreil.ly/E9KVt*) in early 2017 as an annotation library native to Spark to take full advantage of Spark SQL and MLlib modules. The inspiration came from trying to use Spark to distribute other NLP libraries, which were generally not implemented with concurrency or distributed computing in mind.

Spark NLP has the same concepts as any other annotation library but differs in how it stores annotations. Most annotation libraries store the annotations in the document object, but Spark NLP creates columns for the different types of annotations. The annotators are implemented as transformers, estimators, and models. We will look at these in the next section when applying them to our dataset for preprocessing. Before that, let's download and set up Spark NLP on our system.

Setting Up Your Environment

Install Spark NLP via pip:

```
pip3 install spark-nlp==3.2.3
```

Start the PySpark shell:

```
pyspark --packages com.johnsnowlabs.nlp:spark-nlp_2.12:3.4.4
```

Let's import Spark NLP in our PySpark shell:

```
import sparknlp

spark = sparknlp.start()
```

Now, you can import the relevant Spark NLP modules that we'll use:

```
from sparknlp.base import DocumentAssembler, Finisher
from sparknlp.annotator import (Lemmatizer, Stemmer,
                                Tokenizer, Normalizer,
                                StopWordsCleaner)
from sparknlp.pretrained import PretrainedPipeline
```

Now that we have set up our programming environment, let's start working on our dataset. We'll start by parsing the data as a PySpark DataFrame.

Parsing the Data

The output from WikiExtractor can create multiple directories depending on the size of the input dump. We want to import all the data as a single DataFrame. Let's start by specifying the input directory:

```
data_source = 'wikidump/*/*'
```

We import the data using the `wholeTextFiles` method accessible through `sparkCon text`. This method reads the data in as an RDD. We convert it into a DataFrame since that's what we want:

```
raw_data = spark.sparkContext.wholeTextFiles(data_source).toDF()
raw_data.show(1, vertical=True)
...

-RECORD 0------------------
 _1 | file:/home/analyt...
 _2 | <doc id="18831" u...
```

The resulting DataFrame will consist of two columns. The number of records will correspond to the number of files that were read. The first column consists of the filepath and the second contains the corresponding text content. The text contains multiple entries, but we want each row to correspond to a single entry. Based on the entry structure that we had seen earlier, we can separate entries using a couple of PySpark utilities: `split` and `explode`.

```
from pyspark.sql import functions as fun
df = raw_data.withColumn('content', fun.explode(fun.split(fun.col("_2"),
  "</doc>")))
df = df.drop(fun.col('_2')).drop(fun.col('_1'))

df.show(4, vertical=True)
...
-RECORD 0----------------------
 content | <doc id="18831" u...
-RECORD 1----------------------
 content |
<doc id="5627588...
-RECORD 2----------------------
 content |
<doc id="3354393...
-RECORD 3----------------------
 content |
<doc id="5999808...
only showing top 4 rows
```

The `split` function is used to split the DataFrame string `Column` into an array based on matches of a provided pattern. In the previous code, we split the combined document XML string into an array based on the *</doc>* string. This effectively gives us an array of multiple documents. Then, we use `explode` to create new rows for each element in the array returned by the `split` function. This results in rows being created corresponding to each document.

Go through the structure obtained in the `content` column by our previous operation:

```
df.show(1, truncate=False, vertical=True)
...
-RECORD 0

-----------------------------------------------------------------
 content | <doc id="18831" url="?curid=18831" title="Mathematics">
Mathematics

Mathematics (from Greek: ) includes the study of such topics as numbers...
```

We can further split our `content` column by extracting the entries' titles:

```
df = df.withColumn('title', fun.split(fun.col('content'), '\n').getItem(2)) \
       .withColumn('content', fun.split(fun.col('content'), '\n').getItem(4))
df.show(4, vertical=True)
...
-RECORD 0---------------------
 content | In mathematics, a...
 title   | Tertiary ideal
-RECORD 1---------------------
 content | In algebra, a bin...
 title   | Binomial (polynom...
-RECORD 2---------------------
 content | Algebra (from ) i...
 title   | Algebra
-RECORD 3---------------------
 content | In set theory, th...
 title   | Kernel (set theory)
only showing top 4 rows
...
```

Now that we have our parsed dataset, let's move on to preprocessing using Spark NLP.

Preparing the Data Using Spark NLP

We had earlier mentioned that a library based on the document-annotator model such as Spark NLP has the concept of "documents." There does not exist such a concept natively in PySpark. Hence, one of Spark NLP's core design tenets is strong interoperability with MLlib. This is done by providing DataFrame-compatible transformers that convert text columns into documents and convert annotations into PySpark data types.

We start by creating our document column using `DocumentAssembler`:

```
document_assembler = DocumentAssembler() \
    .setInputCol("content") \
    .setOutputCol("document") \
    .setCleanupMode("shrink")

document_assembler.transform(df).select('document').limit(1).collect()
...

Row(document=[Row(annotatorType='document', begin=0, end=289, result='...',
    metadata={'sentence': '0'}, embeddings=[])])
```

> We could have utilized Spark NLP's `DocumentNormalizer` (*https://oreil.ly/UL1vp*) annotator in the parsing section.

We can transform the input dataframe directly as we have done in the previous code. However, we will instead use `DocumentAssembler` and other required annotators as part of an ML pipeline.

We will use the following annotators as part of our preprocessing pipeline: `Tokenizer`, `Normalizer`, `StopWordsCleaner`, and `Stemmer`.

Let's start with the `Tokenizer`:

```
# Split sentence to tokens(array)
tokenizer = Tokenizer() \
    .setInputCols(["document"]) \
    .setOutputCol("token")
```

The `Tokenizer` is a fundamental annotator. Almost all text-based data processing begins with some form of tokenization, which is the process of breaking raw text into small chunks. Tokens can be words, characters, or subwords (n-grams). Most classical NLP algorithms expect tokens as the basic input. Many deep learning algorithms are being developed that take characters as basic input. Most NLP applications still use tokenization.

Next up is the `Normalizer`:

```
# clean unwanted characters and garbage
normalizer = Normalizer() \
    .setInputCols(["token"]) \
    .setOutputCol("normalized") \
    .setLowercase(True)
```

The `Normalizer` cleans out tokens from the previous step and removes all unwanted characters from the text.

Next up is the `StopWordsCleaner`:

```
# remove stopwords
stopwords_cleaner = StopWordsCleaner()\
        .setInputCols("normalized")\
        .setOutputCol("cleanTokens")\
        .setCaseSensitive(False)
```

This annotator removes *stop words* from text. Stop words such as "the," "is," and "at," which are so common that they can be removed without significantly altering the meaning of a text. Removing stop words is useful when one wants to deal with only the most semantically important words in a text and ignore words that are rarely semantically relevant, such as articles and prepositions.

Last up is the `Stemmer`:

```
# stem the words to bring them to the root form.
stemmer = Stemmer() \
        .setInputCols(["cleanTokens"]) \
        .setOutputCol("stem")
```

`Stemmer` returns hard stems out of words with the objective of retrieving the meaningful part of the word. *Stemming* is the process of reducing a word to its root word stem with the objective of retrieving the meaningful part. For example, "picking," "picked," and "picks" all have "pick" as the root.

We are almost done. Before we can complete our NLP pipeline, we need to add the `Finisher`. Spark NLP adds its own structure when we convert each row in the dataframe to a document. `Finisher` is critical because it helps us to bring back the expected structure, an array of tokens:

```
finisher = Finisher() \
        .setInputCols(["stem"]) \
        .setOutputCols(["tokens"]) \
        .setOutputAsArray(True) \
        .setCleanAnnotations(False)
```

Now we have all the required pieces in place. Let's build our pipeline so that each phase can be executed in sequence:

```
from pyspark.ml import Pipeline
nlp_pipeline = Pipeline(
    stages=[document_assembler,
            tokenizer,
            normalizer,
            stopwords_cleaner,
            stemmer,
            finisher])
```

Execute the pipeline and transform the dataframe:

```
nlp_model = nlp_pipeline.fit(df) ❶

processed_df  = nlp_model.transform(df) ❷

processed_df.printSchema()
...

root
 |-- content: string (nullable = true)
 |-- title: string (nullable = true)
 |-- document: array (nullable = true)
 |    |-- element: struct (containsNull = true)
 |    |    |-- annotatorType: string (nullable = true)
 |    |    |-- begin: integer (nullable = false)
 |    |    |-- end: integer (nullable = false)
 |    |    |-- result: string (nullable = true)
 |    |    |-- metadata: map (nullable = true)
 |    |    |    |-- key: string
 |    |    |    |-- value: string (valueContainsNull = true)
 |    |    |-- embeddings: array (nullable = true)
 |    |    |    |-- element: float (containsNull = false)
 |-- token: array (nullable = true)
 |    |-- element: struct (containsNull = true)
 |    |    |-- annotatorType: string (nullable = true)
 |    |    |-- begin: integer (nullable = false)
 |    |    |-- end: integer (nullable = false)
 |    |    |-- result: string (nullable = true)
 |    |    |-- metadata: map (nullable = true)
 |    |    |    |-- key: string
 |    |    |    |-- value: string (valueContainsNull = true)
 |    |    |-- embeddings: array (nullable = true)
 |    |    |    |-- element: float (containsNull = false)
 |-- normalized: array (nullable = true)
 |    |-- element: struct (containsNull = true)
 |    |    |-- annotatorType: string (nullable = true)
 |    |    |-- begin: integer (nullable = false)
 |    |    |-- end: integer (nullable = false)
 |    |    |-- result: string (nullable = true)
 |    |    |-- metadata: map (nullable = true)
 |    |    |    |-- key: string
 |    |    |    |-- value: string (valueContainsNull = true)
 |    |    |-- embeddings: array (nullable = true)
 |    |    |    |-- element: float (containsNull = false)
 |-- cleanTokens: array (nullable = true)
 |    |-- element: struct (containsNull = true)
 |    |    |-- annotatorType: string (nullable = true)
 |    |    |-- begin: integer (nullable = false)
 |    |    |-- end: integer (nullable = false)
 |    |    |-- result: string (nullable = true)
 |    |    |-- metadata: map (nullable = true)
```

```
|    |    |    |-- key: string
|    |    |    |-- value: string (valueContainsNull = true)
|    |    |-- embeddings: array (nullable = true)
|    |    |    |-- element: float (containsNull = false)
|-- stem: array (nullable = true)
|    |-- element: struct (containsNull = true)
|    |    |-- annotatorType: string (nullable = true)
|    |    |-- begin: integer (nullable = false)
|    |    |-- end: integer (nullable = false)
|    |    |-- result: string (nullable = true)
|    |    |-- metadata: map (nullable = true)
|    |    |    |-- key: string
|    |    |    |-- value: string (valueContainsNull = true)
|    |    |-- embeddings: array (nullable = true)
|    |    |    |-- element: float (containsNull = false)
|-- tokens: array (nullable = true)
|    |-- element: string (containsNull = true)
```

❶ Train the pipeline.

❷ Apply the pipeline to transform the dataframe.

The NLP pipeline created intermediary columns that we do not need. Let's remove the redundant columns:

```
tokens_df = processed_df.select('title','tokens')
tokens_df.show(2, vertical=True)
...

-RECORD 0---------------------
 title  | Tertiary ideal
 tokens | [mathemat, tertia...
-RECORD 1---------------------
 title  | Binomial (polynom...
 tokens | [algebra, binomi,...
only showing top 2 rows
```

Next, we will understand the basics of TF-IDF and implement it on the preprocessed dataset, token_df, that we have obtained before building an LDA model.

TF-IDF

Before applying LDA, we need to convert our data into a numeric representation. We will obtain such a representation using the term frequency-inverse document frequency method. Loosely, TF-IDF is used to determine the importance of terms corresponding to given documents. Here's a representation in Python code of the formula. We won't actually end up using this code because PySpark provides its own implementation.

```
import math

def term_doc_weight(term_frequency_in_doc, total_terms_in_doc,
                    term_freq_in_corpus, total_docs):
    tf = term_frequency_in_doc / total_terms_in_doc
    doc_freq = total_docs / term_freq_in_corpus
    idf = math.log(doc_freq)
    tf * idf
}
```

TF-IDF captures two intuitions about the relevance of a term to a document. First, we would expect that the more often a term occurs in a document, the more important it is to that document. Second, not all terms are equal in a global sense. It is more meaningful to encounter a word that occurs rarely in the entire corpus than a word that appears in most of the documents; thus, the metric uses the *inverse* of the word's appearance in documents in the full corpus.

The frequency of words in a corpus tends to be distributed exponentially. A common word might appear ten times as often as a mildly common word, which in turn might appear ten or a hundred times as often as a rare word. Basing a metric on the raw inverse document frequency would give rare words enormous weight and practically ignore the impact of all other words. To capture this distribution, the scheme uses the *log* of the inverse document frequency. This mellows the differences in document frequencies by transforming the multiplicative gaps between them into additive gaps.

The model relies on a few assumptions. It treats each document as a "bag of words," meaning that it pays no attention to the ordering of words, sentence structure, or negations. By representing each term once, the model has difficulty dealing with *polysemy*, the use of the same word for multiple meanings. For example, the model can't distinguish between the use of "band" in "Radiohead is the best band ever" and "I broke a rubber band." If both sentences appear often in the corpus, it may come to associate "Radiohead" with "rubber."

Let's proceed now to the implementation of TF-IDF using PySpark.

Computing the TF-IDFs

First, we'll calculate TF (term frequency; that is, the frequency of each term in a document) with CountVectorizer, which keeps track of the vocabulary that's being created so we can map our topics back to their corresponding words. TF creates a matrix that counts how many times each word in the vocabulary appears in each body of text. This then gives each word a weight based on its frequency. We derive the vocabulary of our data while fitting and get the counts at the transform step:

```
from pyspark.ml.feature import CountVectorizer
cv = CountVectorizer(inputCol="tokens", outputCol="raw_features")
```

```
# train the model
cv_model = cv.fit(tokens_df)

# transform the data. Output column name will be raw_features.
vectorized_tokens = cv_model.transform(tokens_df)
```

Then, we proceed with IDF (the inverse frequency of documents where a term occurred), which reduces the weights of commonly appearing terms:

```
from pyspark.ml.feature import IDF
idf = IDF(inputCol="raw_features", outputCol="features")

idf_model = idf.fit(vectorized_tokens)

vectorized_df = idf_model.transform(vectorized_tokens)
```

This is what the result will look like:

```
vectorized_df = vectorized_df.drop(fun.col('raw_features'))

vectorized_df.show(6)
...

+-------------------+--------------------+--------------------+
|              title|              tokens|            features|
+-------------------+--------------------+--------------------+
|     Tertiary ideal|[mathemat, tertia...|(2451,[1,6,43,56,...|
|Binomial (polynom...|[algebra, binomi,...|(2451,[0,10,14,34...|
|            Algebra|[algebra, on, bro...|(2451,[0,1,5,6,15...|
| Kernel (set theory)|[set, theori, ker...|(2451,[2,3,13,19,...|
|Generalized arith...|[mathemat, gener,...|(2451,[1,2,6,45,4...|
+-------------------+--------------------+--------------------+
```

With all the preprocessing and feature engineering done, we can now create our LDA model. That's what we'll do in the next section.

Creating Our LDA Model

We had mentioned previously that LDA distills a corpus into a set of relevant topics. We will get to have a look at examples of such topics further ahead in this section. Before that, we need to decide on two hyperparameters that our LDA model requires. They are number of topics (referred to as k) and number of iterations.

There are multiple ways that you can go about choosing k. Two popular metrics used for doing this are perplexity and topic coherence. The former is made available by PySpark's implementation. The basic idea is to try to figure out the k where the improvements to these metrics start to become insignificant. If you are familiar with the *elbow method* for finding the number of clusters for K-means, this is similar. Depending on the size of your corpus, it can be a resource-intensive and time-consuming process since you will need to build the model for multiple values of *k*. An alternative could be to try to create a representative sample of the dataset in hand and use it to determine *k*. It is left as an exercise for you to read up on this and try it.

Since you may be working locally right now, we will go ahead and assign reasonable values (*k* as 5 and `max_iter` as 50) for now.

Let's create our LDA model:

```
from pyspark.ml.clustering import LDA

num_topics = 5
max_iter = 50

lda = LDA(k=num_topics, maxIter=max_iter)
model = lda.fit(vectorized_df)

lp = model.logPerplexity(vectorized_df)

print("The upper bound on perplexity: " + str(lp))
...

The upper bound on perplexity: 6.768323190833805
```

Perplexity is a measurement of how well a model predicts a sample. A low perplexity indicates the probability distribution is good at predicting the sample. When comparing different models, go for the one with the lower value of perplexity.

Now that we have created our model, we want to output the topics as human-readable. We will get the vocabulary generated from our preprocessing steps, get the topics from the LDA model, and map both of them.

```
vocab = cv_model.vocabulary  ❶

raw_topics = model.describeTopics().collect()  ❷

topic_inds = [ind.termIndices for ind in raw_topics]  ❸

topics = []
for topic in topic_inds:
    _topic = []
    for ind in topic:
        _topic.append(vocab[ind])
    topics.append(_topic)
```

❶ Create a reference to our vocabulary.

❷ Get topics generated by the LDA model using `describeTopics` and load them into a Python list.

❸ Get indices of the vocabulary terms from our topics.

Let us now generate the mappings from our topic indices to our vocabulary:

```
for i, topic in enumerate(topics, start=1):
    print(f"topic {i}: {topic}")
...

topic 1: ['islam', 'health', 'drug', 'empir', 'medicin', 'polici',...
topic 2: ['formula', 'group', 'algebra', 'gener', 'transform',   ...
topic 3: ['triangl', 'plane', 'line', 'point', 'two', 'tangent',  ...
topic 4: ['face', 'therapeut', 'framework', 'particl', 'interf',  ...
topic 5: ['comput', 'polynomi', 'pattern', 'internet', 'network', ...
```

The previous result is not perfect, but there are some patterns that can be noticed in the topics. Topic 1 is primarily related to health. It also contains references to Islam and empire. Could it be because of them being referenced in medicinal history and vice versa or something else? Topics 2 and 3 are related to mathematics with the latter inclined toward geometry. Topic 5 is a mix of computing and mathematics. Even if you hadn't read any of the documents, you can already guess with a reasonable accuracy about their categories. This is exciting!

We can now also check which topics our input documents are most closely related to. A single document can have multiple topic associations that are significant. For now, we'll only look at the most strongly associated topics.

Let's run the LDA model's transform operation on our input dataframe:

```
lda_df = model.transform(vectorized_df)
lda_df.select(fun.col('title'), fun.col('topicDistribution')).\
                show(2, vertical=True, truncate=False)

...
-RECORD 0------------------------------------
 title             | Tertiary ideal
 topicDistribution | [5.673953573608612E-4,...
-RECORD 1------------------------------------...
 title             | Binomial (polynomial) ...
 topicDistribution | [0.00193743840602051207...
only showing top 2 rows
```

As you can see, each document has a topic probability distribution associated with it. To get the associated topic for each document, we want to find out the topic index with the highest probability score. We can then map it to the topics that we obtained previously.

We will write a PySpark UDF to find the highest topic probability score for each record:

```
from pyspark.sql.types import IntegerType
max_index = fun.udf(lambda x: x.tolist().index(max(x)) + 1, IntegerType())
lda_df = lda_df.withColumn('topic_index',
                    max_index(fun.col('topicDistribution')))
```

```
lda_df.select('title', 'topic_index').show(10, truncate=False)
...

+----------------------------------+-----------+
|title                             |topic_index|
+----------------------------------+-----------+
|Tertiary ideal                    |2          |
|Binomial (polynomial)             |2          |
|Algebra                           |2          |
|Kernel (set theory)               |2          |
|Generalized arithmetic progression|2          |
|Schur algebra                     |2          |
|Outline of algebra                |2          |
|Recurrence relation               |5          |
|Rational difference equation      |5          |
|Polynomial arithmetic             |2          |
+----------------------------------+-----------+
only showing top 11 rows
```

Topic 2, if you remember, was associated with mathematics. The output is in line with our expectations. You can scan more of the dataset to see how it performed. You can select particular topics using the `where` or `filter` commands and compare them against the topic list generated earlier to get a better sense of the clusters that have been created. As promised at the beginning of the chapter, we're able to cluster articles into different topics without reading them!

Where to Go from Here

In this chapter, we performed LDA on the Wikipedia corpus. In the process, we also learned about text preprocessing using the amazing Spark NLP library and the TF-IDF technique. You can further build on this by improving the model by better preprocessing and hyperparameter tuning. In addition, you can even try to recommend similar entries based on document similarity when provided with user input. Such a similarity measure may be obtained by using the probability distribution vector obtained from LDA.

In addition, a variety of other methods exist for understanding large corpora of text. For example, a technique known as latent semantic analysis (LSA) is useful in similar applications and was used in the previous edition of this book on the same dataset. Deep learning, which is explored in Chapter 10, also offers avenues to perform topic modeling. You can explore them on your own.

## CHAPTER 7

Geospatial and Temporal Data Analysis on Taxi Trip Data

Geospatial data refers to data that has location information embedded in it in some form. Such data is being generated currently at a massive scale by billions of sources, such as mobile phones and sensors, every day. Data about movement of humans and machines, and from remote sensing, is significant for our economy and general well-being. Geospatial analytics can provide us with the tools and methods we need to make sense of all that data and put it to use in solving problems we face.

The PySpark and PyData ecosystems have evolved considerably over the last few years when it comes to geospatial analysis. They are being used across industries for handling location-rich data and, in turn, impacting our daily lives. One daily activity where geospatial data manifests itself in a visible way is local transport. The phenomenon of digital cab hailing services becoming popular over the last few years has led to us being more aware of geospatial technology. In this chapter, we'll use our PySpark and data analysis skills in this domain as we work with a dataset containing information about trips taken by cabs in New York City.

One statistic that is important to understanding the economics of taxis is *utilization*: the fraction of time that a cab is on the road and is occupied by one or more passengers. One factor that impacts utilization is the passenger's destination: a cab that drops off passengers near Union Square at midday is much more likely to find its next fare in just a minute or two, whereas a cab that drops someone off at 2 A.M. on Staten Island may have to drive all the way back to Manhattan before it finds its next fare. We'd like to quantify these effects and find out the average time it takes for a cab to find its next fare as a function of the borough in which it dropped its passengers off—Manhattan, Brooklyn, Queens, the Bronx, Staten Island, or none of the above (e.g., if it dropped the passenger off somewhere outside of the city, like Newark Liberty International Airport).

We'll start by setting up our dataset, and then we'll dive into geospatial analysis. We will learn about the GeoJSON format and use tools from the PyData ecosystem in combination with PySpark. We'll use GeoPandas for working with *geospatial information*, like points of longitude and latitude and spatial boundaries. To wrap things up, we will work with temporal features of our data, such as date and time, by performing a type of analysis called sessionization. This will help us understand utilization of New York City cabs. PySpark's DataFrame API provides out-of-the-box data types and methods to handle temporal data.

Let's get going by downloading our dataset and exploring it using PySpark.

Origin Story of the New York City Taxi Trip Dataset

Residents of New York City have all kinds of tips based on their anecdotal experiences about the best times and places to catch a cab, especially during rush hour and when it's raining. But there is one time of day when everyone will recommend that you simply take the subway instead: during the shift change that happens between 4 and 5 P.M. every day. During this time, yellow taxis have to return to their dispatch centers (often in Queens) so that one driver can quit for the day and the next one can start, and drivers who are late to return have to pay fines.

In March of 2014, the New York City Taxi and Limousine Commission shared an infographic on its Twitter account, @nyctaxi (*https://oreil.ly/MAA7t*), that showed the number of taxis on the road and the fraction of those taxis that was occupied at any given time. Sure enough, there was a noticeable dip of taxis on the road from 4 to 6 P.M., and two-thirds of the taxis that were driving were occupied.

This tweet caught the eye of self-described urbanist, mapmaker, and data junkie Chris Whong, who sent a tweet to the @nyctaxi account to find out if the data it used in its infographic was publicly available. Chris gained access to all of the data on taxi rides from January 1 through December 31, 2013. Even better, he posted all of the fare data online, where it has been used as the basis for a number of beautiful visualizations of transportation in New York City. This is the dataset that we will leverage as well in this chapter.

Preparing the Data

For this analysis, we're only going to consider the fare data from January 2013, which will be about 2.5 GB of data after we uncompress it. You can access the data for each month of 2013 (*https://oreil.ly/7m7Ki*), and if you have a sufficiently large PySpark cluster at your disposal, you can re-create the following analysis against all of the data for the year. For now, let's create a working directory on our client machine and take a look at the structure of the fare data:

```
$ mkdir taxidata
$ cd taxidata
$ curl -O https://storage.googleapis.com/aas-data-sets/trip_data_1.csv.zip
$ unzip trip_data_1.csv.zip
$ head -n 5 trip_data_1.csv

...

medallion,hack_license,vendor_id,rate_code,store_and_fwd_flag,...
89D227B655E5C82AECF13C3F540D4CF4,BA96DE419E711691B9445D6A6307C170,CMT,1,...
0BD7C8F5BA12B88E0B67BED28BEA73D8,9FD8F69F0804BDB5549F40E9DA1BE472,CMT,1,...
0BD7C8F5BA12B88E0B67BED28BEA73D8,9FD8F69F0804BDB5549F40E9DA1BE472,CMT,1,...
DFD2202EE08F7A8DC9A57B02ACB81FE2,51EE87E3205C985EF8431D850C786310,CMT,1,...
```

Each row of the file after the header represents a single taxi ride in CSV format. For each ride, we have some attributes of the cab (a hashed version of the medallion number) as well as the driver (a hashed version of the *hack license*, which is what a license to drive a taxi is called), some temporal information about when the trip started and ended, and the longitude/latitude coordinates for where the passengers were picked up and dropped off.

Let's create a *taxidata* directory and copy the trip data into the storage:

```
$ mkdir taxidata
$ mv trip_data_1.csv taxidata/
```

We have used a local filesystem here, but this may not be the case for you. It's more likely nowadays to use a cloud native filesystem such as AWS S3 or GCS. In such a scenario, you will upload the data to S3 or GCS, respectively.

Now start the PySpark shell:

```
$ pyspark
```

Once the PySpark shell has loaded, we can create a dataset from the taxi data and examine the first few lines, just as we have in other chapters:

```
taxi_raw = pyspark.read.option("header", "true").csv("taxidata")
taxi_raw.show(1, vertical=True)

...

RECORD 0---------------------------------
 medallion          | 89D227B655E5C82AE...
 hack_license       | BA96DE419E711691B...
 vendor_id          | CMT
 rate_code          | 1
 store_and_fwd_flag | N
 pickup_datetime    | 2013-01-01 15:11:48
 dropoff_datetime   | 2013-01-01 15:18:10
```

```
 passenger_count      | 4
 trip_time_in_secs    | 382
 trip_distance        | 1.0
 pickup_longitude     | -73.978165
 pickup_latitude      | 40.757977
 dropoff_longitude    | -73.989838
 dropoff_latitude     | 40.751171
only showing top 1 row

...
```

This looks like a well-formatted dataset at first glance. Let's have a look at the DataFrame's schema:

```
taxi_raw.printSchema()
...
root
 |-- medallion: string (nullable = true)
 |-- hack_license: string (nullable = true)
 |-- vendor_id: string (nullable = true)
 |-- rate_code: integer (nullable = true)
 |-- store_and_fwd_flag: string (nullable = true)
 |-- pickup_datetime: string (nullable = true)
 |-- dropoff_datetime: string (nullable = true)
 |-- passenger_count: integer (nullable = true)
 |-- trip_time_in_secs: integer (nullable = true)
 |-- trip_distance: double (nullable = true)
 |-- pickup_longitude: double (nullable = true)
 |-- pickup_latitude: double (nullable = true)
 |-- dropoff_longitude: double (nullable = true)
 |-- dropoff_latitude: double (nullable = true)
...
```

We are representing the pickup_datetime and dropoff_datetime fields as Strings and storing the individual (x,y) coordinates of the pickup and drop-off locations in their own fields as Doubles. We want the datetime fields as timestamps since that will allow us to manipulate and analyze them conveniently.

Converting Datetime Strings to Timestamps

As mentioned previously, PySpark provides out-of-the-box methods for handling temporal data.

Specifically, we will use the to_timestamp function to parse the datetime strings and convert them into timestamps:

```
from pyspark.sql import functions as fun

taxi_raw = taxi_raw.withColumn('pickup_datetime',
                               fun.to_timestamp(fun.col('pickup_datetime'),
                                                "yyyy-MM-dd HH:mm:ss"))
taxi_raw = taxi_raw.withColumn('dropoff_datetime',
```

```
                    fun.to_timestamp(fun.col('dropoff_datetime'),
                                     "yyyy-MM-dd HH:mm:ss"))
```

Let's have a look at the schema again:

```
taxi_raw.printSchema()
...

root
 |-- medallion: string (nullable = true)
 |-- hack_license: string (nullable = true)
 |-- vendor_id: string (nullable = true)
 |-- rate_code: integer (nullable = true)
 |-- store_and_fwd_flag: string (nullable = true)
 |-- pickup_datetime: timestamp (nullable = true)
 |-- dropoff_datetime: timestamp (nullable = true)
 |-- passenger_count: integer (nullable = true)
 |-- trip_time_in_secs: integer (nullable = true)
 |-- trip_distance: double (nullable = true)
 |-- pickup_longitude: double (nullable = true)
 |-- pickup_latitude: double (nullable = true)
 |-- dropoff_longitude: double (nullable = true)
 |-- dropoff_latitude: double (nullable = true)


...
```

The pickup_datetime and dropoff_datetime fields are timestamps now. Well done!

We'd mentioned that this dataset contains trips from January 2013. Don't just take our word for this, though. We can confirm this by sorting the pickup_datetime field to get the latest datetime in the data. For this, we use DataFrame's sort method combined with PySpark column's desc method:

```
taxi_raw.sort(fun.col("pickup_datetime").desc()).show(3, vertical=True)
...

-RECORD 0---------------------------------
 medallion          | EA00A64CBDB68C77D...
 hack_license       | 2045C77002FA0F2E0...
 vendor_id          | CMT
 rate_code          | 1
 store_and_fwd_flag | N
 pickup_datetime    | 2013-01-31 23:59:59
 dropoff_datetime   | 2013-02-01 00:08:39
 passenger_count    | 1
 trip_time_in_secs  | 520
 trip_distance      | 1.5
 pickup_longitude   | -73.970528
 pickup_latitude    | 40.75502
 dropoff_longitude  | -73.981201
 dropoff_latitude   | 40.769104
-RECORD 1---------------------------------
 medallion          | E3F00BB3F4E710383...
```

```
hack_license        | 10A2B96DE39865918...
vendor_id           | CMT
rate_code           | 1
store_and_fwd_flag  | N
pickup_datetime     | 2013-01-31 23:59:59
dropoff_datetime    | 2013-02-01 00:05:16
passenger_count     | 1
trip_time_in_secs   | 317
trip_distance       | 1.0
pickup_longitude    | -73.990685
pickup_latitude     | 40.719158
dropoff_longitude   | -74.003288
dropoff_latitude    | 40.71521
-RECORD 2--------------------------------
medallion           | 83D8E776A05EEF731...
hack_license        | E6D27C8729EF55D20...
vendor_id           | CMT
rate_code           | 1
store_and_fwd_flag  | N
pickup_datetime     | 2013-01-31 23:59:58
dropoff_datetime    | 2013-02-01 00:04:19
passenger_count     | 1
trip_time_in_secs   | 260
trip_distance       | 0.8
pickup_longitude    | -73.982452
pickup_latitude     | 40.77277
dropoff_longitude   | -73.989227
dropoff_latitude    | 40.766754
only showing top 3 rows
...
```

With our data types in place, let's check if there are any inconsistencies in our data.

Handling Invalid Records

Anyone who has been working with large-scale, real-world datasets knows that they invariably contain at least a few records that do not conform to the expectations of the person who wrote the code to handle them. Many PySpark pipelines have failed because of invalid records that caused the parsing logic to throw an exception. When performing interactive analysis, we can get a sense of potential anomalies in the data by focusing on key variables.

In our case, variables containing geospatial and temporal information are worth looking at for inconsistencies. Presence of null values in these columns will definitely throw off our analysis.

```
geospatial_temporal_colnames = ["pickup_longitude", "pickup_latitude", \
                                "dropoff_longitude", "dropoff_latitude", \
                                "pickup_datetime", "dropoff_datetime"]
taxi_raw.select([fun.count(fun.when(fun.isnull(c), c)).\
                            alias(c) for c in geospatial_temporal_colnames]).\
```

```
            show()
   ...

   +----------------+----------------+----------------
   |pickup_longitude|pickup_latitude|dropoff_longitude
   +----------------+----------------+----------------
   |               0|              0|               86
   +----------------+----------------+----------------

   +----------------+----------------+----------------+
   |dropoff_latitude|pickup_datetime|dropoff_datetime|
   +----------------+----------------+----------------+
   |              86|              0|               0|
   +----------------+----------------+----------------+
```

Let's remove the null values from our data:

```
taxi_raw = taxi_raw.na.drop(subset=geospatial_temporal_colnames)
```

Another commonsense check that we can do is for latitude and longitude records where the values are zero. We know that for the region we're concerned with, those would be invalid values:

```
print("Count of zero dropoff, pickup latitude and longitude records")
taxi_raw.groupBy((fun.col("dropoff_longitude") == 0) |
  (fun.col("dropoff_latitude") == 0) |
  (fun.col("pickup_longitude") == 0) |
  (fun.col("pickup_latitude") == 0)).\ ❶
    count().show()
...

Count of zero dropoff, pickoff latitude and longitude records
+---------------+
|  ...  |   count|
+------+--------+
| true |   285909|
| false|14490620|
+---------------+
```

❶ Multiple OR conditions will be true if either of them evaluates to True for any record.

We have quite a few of these. If it looks as if a taxi took a passenger to the South Pole, we can be reasonably confident that the record is invalid and should be excluded from our analysis. We will not remove them but get back to them toward the end of the next section to see how they can affect our analysis.

In production settings, we handle these exceptions one at a time by checking the logs for the individual tasks, figuring out which line of code threw the exception, and then figuring out how to tweak the code to ignore or correct the invalid records. This is a tedious process, and it often feels like we're playing whack-a-mole: just as we get one exception fixed, we discover another one on a record that came later within the partition.

One strategy that experienced data scientists deploy when working with a new dataset is to add a `try-except` block to their parsing code so that any invalid records can be written out to the logs without causing the entire job to fail. If there are only a handful of invalid records in the entire dataset, we might be okay with ignoring them and continuing with our analysis.

Now that we have prepared our dataset, let's get started with geospatial analysis.

Geospatial Analysis

There are two major kinds of geospatial data—vector and raster—and there are different tools for working with each type. In our case, we have latitude and longitude for our taxi trip records, and vector data stored in the GeoJSON format that represents the boundaries of the different boroughs of New York. We've looked at the latitude and longitude points. Let's start by having a look at the GeoJSON data.

Intro to GeoJSON

The data we'll use for the boundaries of boroughs in New York City comes written in a format called *GeoJSON*. The core object in GeoJSON is called a *feature*, which is made up of a *geometry* instance and a set of key-value pairs called *properties*. A geometry is a shape like a point, line, or polygon. A set of features is called a `FeatureCollection`. Let's pull down the GeoJSON data for the NYC borough maps and take a look at its structure.

In the *taxidata* directory on your client machine, download the data and rename the file to something a bit shorter:

```
$ url="https://nycdatastables.s3.amazonaws.com/\
        2013-08-19T18:15:35.172Z/nyc-borough-boundaries-polygon.geojson"
$ curl -O $url
$ mv nyc-borough-boundaries-polygon.geojson nyc-boroughs.geojson
```

Open the file and look at a feature record. Note the properties and the geometry objects—in this case, a polygon representing the boundaries of the borough and the properties containing the name of the borough and other related information.

```
$ head -n 7 data/trip_data_ch07/nyc-boroughs.geojson
...
{
"type": "FeatureCollection",

"features": [{ "type": "Feature", "id": 0, "properties": { "boroughCode": 5, ...
,
{ "type": "Feature", "id": 1, "properties": { "boroughCode": 5, ...
```

GeoPandas

The first thing you should consider when choosing a library to perform geospatial analysis is determine what kind of data you will need to work with. We need a library that can parse GeoJSON data and can handle spatial relationships, like detecting whether a given longitude/latitude pair is contained inside a polygon that represents the boundaries of a particular borough. We will use the GeoPandas library (*https://geopandas.org*) for this task. GeoPandas is an open source project to make working with geospatial data in Python easier. It extends the data types used by the pandas library, which we used in previous chapters, to allow spatial operations on geometric data types.

Install the GeoPandas package using pip:

```
pip3 install geopandas
```

Let us now start examining the geospatial aspects of the taxi data. For each trip, we have longitude/latitude pairs representing where the passenger was picked up and dropped off. We would like to be able to determine which borough each of these longitude/latitude pairs belongs to, and identify any trips that did not start or end in any of the five boroughs. For example, if a taxi took passengers from Manhattan to Newark Liberty International Airport, that would be a valid ride that would be interesting to analyze, even though it would not end within one of the five boroughs.

To perform our borough analysis, we need to load the GeoJSON data we downloaded earlier and stored in the *nyc-boroughs.geojson* file:

```
import geopandas as gdp

gdf = gdp.read_file("./data/trip_data_ch07/nyc-boroughs.geojson")
```

Before we use the GeoJSON features on the taxi trip data, we should take a moment to think about how to organize this geospatial data for maximum efficiency. One option would be to research data structures that are optimized for geospatial lookups, such as quad trees, and then find or write our own implementation. Instead, we will try to come up with a quick heuristic that will allow us to bypass that bit of work.

We will iterate through the gdf until we find a feature whose geometry contains a given point of longitude/latitude. Most taxi rides in NYC begin and end in Manhattan, so if the geospatial features that represent Manhattan are earlier in the sequence, our searches will end relatively quickly. We can use the fact that the boroughCode property of each feature can be used as a sorting key, with the code for Manhattan equal to 1 and the code for Staten Island equal to 5. Within the features for each borough, we want the features associated with the largest polygons to come before those associated with the smaller polygons, because most trips will be to and from the "major" region of each borough.

We will calculate area associated with each feature's geometry and store it as a new column:

```
gdf = gdf.to_crs(3857)

gdf['area'] = gdf.apply(lambda x: x['geometry'].area, axis=1)
gdf.head(5)
...
```

```
   boroughCode  borough         @id        geometry      area
0  5            Staten Island  http://nyc.pediacities.com/Resource/Borough/St...
1  5            Staten Island  http://nyc.pediacities.com/Resource/Borough/St...
2  5            Staten Island  http://nyc.pediacities.com/Resource/Borough/St...
3  5            Staten Island  http://nyc.pediacities.com/Resource/Borough/St...
4  4            Queens         http://nyc.pediacities.com/Resource/Borough/Qu...
```

Sorting the features by the combination of the borough code and the area of each feature's geometry should do the trick:

```
gdf = gdf.sort_values(by=['boroughCode', 'area'], ascending=[True, False])
gdf.head(5)
...
    boroughCode  borough     @id        geometry     area
72  1            Manhattan  http://nyc.pediacities.com/Resource/Borough/Ma...
71  1            Manhattan  http://nyc.pediacities.com/Resource/Borough/Ma...
51  1            Manhattan  http://nyc.pediacities.com/Resource/Borough/Ma...
```

```
69  1              Manhattan  http://nyc.pediacities.com/Resource/Borough/Ma...
73  1              Manhattan  http://nyc.pediacities.com/Resource/Borough/Ma...
```

Note that we're sorting based on area value in descending order because we want the largest polygons to come first, and `sort_values` sorts in ascending order by default.

Now we can broadcast the sorted features in the `gdf` GeoPandas DataFrame to the cluster and write a function that uses these features to find out in which of the five boroughs (if any) a particular trip ended:

```
b_gdf = spark.sparkContext.broadcast(gdf)

def find_borough(latitude,longitude):
    mgdf = b_gdf.value.apply(lambda x: x['borough'] if \
                             x['geometry'].\
                             intersects(gdp.\
                                        points_from_xy(
                                            [longitude], \
                                            [latitude])[0]) \
                             else None, axis=1)
    idx = mgdf.first_valid_index()
    return mgdf.loc[idx] if idx is not None else None

find_borough_udf = fun.udf(find_borough, StringType())
```

To UDF or Not to UDF?

PySpark SQL makes it very easy to convert business logic into functions as we did here with the `find_borough` function. Given this, you might think that it would be a good idea to move all of your business logic into UDFs to make it easy to reuse, test, and maintain. However, there are a few caveats for using UDFs that you should be mindful of before you start sprinkling them throughout your code:

- First, UDFs are opaque to PySpark's SQL query planner and execution engine in a way that standard SQL query syntax is not, so moving logic into a UDF instead of using a literal SQL expression could hurt query performance.

- Second, handling null values in PySpark SQL can get complicated quickly, especially for UDFs that take multiple arguments.

We can apply `find_borough` to the trips in the `taxi_raw` DataFrame to create a histogram of trips by borough:

```
df_with_boroughs = taxi_raw.\
                   withColumn("dropoff_borough", \
                              find_borough_udf(
                                  fun.col("dropoff_latitude"),\
                                  fun.col('dropoff_longitude')))
```

```
df_with_boroughs.groupBy(fun.col("dropoff_borough")).count().show()
...
+----------------------+--------+
|       dropoff_borough |   count|
+----------------------+--------+
|                Queens|  672192|
|                  null| 7942421|
|              Brooklyn|  715252|
|         Staten Island|    3338|
|             Manhattan|12979047|
|                 Bronx|   67434|
+----------------------+--------+
```

As we expected, the vast majority of trips end in the borough of Manhattan, while relatively few trips end in Staten Island. One surprising observation is the number of trips that end outside of any borough; the number of null records is substantially larger than the number of taxi rides that end in the Bronx.

We had talked about handling such invalid records earlier but did not remove them. It is left as an exercise for you to remove such records and create a histogram from the cleaned-up data. Once done, you will notice a reduction in the number of null entries, leaving a much more reasonable number of observations that had drop-offs outside the city.

Having worked with the geospatial aspects of our data, let us now dig deeper into the temporal nature of our data by performing sessionization using PySpark.

Sessionization in PySpark

The kind of analysis, in which we want to analyze a single entity as it executes a series of events over time, is called *sessionization*, and is commonly performed over web logs to analyze the behavior of the users of a website. PySpark provides Window and aggregation functions out of the box that can be used to perform such analysis. These allow us to focus on business logic instead of trying to implement complex data manipulation and calculation. We will use these in the next section to better understand utilization of taxi cabs in our dataset.

Sessionization can be a very powerful technique for uncovering insights in data and building new data products that can be used to help people make better decisions. For example, Google's spell-correction engine is built on top of the sessions of user activity that Google builds each day from the logged records of every event (searches, clicks, maps visits, etc.) occurring on its web properties. To identify likely spell-correction candidates, Google processes those sessions looking for situations where a user typed a query, didn't click anything, typed a slightly different query a few seconds later, and then clicked a result and didn't come back to Google. Then it counts how often this pattern occurs for any pair of queries. If it occurs frequently enough (e.g., if every time we see the query "untied stats," it's followed a few seconds later by the query "united states"), then we assume that the second query is a spell correction of the first.

This analysis takes advantage of the patterns of human behavior that are represented in the event logs to build a spell-correction engine from data that is more powerful than any engine that could be created from a dictionary. The engine can be used to perform spell correction in any language and can correct words that might not be included in any dictionary (e.g., the name of a new startup) or queries like "untied stats" where none of the words are misspelled! Google uses similar techniques to show recommended and related searches, as well as to decide which queries should return a OneBox result that gives the answer to a query on the search page itself, without requiring that the user click through to a different page. There are OneBoxes for weather, scores from sporting events, addresses, and lots of other kinds of queries.

So far, information about the set of events that occurs to each entity is spread out across the DataFrame's partitions, so, for analysis, we need to place these relevant events next to each other and in chronological order. In the next section, we will show how to efficiently construct and analyze sessions using advanced PySpark functionality.

Building Sessions: Secondary Sorts in PySpark

The naive way to create sessions in PySpark is to perform a groupBy on the identifier we want to create sessions for and then sort the events post-shuffle by a timestamp identifier. If we only have a small number of events for each entity, this approach will work reasonably well. However, because this approach requires all the events for any particular entity to be in memory at the same time, it will not scale as the number of events for each entity gets larger and larger. We need a way of building sessions that does not require all of the events for a particular entity to be held in memory at the same time for sorting.

In MapReduce, we can build sessions by performing a *secondary sort*, where we create a composite key made up of an identifier and a timestamp value, sort all of the records on the composite key, and then use a custom partitioner and grouping function to ensure that all of the records for the same identifier appear in the same output partition. Fortunately, PySpark can also support a similar pattern by using Window functions:

```
from pyspark.sql import Window

window_spec = Window.partitionBy("hack_license").\
                orderBy(fun.col("hack_license"),
                        fun.col("pickup_datetime"))
```

First, we use the partitionBy method to ensure that all of the records that have the same value for the license column end up in the same partition. Then, within each of these partitions, we sort the records by their license value (so all trips by the same driver appear together) and then by their pickupTime so that the sequence of trips appears in sorted order within the partition. Now when we aggregate the trip records, we can be sure that the trips are ordered in a way that is optimal for sessions analysis. Because this operation triggers a shuffle and a fair bit of computation and we'll need to use the results more than once, we cache them:

```
window_spec.cache()
```

Executing a sessionization pipeline is an expensive operation, and the sessionized data is often useful for many different analysis tasks that we might want to perform. In settings where one might want to pick up on the analysis later or collaborate with other data scientists, it is a good idea to amortize the cost of sessionizing a large dataset by only performing the sessionization once and then writing the sessionized data to a filesystem such as S3 or HDFS so that it can be used to answer lots of different questions. Performing sessionization once is also a good way to enforce standard rules for session definitions across the entire data science team, which has the same benefits for ensuring apples-to-apples comparisons of results.

At this point, we are ready to analyze our sessions data to see how long it takes for a driver to find his next fare after a drop-off in a particular borough. We will use the lag function along with the window_spec object created earlier to take two trips and compute the duration in seconds between the drop-off time of the first trip and the pickup time of the second:

```
df_ with_ borough_durations = df_with_boroughs.\
        withColumn("trip_time_difference", \
        fun.col("pickup_datetime") - fun.lag(fun.col("pickup_datetime"),
                                    1). \
        over(window_spec)).show(50, vertical=True)
```

Now, we should do a validation check to ensure that most of the durations are nonnegative:

```
df_with_borough_durations.
  selectExpr("floor(seconds / 3600) as hours").
  groupBy("hours").
  count().
  sort("hours").
  show()
...
+-----+--------+
|hours|   count|
+-----+--------+
|   -3|       2|
|   -2|      16|
|   -1|    4253|
|    0|13359033|
|    1|  347634|
```

```
|    2|  76286|
|    3|  24812|
|    4|  10026|
|    5|   4789|
```

Only a few of the records have a negative duration, and when we examine them more closely, there don't seem to be any common patterns to them that we could use to understand the source of the erroneous data. If we exclude these negative duration records from our input dataset and look at the average and standard deviation of the pickup times by borough, we see this:

```
df_with_borough_durations.
  where("seconds > 0 AND seconds < 60*60*4").
  groupBy("borough").
  agg(avg("seconds"), stddev("seconds")).
  show()
...
+-------------+------------------+--------------------+
|      borough|      avg(seconds)|stddev_samp(seconds)|
+-------------+------------------+--------------------+
|       Queens|2380.6603554494727|  2206.6572799118035|
|           NA| 2006.53571169866|  1997.0891370324784|
|     Brooklyn| 1365.394576250576|  1612.9921698951398|
|Staten Island|         2723.5625|  2395.7745475546385|
|    Manhattan| 631.8473780726746|   1042.919915477234|
|        Bronx|1975.9209786770646|   1704.006452085683|
+-------------+------------------+--------------------+
```

As we would expect, the data shows that drop-offs in Manhattan have the shortest amount of downtime for drivers, at around 10 minutes. Taxi rides that end in Brooklyn have a downtime of more than twice that, and the relatively few rides that end in Staten Island take drivers an average of almost 45 minutes to get to their next fare.

As the data demonstrates, taxi drivers have a major financial incentive to discriminate among passengers based on their final destination; drop-offs in Staten Island, in particular, involve an extensive amount of downtime for a driver. The NYC Taxi and Limousine Commission has made a major effort over the years to identify this discrimination and has fined drivers who have been caught rejecting passengers because of where they wanted to go. It would be interesting to attempt to examine the data for unusually short taxi rides that could be indicative of a dispute between the driver and the passenger about where the passenger wanted to be dropped off.

Where to Go from Here

In this chapter, we worked with both temporal and spatial features of a real-world dataset. The familiarity with geospatial analysis that you have gained so far can be used to dive into frameworks such as Apache Sedona or GeoMesa. They will have a steeper learning curve compared to working with GeoPandas and UDFs but will be more efficient. There's also a lot of scope for using data visualization with geospatial and temporal data.

Further, imagine using this same technique on the taxi data to build an application that could recommend the best place for a cab to go after a drop-off based on current traffic patterns and the historical record of next-best locations contained within this data. You could also look at the information from the perspective of someone trying to catch a cab: given the current time, place, and weather data, what is the probability that I will be able to hail a cab from the street within the next five minutes? This sort of information could be incorporated into applications like Google Maps to help travelers decide when to leave and which travel option they should take.

## CHAPTER 8

Estimating Financial Risk

Is there a way to approximate how much you can expect to lose when investing in financial markets? This is the quantity that the financial statistic *value at risk* (VaR) seeks to measure. VaR is a simple measure of investment risk that tries to provide a reasonable estimate of the maximum probable loss in value of an investment portfolio over a particular time period. A VaR statistic depends on three parameters: a portfolio, a time period, and a probability. For example, a VaR value of $1 million with a 5% probability and two weeks indicates the belief that the portfolio stands only a 5% chance of losing more than $1 million over two weeks.

Since its development soon after the stock market crash of 1987, VaR has seen widespread use across financial services organizations. The statistic plays a vital role in the management of these institutions by helping to determine the risk characteristics of their strategies.

Many of the most sophisticated approaches to estimating this statistic rely on computationally intensive simulations of markets under random conditions. The technique behind these approaches, called the Monte Carlo simulation, involves posing thousands or millions of random market scenarios and observing how they tend to affect a portfolio. These scenarios are referred to as *trials*. PySpark is an ideal tool for Monte Carlo simulations. PySpark can leverage thousands of cores to run random trials and aggregate their results. As a general-purpose data transformation engine, it is also adept at performing the pre- and postprocessing steps that surround the simulations. It can transform raw financial data into the model parameters needed to carry out the simulations, as well as support ad hoc analysis of the results. Its simple programming model can drastically reduce development time compared to more traditional approaches that use HPC environments.

We'll also discuss how to compute a related statistic called *conditional value at risk* (CVaR), sometimes known as *expected shortfall*, which the Basel Committee on Banking Supervision proposed as a better risk measure than VaR a few years back. A CVaR statistic has the same three parameters as a VaR statistic but considers the expected average loss instead of providing a probable loss value. A CVaR of $5 million with a 5% *q-value* and two weeks indicates the belief that the average loss in the worst 5% of outcomes is $5 million.

In the process of modeling VaR, we'll introduce a few different concepts, approaches, and packages. We'll start by going over basic financial terminology that will be used throughout the chapter and then learn about the methods used to calculate VaR, including the Monte Carlo simulation technique. After that, we will download and prepare our dataset using PySpark and pandas. We'll be using stock market data from late 2000s and early 2010s, including market indicators such as treasury bond prices along with stock values of various companies. Once done with preprocessing, we will create a linear regression model to calculate change in value for stocks over a time period. We'll also come up with a way to generate sample market indicator values for use in trials when performing a Monte Carlo simulation. Finally, we'll perform the simulation using PySpark and go over our results.

Let's start by defining basic financial terms that we will use.

Terminology

This chapter makes use of a set of terms specific to the finance domain:

Instrument
A tradable asset, such as a bond, loan, option, or stock investment. At any particular time, an instrument is considered to have a *value*, which is the price for which it could be sold.

Portfolio
A collection of instruments owned by a financial institution.

Return
The change in an instrument or portfolio's value over a time period.

Loss
A negative return.

Index
An imaginary portfolio of instruments. For example, the NASDAQ Composite Index includes about 3,000 stocks and similar instruments for major US and international companies.

Market factor
> A value that can be used as an indicator of macro aspects of the financial climate at a particular time—for example, the value of an index, the gross domestic product of the United States, or the exchange rate between the dollar and the euro. We will often refer to market factors as just *factors*.

Methods for Calculating VaR

So far, our definition of VaR has been fairly open ended. Estimating this statistic requires proposing a model for how a portfolio functions and choosing the probability distribution its returns are likely to take. Institutions employ a variety of approaches for calculating VaR, all of which tend to fall under a few general methods.

Variance-Covariance

Variance-covariance is by far the simplest and least computationally intensive method. Its model assumes that the return of each instrument is normally distributed, which allows deriving an estimate analytically.

Historical Simulation

Historical simulation extrapolates risk from historical data by using its distribution directly instead of relying on summary statistics. For example, to determine a 95% VaR for a portfolio, we might look at that portfolio's performance for the last 100 days and estimate the statistic as its value on the fifth-worst day. A drawback of this method is that historical data can be limited and fails to include what-ifs. For example, what if the history we have for the instruments in our portfolio lacks market collapses, and we want to model what happens to our portfolio in these situations? Techniques exist for making historical simulation robust to these issues, such as introducing "shocks" into the data, but we won't cover them here.

Monte Carlo Simulation

Monte Carlo simulation, which the rest of this chapter will focus on, tries to weaken the assumptions in the previous methods by simulating the portfolio under random conditions. When we can't derive a closed form for a probability distribution analytically, we can often estimate its probability density function by repeatedly sampling simpler random variables that it depends on and seeing how it plays out in aggregate. In its most general form, this method:

- Defines a relationship between market conditions and each instrument's returns. This relationship takes the form of a model fitted to historical data.

- Defines distributions for the market conditions that are straightforward to sample from. These distributions are fitted to historical data.

- Poses trials consisting of random market conditions.

- Calculates the total portfolio loss for each trial and uses these losses to define an empirical distribution over losses. This means that if we run 100 trials and want to estimate the 5% VaR, we would choose it as the loss from the trial with the fifth-greatest loss. To calculate the 5% CVaR, we would find the average loss over the five worst trials.

Of course, the Monte Carlo method isn't perfect either. It relies on models for generating trial conditions and for inferring instrument performance, and these models must make simplifying assumptions. If these assumptions don't correspond to reality, then neither will the final probability distribution that comes out.

Our Model

A Monte Carlo risk model typically phrases each instrument's return in terms of a set of market factors. Common market factors might be the value of indexes like the S&P 500, the US GDP, or currency exchange rates. We then need a model that predicts the return of each instrument based on these market conditions. In our simulation, we'll use a simple linear model. By our previous definition of return, a *factor return* is a change in the value of a market factor over a particular time. For example, if the value of the S&P 500 moves from 2,000 to 2,100 over a time interval, its return would be 100. We'll derive a set of features from simple transformations of the factor returns. That is, the market factor vector m_t for a trial t is transformed by some function ϕ to produce a feature vector of possible different length f_t:

$$f_t = \phi(m_t)$$

For each instrument, we'll train a model that assigns a weight to each feature. To calculate r_{it}, the return of instrument i in trial t, we use c_i, the intercept term for the instrument; w_{ij}, the regression weight for feature j on instrument i; and f_{tj}, the randomly generated value of feature j in trial t:

$$r_{it} = c_i + \sum_{j=1}^{|w_i|} w_{ij} * f_{tj}$$

This means that the return of each instrument is calculated as the sum of the returns of the market factor features multiplied by their weights for that instrument. We can fit the linear model for each instrument using historical data (also known as doing linear regression). If the horizon of the VaR calculation is two weeks, the regression treats every (overlapping) two-week interval in history as a labeled point.

It's also worth mentioning that we could have chosen a more complicated model. For example, the model need not be linear: it could be a regression tree or explicitly incorporate domain-specific knowledge.

Now that we have our model for calculating instrument losses from market factors, we need a process for simulating the behavior of market factors. A simple assumption is that each market factor return follows a normal distribution. To capture the fact that market factors are often correlated—when the NASDAQ is down, the Dow is likely to be suffering as well—we can use a multivariate normal distribution with a nondiagonal covariance matrix:

$$m_t \sim \mathcal{N}(\mu, \Sigma)$$

where μ is a vector of the empirical means of the returns of the factors and Σ is the empirical covariance matrix of the returns of the factors.

As before, we could have chosen a more complicated method of simulating the market or assumed a different type of distribution for each market factor, perhaps using distributions with fatter tails.

Getting the Data

Download the historical stock price dataset and place it in a *data/stocks/* directory:

```
$ mkdir stocks && cd stocks
$ url="https://raw.githubusercontent.com/ \
      sryza/aas/master/ch09-risk/data/stocks.zip"
$ wget $url
$ unzip stocks.zip
```

It can be difficult to find large volumes of nicely formatted historical price data. The dataset used in this chapter was downloaded from Yahoo!

We also need historical data for risk factors. For our factors, we'll use the values of:

- iShares 20 Plus Year Treasury Bond ETF (NASDAQ: TLT)
- iShares US Credit Bond ETF (NYSEArca: CRED)
- SPDR Gold Trust (NYSEArca: GLD)

Download and place the factors data:

```
$ cd .. && mkdir factors && cd factors
$ url2 = "https://raw.githubusercontent.com/ \
      sryza/aas/master/ch09-risk/data/factors.zip"
$ wget $url2
$ unzip factors.zip
$ ls factors
```

```
...

NASDAQ%3ATLT.csv  NYSEARCA%3ACRED.csv  NYSEARCA%3AGLD.csv
```

Let's have a look at one of our factors:

```
$ !head -n 5 data/factors/NASDAQ%3ATLT.csv
...

Date,Open,High,Low,Close,Volume
31-Dec-13,102.29,102.55,101.17,101.86,7219195
30-Dec-13,102.15,102.58,102.08,102.51,4491711
27-Dec-13,102.07,102.31,101.69,101.81,4755262
26-Dec-13,102.35,102.36,102.01,102.10,4645323
24-Dec-13,103.23,103.35,102.80,102.83,4897009
```

With our dataset downloaded, we will now prepare it.

Preparing the Data

The first few rows of the Yahoo!-formatted data for GOOGL look like this:

```
$ !head -n 5 data/stocks/GOOGL.csv
...

Date,Open,High,Low,Close,Volume
31-Dec-13,556.68,561.06,553.68,560.92,1358300
30-Dec-13,560.73,560.81,555.06,555.28,1236709
27-Dec-13,560.56,560.70,557.03,559.76,1570140
26-Dec-13,557.56,560.06,554.90,559.29,1338507
24-Dec-13,558.04,558.18,554.60,556.48,734170
```

Let's fire up the PySpark shell:

```
$ pyspark --driver-memory 4g
```

Read in the instruments dataset as a DataFrame:

```
stocks = spark.read.csv("data/stocks/", header='true', inferSchema='true')

stocks.show(2)
...

+----------+----+----+----+-----+------+
|      Date|Open|High| Low|Close|Volume|
+----------+----+----+----+-----+------+
|2013-12-31|4.40|4.48|3.92| 4.07|561247|
|2013-12-30|3.93|4.42|3.90| 4.38|550358|
+----------+----+----+----+-----+------+
```

The DataFrame is missing the instrument symbol. Let's add that using the input filenames corresponding to each row:

```
from pyspark.sql import functions as fun

stocks = stocks.withColumn("Symbol", fun.input_file_name()).\
            withColumn("Symbol",
                fun.element_at(fun.split("Symbol", "/"), -1)).\
            withColumn("Symbol",
                fun.element_at(fun.split("Symbol", "\."), 1))

stocks.show(2)
...
+---------+-------+-------+-------+-------+------+------+
|     Date|   Open|   High|    Low|  Close|Volume|Symbol|
+---------+-------+-------+-------+-------+------+------+
|31-Dec-13|1884.00|1900.00|1880.00| 1900.0|   546|  CLDN|
|30-Dec-13|1889.00|1900.00|1880.00| 1900.0|  1656|  CLDN|
+---------+-------+-------+-------+-------+------+------+
```

We will read in and process the factors dataset in a similar manner:

```
factors = spark.read.csv("data/factors", header='true', inferSchema='true')
factors = factors.withColumn("Symbol", fun.input_file_name()).\
            withColumn("Symbol",
                fun.element_at(fun.split("Symbol", "/"), -1)).\
            withColumn("Symbol",
                fun.element_at(fun.split("Symbol", "\."), 1))
```

We filter out instruments with less than five years of history:

```
from pyspark.sql import Window

stocks = stocks.withColumn('count', fun.count('Symbol').\
            over(Window.partitionBy('Symbol'))).\
            filter(fun.col('count') > 260*5 + 10)
```

Different types of instruments may trade on different days, or the data may have missing values for other reasons, so it is important to make sure that our different histories align. First, we need to trim all of our time series to the same period in time. To do that, we'll first convert the Date column's type from string to date:

```
stocks = stocks.withColumn('Date',
            fun.to_date(fun.to_timestamp(fun.col('Date'),
                                         'dd-MM-yy')))
stocks.printSchema()
...
root
 |-- Date: date (nullable = true)
 |-- Open: string (nullable = true)
 |-- High: string (nullable = true)
 |-- Low: string (nullable = true)
 |-- Close: double (nullable = true)
 |-- Volume: string (nullable = true)
 |-- Symbol: string (nullable = true)
 |-- count: long (nullable = false)
```

Let's trim the time periods of instruments to align:

```
from datetime import datetime

stocks = stocks.filter(fun.col('Date') >= datetime(2009, 10, 23)).\
            filter(fun.col('Date') <= datetime(2014, 10, 23))
```

We will convert the `Date` column's type and trim the time period in our factors DataFrame too:

```
factors = factors.withColumn('Date',
                    fun.to_date(fun.to_timestamp(fun.col('Date'),
                                                 'dd-MMM-yy')))

factors = factors.filter(fun.col('Date') >= datetime(2009, 10, 23)).\
            filter(fun.col('Date') <= datetime(2014, 10, 23))
```

The histories of a few thousand instruments and three factors are small enough to read and process locally. This remains the case even for larger simulations with hundreds of thousands of instruments and thousands of factors. Even though we have used PySpark for preprocessing our data so far, the need arises for a distributed system such as PySpark when we're actually running the simulations, which can require massive amounts of computation on each instrument. We can convert our PySpark DataFrame into a pandas DataFrame and still continue working with it easily by performing in-memory operations.

```
stocks_pd_df = stocks.toPandas()
factors_pd_df = factors.toPandas()

factors_pd_df.head(5)
...
        Date      Open    High    Low     Close   Volume  Symbol
0       2013-12-31        102.29  102.55  101.17  101.86  7219195
        NASDAQ%253ATLT
1       2013-12-30        102.15  102.58  102.08  102.51  4491711
        NASDAQ%253ATLT
2       2013-12-27        102.07  102.31  101.69  101.81  4755262
        NASDAQ%253ATLT
3       2013-12-26        102.35  102.36  102.01  102.10  4645323
        NASDAQ%253ATLT
4       2013-12-24        103.23  103.35  102.80  102.83  4897009
        NASDAQ%253ATLT
```

We will use these pandas DataFrames in the next section as we try to fit a linear regression model to predict instrument returns based on factor returns.

Determining the Factor Weights

Recall that VaR deals with losses *over a particular time horizon*. We are not concerned with the absolute prices of instruments, but with how those prices move over a given length of time. In our calculation, we will set that length to two weeks. The following function makes use of the pandas `rolling` method to transform a time series of prices into an overlapping sequence of price movements over two-week intervals. Note that we use 10 instead of 14 to define the window because financial data does not include weekends:

```
n_steps = 10
def my_fun(x):
    return ((x.iloc[-1] - x.iloc[0]) / x.iloc[0])

stock_returns = stocks_pd_df.groupby('Symbol').Close.\
                            rolling(window=n_steps).apply(my_fun)
factors_returns = factors_pd_df.groupby('Symbol').Close.\\
                            rolling(window=n_steps).apply(my_fun)

stock_returns = stock_returns.reset_index().\
                            sort_values('level_1').\
                            reset_index()
factors_returns = factors_returns.reset_index().\
                                sort_values('level_1').\
                                reset_index()
```

With these return histories in hand, we can turn to our goal of training predictive models for the instrument returns. For each instrument, we want a model that predicts its two-week return based on the returns of the factors over the same time period. For simplicity, we will use a linear regression model.

To model the fact that instrument returns may be nonlinear functions of the factor returns, we can include some additional features in our model that we derive from nonlinear transformations of the factor returns. As an example, we will add one additional feature for each factor return: square. Our model is still a linear model in the sense that the response variable is a linear function of the features. Some of the features just happen to be determined by nonlinear functions of the factor returns. Keep in mind that this particular feature transformation is meant to demonstrate some of the options available—it shouldn't be perceived as a state-of-the-art practice in predictive financial modeling.

```
# Create combined stocks DF
stocks_pd_df_with_returns = stocks_pd_df.\
                            assign(stock_returns = \
                                stock_returns['Close'])

# Create combined factors DF
factors_pd_df_with_returns = factors_pd_df.\
                            assign(factors_returns = \
                                factors_returns['Close'],
                                factors_returns_squared = \
                                factors_returns['Close']**2)

factors_pd_df_with_returns = factors_pd_df_with_returns.\
```

```
                                pivot(index='Date',
                                      columns='Symbol',
                                      values=['factors_returns', \
                                              'factors_returns_squared'])  ❶

    factors_pd_df_with_returns.columns = factors_pd_df_with_returns.\
                                         columns.\
                                         to_series().\
                                         str.\
                                         join('_').\
                                         reset_index()[0]  ❷

    factors_pd_df_with_returns = factors_pd_df_with_returns.\
                                 reset_index()

    print(factors_pd_df_with_returns.head(1))
    ...
    0        Date  factors_returns_NASDAQ%253ATLT   \
    0  2009-10-23                         0.01834

    0  factors_returns_NYSEARCA%253ACRED
    0                          -0.006594

    0 factors_returns_NYSEARCA%253AGLD   \
    0                        - 0.032623

    0   factors_returns_squared_NASDAQ%253ATLT   \
    0                               0.000336

    0   factors_returns_squared_NYSEARCA%253ACRED   \
    0                               0.000043

    0   factors_returns_squared_NYSEARCA%253AGLD
    0                               0.001064
    ...

    print(factors_pd_df_with_returns.columns)
    ...
    Index(['Date', 'factors_returns_NASDAQ%253ATLT',
           'factors_returns_NYSEARCA%253ACRED', 'factors_returns_NYSEARCA%253AGLD',
           'factors_returns_squared_NASDAQ%253ATLT',
           'factors_returns_squared_NYSEARCA%253ACRED',
           'factors_returns_squared_NYSEARCA%253AGLD'],
          dtype='object', name=0)
    ...
```

❶ Convert factors dataframe from long to wide format so that all factors for a period are in one row

❷ Flatten multi-index dataframe and fix column names

Even though we will be carrying out many regressions—one for each instrument—
the number of features and data points in each regression is small, meaning that we
don't need to make use of PySpark's distributed linear modeling capabilities. Instead,
we'll use the ordinary least squares regression offered by the scikit-learn package:

```
from sklearn.linear_model import LinearRegression

# For each stock, create input DF for linear regression training

stocks_factors_combined_df = pd.merge(stocks_pd_df_with_returns,
                                      factors_pd_df_with_returns,
                                      how="left", on="Date")

feature_columns = list(stocks_factors_combined_df.columns[-6:])

with pd.option_context('mode.use_inf_as_na', True):
    stocks_factors_combined_df = stocks_factors_combined_df.\
                                    dropna(subset=feature_columns \
                                        + ['stock_returns'])


def find_ols_coef(df):
    y = df[['stock_returns']].values
    X = df[feature_columns]

    regr = LinearRegression()
    regr_output = regr.fit(X, y)

    return list(df[['Symbol']].values[0]) + \
                list(regr_output.coef_[0])

coefs_per_stock = stocks_factors_combined_df.\
                    groupby('Symbol').\
                    apply(find_ols_coef)


coefs_per_stock = pd.DataFrame(coefs_per_stock).reset_index()
coefs_per_stock.columns = ['symbol', 'factor_coef_list']

coefs_per_stock = pd.DataFrame(coefs_per_stock.\
                                factor_coef_list.tolist(),
                                index=coefs_per_stock.index,
                                columns = ['Symbol'] + feature_columns)

coefs_per_stock
```

We now have a dataframe where each row is the set of model parameters (coefficients, weights, covariants, regressors, or whatever you wish to call them) for an
instrument.

At this point in any real-world pipeline it would be useful to understand how well these models fit the data. Because the data points are drawn from time series, and especially because the time intervals are overlapping, it is very likely that the samples are autocorrelated. This means that common measures like R^2 are likely to overestimate how well the models fit the data. The Breusch-Godfrey test (*https://oreil.ly/9cwg6*) is a standard test for assessing these effects. One quick way to evaluate a model is to separate a time series into two sets, leaving out enough data points in the middle so that the last points in the earlier set are not autocorrelated with the first points in the later set. Then train the model on one set and look at its error on the other.

With our models that map factor returns to instrument returns in hand, we now need a procedure for simulating market conditions by generating random factor returns. That's what we'll do next.

Sampling

To come up with a way for generating random factor returns, we need to decide on a probability distribution over factor return vectors and sample from it. What distribution does the data actually take? It can often be useful to start answering this kind of question visually.

A nice way to visualize a probability distribution over continuous data is a density plot that plots the distribution's domain versus its probability density function. Because we don't know the distribution that governs the data, we don't have an equation that can give us its density at an arbitrary point, but we can approximate it through a technique called *kernel density estimation* (KDE). In a loose way, kernel density estimation is a way of smoothing out a histogram. It centers a probability distribution (usually a normal distribution) at each data point. So a set of two-week-return samples would result in multiple normal distributions, each with a different mean. To estimate the probability density at a given point, it evaluates the PDFs of all the normal distributions at that point and takes their average. The smoothness of a kernel density plot depends on its *bandwidth*, the standard deviation of each of the normal distributions.

We'll use one of pandas DataFrame's built-in methods to calculate and draw a KDE plot. The following snippet creates a density plot for one of our factors:

```
samples = factors_returns.loc[factors_returns.Symbol == \
                              factors_returns.Symbol.unique()[0]]['Close']
samples.plot.kde()
```

Figure 8-1 shows the distribution (probability density function) of two-week returns for the 20+ Year Treasury Bond ETF in our history.

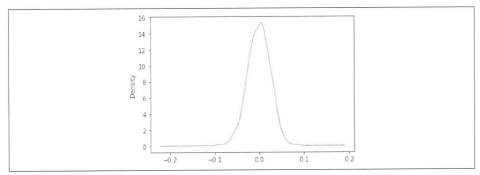

Figure 8-1. Two-week 20+ Year Treasury Bond ETF distribution

Figure 8-2 shows the same for two-week returns of US Credit Bonds.

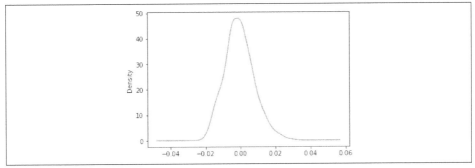

Figure 8-2. Two-week US Credit Bond ETF returns distribution

We will fit a normal distribution to the returns of each factor. Looking for a more exotic distribution, perhaps with fatter tails, that more closely fits the data is often worthwhile. However, for the sake of simplicity, we'll avoid tuning our simulation in this way.

The simplest way to sample factors' returns would be to fit a normal distribution to each of the factors and sample from these distributions independently. However, this ignores the fact that market factors are often correlated. If the Treasury Bond ETF is down, the Credit Bond ETF is likely to be down as well. Failing to take these correlations into account can give us a much rosier picture of our risk profile than its reality. Are the returns of our factors correlated? The Pearson's correlation implementation in pandas can help us find out:

```
f_1 = factors_returns.loc[factors_returns.Symbol == \
                    factors_returns.Symbol.unique()[0]]['Close']
f_2 = factors_returns.loc[factors_returns.Symbol == \
                    factors_returns.Symbol.unique()[1]]['Close']
f_3 = factors_returns.loc[factors_returns.Symbol == \
                    factors_returns.Symbol.unique()[2]]['Close']
```

```
pd.DataFrame({'f1': list(f_1), 'f2': list(f_2), 'f3': list(f_3)}).corr()
...
```

```
        f1          f2          f3
f1   1.000000              0.530550              0.074578
f2   0.530550              1.000000              0.206538
f3   0.074578              0.206538              1.000000
```

Because we have nonzero elements off the diagonals, it doesn't look like it.

The Multivariate Normal Distribution

The multivariate normal distribution can help here by taking the correlation information between the factors into account. Each sample from a multivariate normal is a vector. Given values for all of the dimensions but one, the distribution of values along that dimension is normal. But, in their joint distribution, the variables are not independent.

The multivariate normal is parameterized with a mean along each dimension and a matrix describing the covariances between each pair of dimensions. With N dimensions, the covariance matrix is N by N because we want to capture the covariances between each pair of dimensions. When the covariance matrix is diagonal, the multivariate normal reduces to sampling along each dimension independently, but placing nonzero values in the off-diagonals helps capture the relationships between variables.

The VaR literature often describes a step in which the factor weights are transformed (decorrelated) so that sampling can proceed. This is normally accomplished with a Cholesky decomposition or eigendecomposition. NumPy package's `Multivariate NormalDistribution` takes care of this step for us under the covers using an eigendecomposition.

To fit a multivariate normal distribution to our data, first we need to find its sample means and covariances:

```
factors_returns_cov = pd.DataFrame({'f1': list(f_1),
                                    'f2': list(f_2[:-1]),
                                    'f3': list(f_3[:-2])})\
                                    .cov().to_numpy()
factors_returns_mean = pd.DataFrame({'f1': list(f_1),
                                     'f2': list(f_2[:-1]),
                                     'f3': list(f_3[:-2])}).\
                                     mean()
```

Then we can simply create a distribution parameterized with them and sample a set of market conditions from it:

```
from numpy.random import multivariate_normal

multivariate_normal(factors_returns_mean, factors_returns_cov)
```

```
...
array([ 0.02234821,  0.01838763, -0.01107748])
```

With the per-instrument models and a procedure for sampling factor returns, we now have the pieces we need to run the actual trials. Let's start working on our simulation and run the trials.

Running the Trials

Because running the trials is computationally intensive, we'll turn to PySpark to help us parallelize them. In each trial, we want to sample a set of risk factors, use them to predict the return of each instrument, and sum all those returns to find the full trial loss. To achieve a representative distribution, we want to run thousands or millions of these trials.

We have a few choices for how to parallelize the simulation. We can parallelize along trials, instruments, or both. To parallelize along both, we would create a dataset of instruments and a dataset of trial parameters and then use the crossJoin transformation to generate a dataset of all the pairs. This is the most general approach, but it has a couple of disadvantages. First, it requires explicitly creating a DataFrame of trial parameters, which we can avoid by using some tricks with random seeds. Second, it requires a shuffle operation.

Partitioning along instruments would look something like this:

```
random_seed = 1496
instruments_dF = ...
def trialLossesForInstrument(seed, instrument):
    ...

instruments_DF.rdd.\
  flatMap(trialLossesForInstrument(random_seed, _)).\
  reduceByKey(_ + _)
```

With this approach, the data is partitioned across a DataFrame of instruments, and for each instrument a flatMap transformation computes and yields the loss against every trial. Using the same random seed across all tasks means that we will generate the same sequence of trials. reduceByKey sums together all the losses corresponding to the same trials. A disadvantage of this approach is that it still requires shuffling $O(|\text{instruments}| * |\text{trials}|)$ data.

Our model data for our few thousand instruments is small enough to fit in memory on every executor, and some back-of-the-envelope calculations reveal that this is probably still the case even with a million or so instruments and hundreds of factors. A million instruments times 500 factors times the 8 bytes needed for the double that stores each factor weight equals roughly 4 GB, small enough to fit in each executor on most modern-day cluster machines. This means that a good option is to distribute the instrument data in a broadcast variable. The advantage of each executor having a full copy of the instrument data is that total loss for each trial can be computed on a single machine. No aggregation is necessary. We also broadcast some other data required for trial return calculation.

```
b_coefs_per_stock = spark.sparkContext.broadcast(coefs_per_stock)
b_feature_columns = spark.sparkContext.broadcast(feature_columns)
b_factors_returns_mean = spark.sparkContext.broadcast(factors_returns_mean)
b_factors_returns_cov = spark.sparkContext.broadcast(factors_returns_cov)
```

With the partition-by-trials approach (which we will use), we start out with a Data-Frame of seeds. We want a different seed in each partition so that each partition generates different trials:

```
from pyspark.sql.types import IntegerType

parallelism = 1000
num_trials = 1000000
base_seed = 1496

seeds = [b for b in range(base_seed,
                          base_seed + parallelism)]
seedsDF = spark.createDataFrame(seeds, IntegerType())

seedsDF = seedsDF.repartition(parallelism)
```

Random number generation is a time-consuming and CPU-intensive process. While we don't employ this trick here, it can often be useful to generate a set of random numbers in advance and use it across multiple jobs. The same random numbers should *not* be used within a single job, because this would violate the Monte Carlo assumption that the random values are independently distributed.

For each seed, we want to generate a set of trial parameters and observe the effects of these parameters on all the instruments. We will write a function that calculates the full return of instruments for multiple trials. We start by simply applying the linear model that we trained earlier for each instrument. Then we average over the returns of all the instruments. This assumes that we're holding an equal value of each instrument in the portfolio. A weighted average would be used if we held different amounts of each stock. Lastly, we need to generate a bunch of trials in each task. Because choosing random numbers is a big part of the process, it is important to use a strong random number generator. Python's in-built random library includes a Mersenne Twister implementation that is good for this. We use it to sample from a multivariate normal distribution as described previously:

```
import random

from pyspark.sql.types import LongType, ArrayType
from pyspark.sql.functions import udf
```

```
def calculate_trial_return(x):
#      return x
    trial_return_list = []

    for i in range(num_trials/parallelism):
        random_int = random.randint(0, num_trials*num_trials)

        seed(x)

        random_factors = multivariate_normal(b_factors_returns_mean.value,
          b_factors_returns_cov.value)

        coefs_per_stock_df = b_coefs_per_stock.value
        returns_per_stock = coefs_per_stock_df[b_feature_columns.value] *
          (list(random_factors) + list(random_factors**2))

        trial_return_list.append(float(returns_per_stock.sum(axis=1).sum()/b_coefs_
          per_stock.value.size))

    return trial_return_list

udf_return = udf(calculate_trial_return, ArrayType(DoubleType()))
```

With our scaffolding complete, we can use it to compute a DataFrame where each element is the total return from a single trial:

```
from pyspark.sql.functions import col, explode

trials = seedsDF.withColumn("trial_return", udf_return(col("value")))
trials = trials.select('value', explode('trial_return')) ❶

trials.cache()
```

❶ Split array of trial returns into individual DataFrame rows

If you recall, the whole reason we've been messing around with all these numbers is to calculate VaR. trials now forms an empirical distribution over portfolio returns. To calculate 5% VaR, we need to find a return that we expect to underperform 5% of the time, and a return that we expect to outperform 5% of the time. With our empirical distribution, this is as simple as finding the value that 5% of trials are worse than and 95% of trials are better than. We can accomplish this by pulling the worst 5% of trials into the driver. Our VaR is the return of the best trial in this subset:

```
trials.approxQuantile('trial_return', [0.05], 0.0)
...
-0.010831826593164014
```

We can find the CVaR with a nearly identical approach. Instead of taking the best trial return from the worst 5% of trials, we take the average return from that set of trials:

```
trials.orderBy(col('trial_return').asc()).\
  limit(int(trials.count()/20)).\
```

```
        agg(fun.avg(col("trial_return"))).show()
...
+-------------------+
|  avg(trial_return)|
+-------------------+
|-0.09002629251426077|
+-------------------+
```

Visualizing the Distribution of Returns

In addition to calculating VaR at a particular confidence level, it can be useful to look at a fuller picture of the distribution of returns. Are they normally distributed? Do they spike at the extremities? As we did for the individual factors, we can plot an estimate of the probability density function for the joint probability distribution using kernel density estimation (see Figure 8-3):

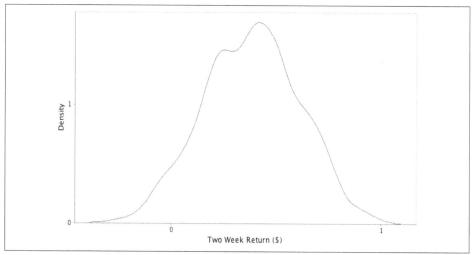

Figure 8-3. Two-week returns distribution

Where to Go from Here

The model laid out in this exercise is a very rough first cut of what would be used in an actual financial institution. In building an accurate VaR model, we glossed over a few very important steps. Curating the set of market factors can make or break a model, and it is not uncommon for financial institutions to incorporate hundreds of factors in their simulations. Picking these factors requires both running numerous experiments on historical data and a heavy dose of creativity. Choosing the predictive model that maps market factors to instrument returns is also important. Although we used a simple linear model, many calculations use nonlinear functions or simulate the path over time with Brownian motion.

Lastly, it is worth putting care into the distribution used to simulate the factor returns. Kolmogorov-Smirnov tests and chi-squared tests are useful for testing an empirical distribution's normality. Q-Q plots are useful for comparing distributions visually. Usually, financial risk is better mirrored by a distribution with fatter tails than the normal distribution that we used. Mixtures of normal distributions are one good way to achieve these fatter tails. "Financial Economics, Fat-tailed Distributions" (*https://oreil.ly/XSxhB*), an article by Markus Haas and Christian Pigorsch, provides a nice reference on some of the other fat-tailed distributions out there.

Banks use PySpark and large-scale data processing frameworks for calculating VaR with historical methods as well. "Evaluation of Value-at-Risk Models Using Historical Data" (*https://oreil.ly/0JoXu*), by Darryll Hendricks, provides a good overview and performance comparison of historical VaR methods.

Monte Carlo risk simulations can be used for more than calculating a single statistic. The results can be used to proactively reduce the risk of a portfolio by shaping investment decisions. For example, if in the trials with the poorest returns, a particular set of instruments tends to come up losing money repeatedly, we might consider dropping those instruments from the portfolio or adding instruments that tend to move in the opposite direction from them.

## CHAPTER 9

Analyzing Genomics Data
and the BDG Project

The advent of next-generation DNA sequencing (NGS) technology has rapidly transformed the life sciences into a data-driven field. However, making the best use of this data is butting up against a traditional computational ecosystem that builds on difficult-to-use, low-level primitives for distributed computing and a jungle of semistructured text-based file formats.

This chapter will serve two primary purposes. First, we introduce a set of popular serialization and file formats (Avro and Parquet) that simplify many problems in data management. These serialization technologies enable us to convert data into compact, machine-friendly binary representations. This helps with movement of data across networks and helps with cross-compatibility across programming languages. Although we will use data serialization techniques with genomics data, the concepts will be useful whenever processing large amounts of data.

Second, we show how to perform typical genomics tasks in the PySpark ecosystem. Specifically, we'll use PySpark and the open source ADAM library to manipulate large quantities of genomics data and process data from multiple sources to create a dataset for predicting transcription factor (TF) binding sites. For this, we will join genome annotations from the ENCODE dataset (*https://oreil.ly/h0yOq*). This chapter will serve as a tutorial to the ADAM project, which comprises a set of genomics-specific Avro schemas, PySpark-based APIs, and command-line tools for large-scale genomics analysis. Among other applications, ADAM provides a natively distributed implementation of the Genome Analysis Toolkit (GATK) (*https://oreil.ly/k2YZH*) using PySpark.

We'll start by talking about the various data formats used in the bioinformatics domain, associated challenges, and how serialization formats can help. After that, we'll install the ADAM project and explore its API using a sample dataset. We will then work with multiple genomics datasets to prepare a dataset that can be used for predicting binding sites in DNA sequences for a particular type of protein—CTCF transcription factor. The datasets will be obtained from the publicly available ENCODE dataset. Because the genome implies a 1D coordinate system, many genomics operations are spatial in nature. The ADAM project provides a genomics-targeted API for performing distributed spatial joins that we will use.

 For those interested, a great introduction to biology is Eric Lander's EdX course (*https://oreil.ly/WIky1*). For an introduction to bioinformatics, see Arthur Lesk's *Introduction to Bioinformatics* (Oxford University Press).

Decoupling Storage from Modeling

Bioinformaticians spend a disproportionate amount of time worrying about file formats—*.fasta*, *.fastq*, *.sam*, *.bam*, *.vcf*, *.gvcf*, *.bcf*, *.bed*, *.gff*, *.gtf*, *.narrowPeak*, *.wig*, *.bigWig*, *.bigBed*, *.ped*, and *.tped*, to name a few. Some scientists also feel it is necessary to specify their own custom format for their custom tool. On top of that, many of the format specifications are incomplete or ambiguous (which makes it hard to ensure implementations are consistent or compliant) and specify ASCII-encoded data. ASCII data is very common in bioinformatics, but it is inefficient and compresses relatively poorly. In addition, the data must always be parsed, necessitating additional compute cycles.

This is particularly troubling because all of these file formats essentially store just a few common object types: an aligned sequence read, a called genotype, a sequence feature, and a phenotype. (The term *sequence feature* is slightly overloaded in genomics, but in this chapter we mean it in the sense of an element from a track of the UCSC Genome Browser.) Libraries like biopython (*http://biopython.org*) are popular because they are chock-full of parsers (e.g., Bio.SeqIO) that attempt to read all the file formats into a small number of common in-memory models (e.g., Bio.Seq, Bio.SeqRecord, Bio.SeqFeature).

We can solve all of these problems in one shot using a serialization framework like Apache Avro. The key lies in Avro's separation of the data model (i.e., an explicit schema) from the underlying storage file format and also the language's in-memory representation. Avro specifies how data of a certain type should be communicated between processes, whether that's between running processes over the internet, or a process trying to write the data into a particular file format. For example, a Java program that uses Avro can write the data into multiple underlying file formats that are all compatible with Avro's data model. This allows each process to stop worrying about compatibility with multiple file formats: the process only needs to know how to read Avro, and the filesystem needs to know how to supply Avro.

Let's take the sequence feature as an example. We begin by specifying the desired schema for the object using the Avro interface definition language (IDL):

```
enum Strand {
  Forward,
  Reverse,
  Independent
}

record SequenceFeature {
  string featureId;
  string featureType;  ❶
  string chromosome;
  long startCoord;
  long endCoord;
  Strand strand;
  double value;
  map<string> attributes;
}
```

❶ For example, "conservation," "centipede," "gene"

This data type could be used to encode, for example, conservation level, the presence of a promoter or ribosome binding site, a TF binding site, and so on at a particular location in the genome. One way to think about it is as a binary version of JSON, but more restricted and with higher performance. Given a particular data schema, the Avro spec then determines the precise binary encoding for the object so that it can be easily communicated between processes (even if written in different programming languages), over the network, or onto disk for storage. The Avro project includes modules for processing Avro-encoded data from many languages, including Java, C/C++, Python, and Perl; after that, the language is free to store the object in memory in whichever way is deemed most advantageous. The separation of data modeling from the storage format provides another level of flexibility/abstraction; Avro data can be stored as Avro-serialized binary objects (Avro container file), in a columnar file format for fast queries (Parquet file), or as text JSON data for maximum flexibility (minimum efficiency). Finally, Avro supports schema evolution, allowing the user to add new fields as they become necessary, while the software gracefully deals with new/old versions of the schema.

Overall, Avro is an efficient binary encoding that allows you to specify evolvable data schemas, process the same data from many programming languages, and store the data using many formats. Deciding to store your data using Avro schemas frees you from perpetually working with more and more custom data formats, while simultaneously increasing the performance of your computations.

Serialization/RPC Frameworks

There are a large number of serialization and remote procedure call frameworks in the wild. The most commonly used frameworks in the big data community are Apache Avro and Google's Protocol Buffers (protobuf). At the core, they all provide an interface definition language for specifying the schemas of object/message types, and they all compile into a variety of programming languages. (Google's RPC framework for protobuf is now the open source project gRPC.) On top of IDL and RPC, Avro adds a file format specification for storing the data on-disk.

It's difficult to make generalizations about which framework is appropriate in what circumstances because they all support different languages and have different performance characteristics for the various languages.

The particular `SequenceFeature` model used in the preceding example is a bit simplistic for real data, but the Big Data Genomics (BDG) project has already defined Avro schemas to represent the following objects, as well as many others:

- `AlignmentRecord` for reads
- `Variant` for known genome variants and metadata
- `Genotype` for a called genotype at a particular locus
- `Feature` for a sequence feature (annotation on a genome segment)

The actual schemas can be found in the `bdg-formats` GitHub repo (*https://oreil.ly/ gCf1f*). The BDG formats can function as a replacement of the ubiquitous "legacy" formats (like BAM and VCF), but more commonly function as high-performance "intermediate" formats. (The original goal of these BDG formats was to replace the use of BAM and VCF, but their stubborn ubiquity has proved this goal to be difficult to attain.) Avro provides many performance and data modeling benefits over the custom ASCII status quo.

In the remainder of the chapter, we'll use some of the BDG schemas to accomplish some typical genomics tasks. Before we can do that, we will need to install the ADAM project. That's what we'll do in the next section.

Setting Up ADAM

BDG's core set of genomics tools is called ADAM. Starting from a set of mapped reads, this core includes tools that can perform mark-duplicates, base quality score recalibration, indel realignment, and variant calling, among other tasks. ADAM also contains a command-line interface that wraps the core for ease of use. In contrast to traditional HPC tools, ADAM can automatically parallelize across a cluster without having to split files or schedule jobs manually.

We can start by installing ADAM using pip:

```
pip3 install bdgenomics.adam
```

Alternative installation methods can be found on the GitHub page (*https://oreil.ly/ 4eFnX*).

ADAM also comes with a submission script that facilitates interfacing with Spark's `spark-submit` script:

```
adam-submit
...

Using ADAM_MAIN=org.bdgenomics.adam.cli.ADAMMain
Using spark-submit=/home/analytical-monk/miniconda3/envs/pyspark/bin/spark-submit

        e        888~-_         e          e    e
       d8b       888   \       d8b        d8b  d8b
      /Y88b      888    |      /Y88b     d888bdY88b
     /  Y88b     888    |     /  Y88b   /  Y88Y Y888b
    /____Y88b    888    /    /____Y88b  /   YY   Y888b
   /      Y88b   888_-~    /       Y88b /         Y888b

Usage: adam-submit [<spark-args> --] <adam-args>

Choose one of the following commands:

ADAM ACTIONS
            countKmers : Counts the k-mers/q-mers from a read dataset...
       countSliceKmers : Counts the k-mers/q-mers from a slice dataset...
    transformAlignments : Convert SAM/BAM to ADAM format and optionally...
      transformFeatures : Convert a file with sequence features into...
     transformGenotypes : Convert a file with genotypes into correspondi...
     transformSequences : Convert a FASTA file as sequences into corresp...
        transformSlices : Convert a FASTA file as slices into correspond...
      transformVariants : Convert a file with variants into correspondin...
            mergeShards : Merges the shards of a fil...
               coverage : Calculate the coverage from a given ADAM fil...
CONVERSION OPERATION
            adam2fastq : Convert BAM to FASTQ file
     transformFragments : Convert alignments into fragment records
PRIN
                  print : Print an ADAM formatted fil
               flagstat : Print statistics on reads in an ADAM file...
                   view : View certain reads from an alignment-record file.
```

At this point, you should be able to run ADAM from the command line and get the usage message. As noted in the usage message, Spark arguments are given before ADAM-specific arguments.

With ADAM set up, we can start working with genomic data. We will explore ADAM's API by working with a sample dataset next.

Introduction to Working with Genomics Data Using ADAM

We'll start by taking a *.bam* file containing some mapped NGS reads, converting them to the corresponding BDG format (AlignedRecord in this case), and saving them to HDFS. First, we get our hands on a suitable *.bam* file:

```
# Note: this file is 16 GB
curl -O ftp://ftp.ncbi.nlm.nih.gov/1000genomes/ftp/phase3/data\
/HG00103/alignment/HG00103.mapped.ILLUMINA.bwa.GBR\
.low_coverage.20120522.bam

# or using Aspera instead (which is *much* faster)
ascp -i path/to/asperaweb_id_dsa.openssh -QTr -l 10G \
anonftp@ftp.ncbi.nlm.nih.gov:/1000genomes/ftp/phase3/data\
/HG00103/alignment/HG00103.mapped.ILLUMINA.bwa.GBR\
.low_coverage.20120522.bam .
```

Move the downloaded file into a directory where we'll store all data for this chapter:

```
mv HG00103.mapped.ILLUMINA.bwa.GBR\
.low_coverage.20120522.bam data/genomics
```

Next up, we'll use the ADAM CLI.

File Format Conversion with the ADAM CLI

We can then use the ADAM transform command to convert the *.bam* file to Parquet format (described in "Parquet Format and Columnar Storage" on page 171). This would work both on a cluster and in local mode:

```
adam-submit \
  --master yarn \ ❶
  --deploy-mode client \
  --driver-memory 8G \
  --num-executors 6 \
  --executor-cores 4 \
  --executor-memory 12G \
  -- \
  transform \ ❷
  data/genomics/HG00103.mapped.ILLUMINA.bwa.GBR\
.low_coverage.20120522.bam \
  data/genomics/HG00103
```

❶ Example Spark args for running on YARN

❷ The ADAM subcommand itself

This should kick off a pretty large amount of output to the console, including the URL to track the progress of the job.

The resulting dataset is the concatenation of all the files in the *data/genomics/reads/HG00103/* directory, where each *part-*.parquet* file is the output from one of the PySpark tasks. You'll also notice that the data has been compressed more efficiently than the initial *.bam* file (which is gzipped underneath) thanks to the columnar storage (see "Parquet Format and Columnar Storage" on page 171).

```
$ du -sh data/genomics/HG00103*bam
16G  data/genomics/HG00103. [...] .bam

$ du -sh data/genomics/HG00103/
13G  data/genomics/HG00103
```

Let's see what one of these objects looks like in an interactive session.

Ingesting Genomics Data Using PySpark and ADAM

First, we start up the PySpark shell using the ADAM helper command. It loads all of the JARs that are necessary.

```
pyadam

...

[...]
Welcome to
      ____              __
     / __/__  ___ _____/ /__
    _\ \/ _ \/ _ `/ __/  '_/
   /__ / .__/\_,_/_/ /_/\_\   version 3.2.1
      /_/
```

```
Using Python version 3.6.12 (default, Sep  8 2020 23:10:56)
Spark context Web UI available at http://192.168.29.60:4040
Spark context available as 'sc'.
SparkSession available as 'spark'.
```

>>>

 In some cases, you can encounter a TypeError error with a mention of JavaPackage object not being when trying to use ADAM with PySpark. It is a known issue and is documented here (*https://oreil.ly/67uBd*).

In such a scenario, please try the solutions suggested in the thread. One could be running the following command to start PySpark shell with ADAM:

```
!pyspark --conf spark.serializer=org.apache.spark.
serializer.KryoSerializer --conf spark.kryo.registrator=
org.bdgenomics.adam.serialization.ADAMKryoRegistrator
--jars `find-adam-assembly.sh` --driver-class-path
`find-adam-assembly.sh`
```

Now we'll load the aligned read data as an `AlignmentDataset`:

```
from bdgenomics.adam.adamContext import ADAMContext

ac = ADAMContext(spark)

readsData = ac.loadAlignments("data/HG00103")

readsDataDF = readsData.toDF()
readsDataDF.show(1, vertical=True)

...

-RECORD 0---------------------------------------
 referenceName        | hs37d5
 start                | 21810734
 originalStart        | null
 end                  | 21810826
 mappingQuality       | 0
 readName             | SRR062640.14600566
 sequence             | TCCATTCCACTCAGTTT...
 qualityScores        | /MOONNCRQPIQIKRGL...
 cigar                | 92M8S
 originalCigar        | null
 basesTrimmedFromStart| 0
 basesTrimmedFromEnd  | 0
 readPaired           | true
 properPair           | false
 readMapped           | false
 mateMapped           | true
```

```
failedVendorQualityChecks |  false
duplicateRead             |  false
readNegativeStrand        |  false
mateNegativeStrand        |  false
primaryAlignment          |  true
secondaryAlignment        |  false
supplementaryAlignment    |  false
mismatchingPositions      |  null
originalQualityScores     |  null
readGroupId               |  SRR062640
readGroupSampleId         |  HG00103
mateAlignmentStart        |  21810734
mateReferenceName         |  hs37d5
insertSize                |  null
readInFragment            |  1
attributes                |  RG:Z:SRR062640\tX...
only showing top 1 row
```

You may get a different read because the partitioning of the data may be different on your system, so there is no guarantee which read will come back first.

Now we can interactively ask questions about our dataset, all while executing the computations across a cluster in the background. How many reads do we have in this dataset?

```
readsData.toDF().count()
...
160397565
```

Do the reads in this dataset derive from all human chromosomes?

```
unique_chr = readsDataDF.select('referenceName').distinct().collect()
unique_chr = [u.referenceName for u in unique_chr]

unique_chr.sort()
...
1
10
11
12
[...]
GL000249.1
MT
NC_007605
X
Y
hs37d5
```

Yep, we observe reads from chromosomes 1 through 22, X and Y, along with some other chromosomal chunks that are not part of the "main" chromosomes or whose locations are unknown. Let's analyze the code a little more closely:

```
readsData = ac.loadAlignments("data/HG00103") ❶

readsDataDF = readsData.toDF() ❷

unique_chr = readsDataDF.select('referenceName').distinct(). \ ❸
                collect() ❹
```

❶ `AlignmentDataset`: an ADAM type that contains all our data.

❷ `DataFrame`: the underlying Spark DataFrame.

❸ This will aggregate all the distinct contig names; it will be small.

❹ This triggers the computation and brings the data in the DataFrame back to the client app (the shell).

For a more clinical example, say we are testing an individual's genome to check whether they carry any gene variants that put them at risk for having a child with cystic fibrosis (CF). Our genetic test uses next-generation DNA sequencing to generate reads from multiple relevant genes, such as the CFTR gene (whose mutations can cause CF). After running our data through our genotyping pipeline, we determine that the CFTR gene appears to have a premature stop codon that destroys its function. However, this mutation has never been reported before in the Human Gene Mutation Database (*https://oreil.ly/wULRR*), nor is it in the Sickkids CFTR database (*https://oreil.ly/u1L0j*), which aggregates CF gene variants. We want to go back to the raw sequencing data to see if the potentially deleterious genotype call is a false positive. To do so, we need to manually analyze all the reads that map to that variant locus, say, chromosome 7 at 117149189 (see Figure 9-1):

```
from pyspark.sql import functions as fun
cftr_reads = readsDataDF.where("referenceName == 7").\
                where(fun.col("start") <= 117149189).\
                where(fun.col("end") > 117149189)

cftr_reads.count()
...

9
```

It is now possible to manually inspect these nine reads, or process them through a custom aligner, for example, and check whether the reported pathogenic variant is a false positive.

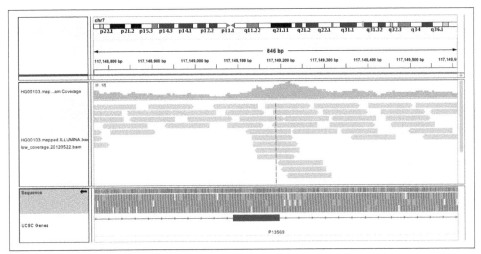

Figure 9-1. Integrative Genomic Viewer visualization of the HG00103 at chr7:117149189 in the CFTR gene

Say we're running a clinical lab that is performing such carrier screening as a service to clinicians. Archiving the raw data using a cloud storage system such as AWS S3 ensures that the data stays relatively warm (compared with, say, tape archive). In addition to having a reliable system for actually performing the data processing, we can easily access all of the past data for quality control or for cases where there needs to be manual interventions, like the CFTR example presented earlier. In addition to the rapid access to the totality of the data, the centrality also makes it easy to perform large analytical studies, like population genetics, large-scale quality-control analyses, and so on.

Now that we are familiar with the ADAM API, let's start work on creation of our transcription factor prediction dataset.

Parquet Format and Columnar Storage

In the previous section, we saw how we can manipulate a potentially large amount of sequencing data without worrying about the specifics of the underlying storage or the parallelization of the execution. However, it's worth noting that the ADAM project makes use of the Parquet file format, which confers some considerable performance advantages that we introduce here.

Parquet is an open source file format specification and a set of reader/writer implementations that we recommend for general use for data that will be used in analytical queries (write once, read many times). It is largely based on the underlying data storage format used in Google's Dremel system (see "Dremel: Interactive Analysis of Web-scale Datasets" (*https://oreil.ly/iObP5*), Proc. VLDB, 2010, by Melnik et al.)

and has a data model that is compatible with Avro, Thrift, and Protocol Buffers. Specifically, it supports most of the common database types (int, double, string, etc.), along with arrays and records, including nested types. Significantly, it is a columnar file format, meaning that values for a particular column from many records are stored contiguously on disk (see Figure 9-2). This physical data layout allows for far more efficient data encoding/compression, and significantly reduces query times by minimizing the amount of data that must be read/deserialized (*https://oreil.ly/ GciCh*). Parquet supports specifying different compression schemes for each column, as well as column-specific encoding schemes such as run-length encoding, dictionary encoding, and delta encoding.

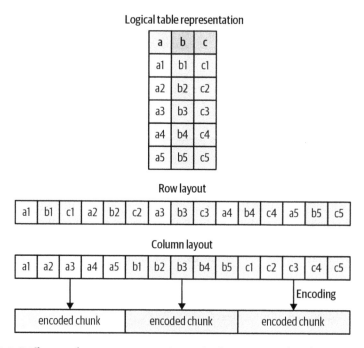

Figure 9-2. Differences between a row-major and column-major data layout

Another useful feature of Parquet for increasing performance is *predicate pushdown*. A *predicate* is some expression or function that evaluates to true or false based on the data record (or equivalently, the expressions in a SQL WHERE clause). In our earlier CFTR query, Spark had to deserialize/materialize each AlignmentRecord before deciding whether or not it passed the predicate. This leads to a significant amount of wasted I/O and CPU time. The Parquet reader implementations allow us to provide a predicate class that only deserializes the necessary columns for making the decision, before materializing the full record.

Predicting Transcription Factor Binding Sites from ENCODE Data

In this example, we will use publicly available sequence feature data to build a simple model for transcription factor binding. TFs are proteins that bind to specific DNA sequences in the genome and help control the expression of different genes. As a result, they are critical in determining the phenotype of a particular cell and are involved in many physiological and disease processes. ChIP-seq is an NGS-based assay that allows the genome-wide characterization of binding sites for a particular TF in a particular cell/tissue type. However, in addition to ChIP-seq's cost and technical difficulty, it requires a separate experiment for each tissue/TF pair. In contrast, DNase-seq is an assay that finds regions of open chromatin genome-wide and needs to be performed only once per tissue type. Instead of assaying TF binding sites by performing a ChIP-seq experiment for each tissue/TF combination, we'd like to predict TF binding sites in a new tissue type assuming only the availability of DNase-seq data.

In particular, we will predict the binding sites for the CTCF TF using DNase-seq data along with known sequence motif data (from HT-SELEX (*https://oreil.ly/t5OEkL*)) and other data from the publicly available ENCODE dataset (*https://oreil.ly/eFJ9n*). We have chosen six different cell types that have available DNase-seq and CTCF ChIP-seq data for training. A training example will be a DNase hypersensitivity (HS) peak (a segment of the genome), and the binary label for whether the TF is bound/unbound will be derived from the ChIP-seq data.

To summarize the overall data flow: the main training/test examples will be derived from the DNase-seq data. Each region of open chromatin (an interval on the genome) will be used to generate a prediction of whether a particular TF in a particular tissue type will be bound there. To do so, we spatially join the ChIP-seq data to the DNase-seq data; every overlap is a positive label for the DNase seq objects. Finally, to improve the prediction accuracy, we generate an additional feature at each interval in the DNase-seq data—distance to a transcription start site (using the GENCODE dataset). The feature is added into the training examples by performing a spatial join (with a possible aggregation).

We will use data from the following cell lines:

GM12878
Commonly studied lymphoblastoid cell line

K562
Female chronic myelogenous leukemia

BJ
Skin fibroblast

HEK293

Embryonic kidney

H54

Glioblastoma

HepG2

Hepatocellular carcinoma

First, we download the DNase data for each cell line in *.narrowPeak* format:

```
mkdir data/genomics/dnase

curl -O -L "https://www.encodeproject.org/ \
            files/ENCFF001UVC/@@download/ENCFF001UVC.bed.gz" | \
            gunzip > data/genomics/dnase/GM12878.DNase.narrowPeak ❶
curl -O -L "https://www.encodeproject.org/ \
            files/ENCFF001UWQ/@@download/ENCFF001UWQ.bed.gz" | \
            gunzip > data/genomics/dnase/K562.DNase.narrowPeak
curl -O -L "https://www.encodeproject.org/ \
            files/ENCFF001WEI/@@download/ENCFF001WEI.bed.gz" | \
            gunzip > data/genomics/dnase/BJ.DNase.narrowPeak
curl -O -L "https://www.encodeproject.org/ \
            files/ENCFF001UVQ/@@download/ENCFF001UVQ.bed.gz" | \
            gunzip > data/genomics/dnase/HEK293.DNase.narrowPeak
curl -O -L "https://www.encodeproject.org/ \
            files/ENCFF001SOM/@@download/ENCFF001SOM.bed.gz" | \
            gunzip > data/genomics/dnase/H54.DNase.narrowPeak
curl -O -L "https://www.encodeproject.org/ \
            files/ENCFF001UVU/@@download/ENCFF001UVU.bed.gz" | \
            gunzip > data/genomics/dnase/HepG2.DNase.narrowPeak

[...]
```

❶ Streaming decompression

Next, we download the ChIP-seq data for the CTCF TF, also in *.narrowPeak* format, and the GENCODE data, in GTF format:

```
mkdir data/genomics/chip-seq

curl -O -L "https://www.encodeproject.org/ \
            files/ENCFF001VED/@@download/ENCFF001VED.bed.gz" | \
            gunzip > data/genomics/chip-seq/GM12878.ChIP-seq.CTCF.narrowPeak
curl -O -L "https://www.encodeproject.org/ \
            files/ENCFF001VMZ/@@download/ENCFF001VMZ.bed.gz" | \
            gunzip > data/genomics/chip-seq/K562.ChIP-seq.CTCF.narrowPeak
curl -O -L "https://www.encodeproject.org/ \
            files/ENCFF001XMU/@@download/ENCFF001XMU.bed.gz" | \
            gunzip > data/genomics/chip-seq/BJ.ChIP-seq.CTCF.narrowPeak
curl -O -L "https://www.encodeproject.org/ \
            files/ENCFF001XQU/@@download/ENCFF001XQU.bed.gz" | \
```

```
                    gunzip > data/genomics/chip-seq/HEK293.ChIP-seq.CTCF.narrowPeak
    curl -O -L "https://www.encodeproject.org/ \
                files/ENCFF001USC/@@download/ENCFF001USC.bed.gz" | \
                gunzip> data/genomics/chip-seq/H54.ChIP-seq.CTCF.narrowPeak
    curl -O -L "https://www.encodeproject.org/ \
                files/ENCFF001XRC/@@download/ENCFF001XRC.bed.gz" | \
                gunzip> data/genomics/chip-seq/HepG2.ChIP-seq.CTCF.narrowPeak

    curl -s -L "http://ftp.ebi.ac.uk/pub/databases/gencode/\
                Gencode_human/release_18/gencode.v18.annotation.gtf.gz" | \
                gunzip > data/genomics/gencode.v18.annotation.gtf
    [...]
```

Note how we unzip the stream of data with `gunzip` on the way to depositing it in our filesystem.

From all of this raw data, we want to generate a training set with a schema like the following:

1. Chromosome

2. Start

3. End

4. Distance to closest transcription start site (TSS)

5. TF identity (always "CTCF" in this case)

6. Cell line

7. TF binding status (boolean; the target variable)

This dataset can easily be converted into a DataFrame to carry into a machine learning library. Since we need to generate the data for multiple cell lines, we will define a DataFrame for each cell line individually and concatenate them at the end:

```
cell_lines = ["GM12878", "K562", "BJ", "HEK293", "H54", "HepG2"]
for cell in cell_lines:
## For each cell line…
  ## …generate a suitable DataFrame
## Concatenate the DataFrames and carry through into MLlib, for example
```

We define a utility function and a broadcast variable that will be used to generate the features:

```
local_prefix = "data/genomics"
import pyspark.sql.functions as fun

## UDF for finding closest transcription start site
## naive; exercise for reader: make this faster
def distance_to_closest(loci, query):
  return min([abs(x - query) for x in loci])
distance_to_closest_udf = fun.udf(distance_to_closest)
```

```
## build in-memory structure for computing distance to TSS
## we are essentially implementing a broadcast join here
tss_data = ac.loadFeatures("data/genomics/gencode.v18.annotation.gtf")
tss_df = tss_data.toDF().filter(fun.col("featureType") == 'transcript')
b_tss_df = spark.sparkContext.broadcast(tss_df.groupBy('referenceName').\
                agg(fun.collect_list("start").alias("start_sites")))
```

Now that we have loaded the data necessary for defining our training examples, we define the body of the "loop" for computing the data on each cell line. Note how we read the text representations of the ChIP-seq and DNase data, because the datasets are not so large that they will hurt performance.

To do so, we load the DNase and ChIP-seq data:

```
current_cell_line = cell_lines[0]

dnase_path = f'data/genomics/dnase/{current_cell_line}.DNase.narrowPeak'
dnase_data = ac.loadFeatures(dnase_path) ❶
dnase_data.toDF().columns ❷
...
['featureId', 'sampleId', 'name', 'source', 'featureType', 'referenceName',
 'start', 'end', 'strand', 'phase', 'frame', 'score', 'geneId', 'transcriptId',
 'exonId', 'proteinId', 'aliases', 'parentIds', 'target', 'gap', 'derivesFrom',
 'notes', 'dbxrefs', 'ontologyTerms', 'circular', 'attributes']

...

chip_seq_path = f'data/genomics/chip-seq/ \
                {current_cell_line}.ChIP-seq.CTCF.narrowPeak'
chipseq_data = ac.loadFeatures(chipseq_path) ❶
```

❶ FeatureDataset

❷ Columns in Dnase DataFrame

Sites that overlap a ChIP-seq peak, as defined by a `ReferenceRegion` in `chip seq_data`, have TF binding sites and are therefore labeled `true`, while the rest of the sites are labeled `false`. This is accomplished using the 1D spatial join primitives provided in the ADAM API. The join functionality requires an RDD that is keyed by a `ReferenceRegion` and will produce tuples that have overlapping regions, according to usual join semantics (e.g., inner versus outer).

```
dnase_with_label = dnase_data.leftOuterShuffleRegionJoin(chipseq_data)
dnase_with_label_df = dnase_with_label.toDF()
...

-RECORD 0-------------------------------------------------------------------..
 _1  | {null, null, chr1.1, null, null, chr1, 713841, 714424, INDEPENDENT, null..
 _2  | {null, null, null, null, null, chr1, 713945, 714492, INDEPENDENT, null, ..
```

```
-RECORD 1-----------------------------------------------------------------..
 _1 | {null, null, chr1.2, null, null, chr1, 740179, 740374, INDEPENDENT, null..
 _2 | {null, null, null, null, null, chr1, 740127, 740310, INDEPENDENT, null, ..
-RECORD 2-----------------------------------------------------------------..
 _1 | {null, null, chr1.3, null, null, chr1, 762054, 763213, INDEPENDENT, null..
 _2 | null...
only showing top 3 rows
...

dnase_with_label_df = dnase_with_label_df.\
                    withColumn("label", \
                              ~fun.col("_2").isNull())
dnase_with_label_df.show(5)
```

Now we compute the final set of features on each DNase peak:

```
## build final training DF
training_df = dnase_with_label_df.withColumn(
    "contig", fun.col("_1").referenceName).withColumn(
    "start", fun.col("_1").start).withColumn(
    "end", fun.col("_1").end).withColumn(
    "tf", fun.lit("CTCF")).withColumn(
    "cell_line", fun.lit(current_cell_line)).drop("_1", "_2")

training_df = training_df.join(b_tss_df,
                                training_df.contig == b_tss_df.referenceName,
                                "inner") ❶

training_df.withColumn("closest_tss",
                    fun.least(distance_to_closest_udf(fun.col("start_sites"),
                                                      fun.col("start")),
                            distance_to_closest_udf(fun.col("start_sites"),
                                                      fun.col("end")))) ❷
```

❶ Left join with `tss_df` created earlier.

❷ Get the closest TSS distance.

This final DF is computed in each pass of the loop over the cell lines. Finally, we union each DF from each cell line and cache this data in memory in preparation for training models off of it:

```
preTrainingData = data_by_cellLine.union(...)
preTrainingData.cache()

preTrainingData.count()
preTrainingData.filter(fun.col("label") == true).count()
```

At this point, the data in `preTrainingData` can be normalized and converted into a DataFrame for training a classifier, as described in "Random Forests" on page 82. Note that you should perform cross-validation, where in each fold, you hold out the data from one of the cell lines.

Where to Go from Here

Many computations in genomics fit nicely into the PySpark computational paradigm. When you're performing ad hoc analysis, the most valuable contribution that projects like ADAM provide is the set of Avro schemas that represents the underlying analytical objects (along with the conversion tools). We saw how once data is converted into the corresponding Avro schemas, many large-scale computations become relatively easy to express and distribute.

While there may still be a relative dearth of tools for performing scientific research on PySpark, there do exist a few projects that could help avoid reinventing the wheel. We explored the core functionality implemented in ADAM, but the project already has implementations for the entire GATK best-practices pipeline, including indel realignment, and deduplication. In addition to ADAM, the Broad Institute is now developing major software projects using Spark, including the newest version of the GATK4 (*https://oreil.ly/hGR87*) and a project called Hail (*https://oreil.ly/V6Wpl*) for large-scale population genetics computations. All of these tools are open source, so if you start using them in your own work, please consider contributing improvements!

## CHAPTER 10

Image Similarity Detection with Deep Learning and PySpark LSH

Whether you encounter them on social media or e-commerce stores, images are integral to our digital lives. In fact, it was an image dataset—ImageNet—which was a key component for sparking the current deep learning revolution. A remarkable performance by a classification model in the ImageNet 2012 challenge was an important milestone and led to widespread attention. It is no wonder then that you are likely to encounter image data at some point as a data science practitioner.

In this chapter, you will gain experience scaling a deep learning workflow for a visual task, namely, image similarity detection, with PySpark. The task of identifying images that are similar to each other comes intuitively to humans, but it is a complex computational task. At scale, it becomes even more difficult. In this chapter, we will introduce an approximate method for finding similar items called locality sensitive hashing, or LSH, and apply it to images. We'll use deep learning to convert image data into a numerical vector representation. PySpark's LSH algorithm will be applied to the resulting vectors, which will allow us to find similar images given a new input image.

On a high level, this example mirrors one of the approaches used by photo sharing apps such as Instagram and Pinterest for image similarity detection. This helps their users make sense of the deluge of visual data that exists on their platforms. This also depicts how a deep learning workflow can benefit from PySpark's scalability.

We'll start by briefly introducing PyTorch, a deep learning framework. It has gained prominence in recent years for its relatively easier learning curve compared to other major low-level deep learning libraries. Then we'll download and prepare our dataset. The dataset being used for our task is the Cars dataset released in 2013 by Stanford AI Lab. PyTorch will be used for image preprocessing. This will be followed by conversion of our input image data into a vector representation (image embeddings).

We'll then import the resulting embeddings into PySpark and transform them using the LSH algorithm. We'll finish up by taking a new image and performing a nearest neighbors search using our LSH-transformed dataset to find similar images.

Let's start by introducing and setting up PyTorch.

PyTorch

PyTorch is a library for building deep learning projects. It emphasizes flexibility and allows deep learning models to be expressed in idiomatic Python. It found early adopters in the research community. Recently, it has grown into one of the most prominent deep learning tools across a broad range of applications due to its ease of use. Along with TensorFlow, it is the most popular library for deep learning as of now.

PyTorch's simple and flexible interface enables fast experimentation. You can load data, apply transforms, and build models with a few lines of code. Then, you have the flexibility to write customized training, validation, and test loops and deploy trained models with ease. It is consistently being used in professional contexts for real-world, mission-critical work. Being able to use GPUs (graphical processing units) for training resource-intensive models has been a big factor for making deep learning popular. PyTorch provides great GPU support, although we won't need that for our task.

Installation

On the PyTorch website (*https://oreil.ly/CHkJo*), you can easily obtain the installation instructions based on your system configuration, as shown in Figure 10-1.

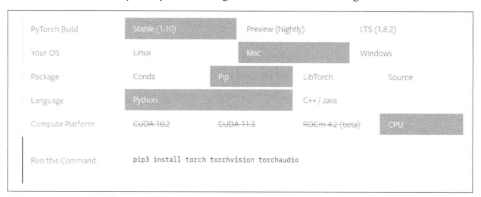

Figure 10-1. PyTorch installation, CPU support

Execute the provided command and follow the instructions for your configuration:

```
$ pip3 install torch torchvision
```

We will not be relying on a GPU and, hence, will choose CPU as a compute platform. If you have a GPU setup that you want to use, choose options accordingly to obtain the required instructions. We will not be needing Torchaudio for this chapter either, so we skip its installation.

Preparing the Data

We will be using the Stanford Cars dataset (*https://oreil.ly/gxo8Q*). It was released as part of the ICCV 2013 paper "3D Object Representations for Fine-Grained Categorization" by Jonathan Krause, Michael Stark, Jia Deng, and Li Fei-Fei.

You can download the images from Kaggle or using the source link provided by Stanford AI Lab.

```
wget http://ai.stanford.edu/~jkrause/car196/car_ims.tgz
```

Once it's downloaded, unzip the train and test image directories and place them in a directory called *cars_data*:

```
data_directory = "cars_data"
train_images = "cars_data/cars_train/cars_train"
```

You can get a CSV file containing labels for the training dataset here (*https://oreil.ly/UoHXh*). Download it, rename it to *cars_train_data.csv*, and place it in the data directory. Let's have a look at it:

```
import pandas as pd

train_df = pd.read_csv(data_directory+"/cars_train_data.csv")

train_df.head()
...
```

	Unnamed: 0	x1	y1	x2	y2	Class	image
0	0	39	116	569	375	14	00001.jpg
1	1	36	116	868	587	3	00002.jpg
2	2	85	109	601	381	91	00003.jpg
3	3	621	393	1484	1096	134	00004.jpg
4	4	14	36	133	99	106	00005.jpg

Ignore all columns other than `Class` and `image`. The other columns are related to the original research project that this dataset was derived from and will not be used for our task.

Resizing Images Using PyTorch

Before we head further, we'll need to preprocess our images. Preprocessing data is very common in machine learning since deep learning models (neural networks) expect the input to meet certain requirements.

We need to apply a series of preprocessing steps, called *transforms*, to convert input images into the proper format for the models. In our case, we need them to be 224 x 224-pixel JPEG-formatted images, since that is a requirement for the ResNet-18 model that we'll use in the next section. We perform this transformation using PyTorch's Torchvision package in the following code:

```
import os
from PIL import Image
from torchvision import transforms

# needed input dimensions for the CNN
input_dim = (224,224)
input_dir_cnn = data_directory + "/images/input_images_cnn"

os.makedirs(input_dir_cnn, exist_ok = True)

transformation_for_cnn_input = transforms.Compose([transforms.Resize(input_dim)])

for image_name in os.listdir(train_images):
    I = Image.open(os.path.join(train_images, image_name))
    newI = transformation_for_cnn_input(I)

    newI.save(os.path.join(input_dir_cnn, image_name))

    newI.close()
    I.close()
```

Here we use a single transformation that resizes the image to fit within the neural networks. However, we can use the Compose transform to define a series of transforms used to preprocess our image too.

Our dataset is in place now. In the next section, we will convert our image data into a vector representation fit for use with PySpark's LSH algorithm.

Deep Learning Model for Vector Representation of Images

Convolutional neural networks, or CNNs, are the standard neural network architectures used for prediction when the input observations are images. We won't be using them for any prediction task but rather for generating a vector representation of images. Specifically, we will use the ResNet-18 architecture.

Residual Network (ResNet) was introduced by Shaoqing Ren, Kaiming He, Jian Sun, and Xiangyu Zhang in their 2015 paper "Deep Residual Learning for Image Recognition." The 18 in ResNet-18 stands for the number of layers that exist in the neural network architecture. Other popular variants of ResNet include 34 and 50 layers. A larger number of layers results in improved performance at the cost of increased computation.

Image Embeddings

An *image embedding* is a representation of an image in a vector space. The basic idea is that if a given image is close to another image, their embedding will also be similar and close in the spatial dimension.

The image in Figure 10-2, released by Andrej Karpathy (*https://oreil.ly/YRhhT*), shows how images can be represented in a lower dimensional space. As an example, you can notice vehicles near the top and birds in the bottom-left space.

Figure 10-2. ILSVRC 2012 image embeddings in a 2-D space

We can obtain image embeddings from ResNet-18 by taking the output of its second-to-last, fully connected layer, which has a dimension of 512. Next, we create a class that, provided an image, can return its numeric vector form representation.

```
import torch
from torchvision import models

class Img2VecResnet18():
    def __init__(self):
        self.device = torch.device("cpu")
        self.numberFeatures = 512
        self.modelName = "resnet-18"
        self.model, self.featureLayer = self.getFeatureLayer()
        self.model = self.model.to(self.device)
        self.model.eval()
        self.toTensor = transforms.ToTensor()    ❶
        self.normalize = transforms.Normalize(mean=[0.485, 0.456, 0.406],
                                              std=[0.229, 0.224, 0.225])    ❷

    def getFeatureLayer(self):
        cnnModel = models.resnet18(pretrained=True)
        layer = cnnModel._modules.get('avgpool')
        self.layer_output_size = 512

        return cnnModel, layer

    def getVec(self, img):
        image = self.normalize(self.toTensor(img)).unsqueeze(0).to(self.device)
        embedding = torch.zeros(1, self.numberFeatures, 1, 1)
        def copyData(m, i, o): embedding.copy_(o.data)
        h = self.featureLayer.register_forward_hook(copyData)
        self.model(image)
        h.remove()
        return embedding.numpy()[0, :, 0, 0]
```

❶ Convert images into the PyTorch tensor format.

❷ Rescale the range of pixel values between 0 and 1. The values for the mean and standard deviation (std) were precomputed based on the data used to train the model. Normalizing the image improves the accuracy of the classifier.

We now initialize the `Img2VecResnet18` class and apply the `getVec` method to all of the images to obtain their image embeddings.

```
import tqdm

img2vec = Img2VecResnet18()
allVectors = {}
for image in tqdm(os.listdir(input_dir_cnn)):
    I = Image.open(os.path.join(input_dir_cnn, image))
    vec = img2vec.getVec(I)
    allVectors[image] = vec
    I.close()
```

For a larger dataset, you may want to sequentially write the vector output to a file rather than keeping it in memory to avoid an out-of-memory error. The data is manageable here, so we create a dictionary, which we save as a CSV file in the next step:

```
import pandas as pd

pd.DataFrame(allVectors).transpose().\
    to_csv(data_folder + '/input_data_vectors.csv')
```

 Since we are working locally, we went with the CSV format for saving the vector output. However, Parquet format is more appropriate for data of this nature. You could easily save the data in Parquet format by replacing to_csv with to_parquet in the previous code.

Now that we have the required image embeddings, we can import them into PySpark.

Import Image Embeddings into PySpark

Start the PySpark shell:

```
$ pyspark --driver-memory 4g
```

Import the image embeddings:

```
input_df = spark.read.option('inferSchema', True).\
                    csv(data_directory + '/input_data_vectors.csv')
input_df.columns
...

['_c0',
 '_c1',
 '_c2',
 '_c3',
 '_c4',
 [...]
 '_c509',
 '_c510',
 '_c511',
 '_c512']
```

PySpark's LSH implementation requires a vector column as an input. We can create one by combining the relevant columns in our dataframe using the VectorAssembler transform:

```
from pyspark.ml.feature import VectorAssembler

vector_columns = input_df.columns[1:]
assembler = VectorAssembler(inputCols=vector_columns, outputCol="features")
```

```
output = assembler.transform(input_df)
output = output.select('_c0', 'features')

output.show(1, vertical=True)
...

-RECORD 0-----------------------
 _c0      | 01994.jpg
 features | [0.05640895,2.709...

...

output.printSchema()
...

root
 |-- _c0: string (nullable = true)
 |-- features: vector (nullable = true)
```

In the next section, we will use the LSH algorithm to create a way for us to find similar images from our dataset.

Image Similarity Search Using PySpark LSH

Locality sensitive hashing is an important class of hashing techniques, which is commonly used in clustering, approximate nearest neighbor search, and outlier detection with large datasets. Locality sensitive functions take two data points and decide whether or not they should be a candidate pair.

The general idea of LSH is to use a family of functions ("LSH families") to hash data points into buckets so that the data points that are close to each other are in the same buckets with high probability, while data points that are far away from each other are very likely in different buckets. The data points that map to the same buckets are considered a candidate pair.

In PySpark, different LSH families are implemented in separate classes (e.g., MinHash and BucketedRandomProjection), and APIs for feature transformation, approximate similarity join, and approximate nearest neighbor are provided in each class.

We'll use the BucketedRandomProjection implementation of LSH.

Let's first create our model object:

```
from pyspark.ml.feature import BucketedRandomProjectionLSH

brp = BucketedRandomProjectionLSH(inputCol="features", outputCol="hashes",
                                  numHashTables=200, bucketLength=2.0)
model = brp.fit(output)
```

In the BucketedRandomProjection LSH implementation, the bucket length can be used to control the average size of hash buckets (and thus the number of buckets). A larger bucket length (i.e., fewer buckets) increases the probability of features being hashed to the same bucket (increasing the number of true and false positives).

We now transform the input DataFrame using the newly created LSH model object. The resulting DataFrame will contain a hashes column containing hashed representation of the image embeddings:

```
lsh_df = model.transform(output)
lsh_df.show(5)
```

```
...
+---------+--------------------+--------------------+
|      _c0|            features|              hashes|
+---------+--------------------+--------------------+
|01994.jpg|[0.05640895,2.709...|[[0.0], [-2.0], [...|
|07758.jpg|[2.1690884,3.4647...|[[0.0], [-1.0], [...|
|05257.jpg|[0.7666548,3.7960...|[[-1.0], [-1.0], ...|
|07642.jpg|[0.86353475,2.993...|[[-1.0], [-1.0], ...|
|00850.jpg|[0.49161428,2.172...|[[-1.0], [-2.0], ...|
+---------+--------------------+--------------------+
only showing top 5 rows
```

With our LSH-transformed dataset ready, we'll put our work to the test in the next section.

Nearest Neighbor Search

Let's try to find a similar image using a new image. For now, we will pick one from the input dataset itself (Figure 10-3):

```
from IPython.display import display
from PIL import Image

input_dir_cnn = data_folder + "/images/input_images_cnn"

test_image = os.listdir(input_dir_cnn)[0]
test_image = os.path.join(input_dir_cnn, test_image)
print(test_image)
display(Image.open(test_image))
...
cars_data/images/input_images_cnn/01994.jpg
```

Figure 10-3. Randomly picked car image from our dataset

First, we'll need to convert the input image into a vector format using our `Img2Vec Resnet18` class:

```
img2vec = Img2VecResnet18()
I = Image.open(test_image)
test_vec = img2vec.getVec(I)
I.close()

print(len(test_vec))
print(test_vec)
...

512
[5.64089492e-02 2.70972490e+00 2.15519500e+00 1.43926993e-01
 2.47581363e+00 1.36641121e+00 1.08204508e+00 7.62105465e-01
 [...]
5.62133253e-01 4.33687061e-01 3.95899676e-02 1.47889364e+00
 2.89110214e-01 6.61322474e-01 1.84713617e-01 9.42268595e-02]
...

test_vector = Vectors.dense(test_vec)
```

Now we perform an approximate nearest neighbor search:

```
print("Approximately searching lsh_df for 5 nearest neighbors \
        of input vector:")
result = model.approxNearestNeighbors(lsh_df, test_vector, 5)

result.show()
...
+---------+--------------------+--------------------+--------------------+
|      _c0|            features|              hashes|             distCol|
+---------+--------------------+--------------------+--------------------+
|01994.jpg|[0.05640895,2.709...|[[0.0], [-2.0], [...|3.691941786298668...|
|00046.jpg|[0.89430475,1.992...|[[0.0], [-2.0], [...|   10.16105522433224|
|04232.jpg|[0.71477133,2.582...|[[-1.0], [-2.0], ...|  10.255391011678762|
|05146.jpg|[0.36903867,3.410...|[[-1.0], [-2.0], ...|  10.264572173322843|
|00985.jpg|[0.530428,2.87453...|[[-1.0], [-2.0], ...|  10.474841359816633|
+---------+--------------------+--------------------+--------------------+
```

You can check the images in Figures 10-4 through 10-8 to see that the model gets it somewhat right already:

```
for i in list(result.select('_c0').toPandas()['_c0']):
    display(Image.open(os.path.join(input_dir_cnn, i)))
```

Figure 10-4. Result image 1

Figure 10-5. Result image 2

Figure 10-6. Result image 3

Figure 10-7. Result image 4

Figure 10-8. Result image 5

The input image is on top of the list as one would expect.

Where to Go from Here

In this chapter, we learned how PySpark can be combined with a modern deep learning framework to scale an image similarity detection workflow.

There are multiple ways to improve this implementation. You can try using a better model or improving the preprocessing to get better quality of embeddings. Further, the LSH model can be tweaked. In a real-life setting, you may need to update the reference dataset consistently to account for new images coming into the system. The simplest way to do this is by running a batch job at periodic intervals to create new LSH models. You can explore all of these depending on your need and interest.

## CHAPTER 11

Managing the Machine Learning Lifecycle with MLflow

As machine learning gains prominence across industries and is deployed in production environments, the level of collaboration and complexity surrounding it has increased as well. Thankfully, platforms and tools have cropped up to help manage the machine learning lifecycle in a structured manner. One such platform that works well with PySpark is MLflow. In this chapter, we will show how MLflow can be used with PySpark. Along the way, we'll introduce key practices that you can incorporate in your data science workflow.

Rather than starting from scratch, we'll build upon the work that we did in Chapter 4. We will revisit our decision tree implementation using the Covtype dataset. Only this time, we'll use MLflow for managing the machine learning lifecycle.

We'll start by explaining the challenges and processes that encompass the machine learning lifecycle. We will then introduce MLflow and its components, as well as cover MLflow's support for PySpark. This will be followed by an introduction to tracking machine learning training runs using MLflow. We'll then learn how to manage machine learning models using MLflow Models. Then we'll discuss deployment of our PySpark model and do an implementation for it. We'll end the chapter by creating an MLflow Project. This will show how we can make our work so far reproducible for collaborators. Let's get started by discussing the machine learning lifecycle.

Machine Learning Lifecycle

There are multiple ways to describe the machine learning lifecycle. One simple way is to break it down into various components or steps, as shown in Figure 11-1. These steps may not necessarily be in sequence for every project, and the lifecycle is cyclic more often than not.

- Business project definition and stakeholder alignment
- Data acquisition and exploration
- Data modeling
- Interpretation and communication of results
- Model implementation and deployment

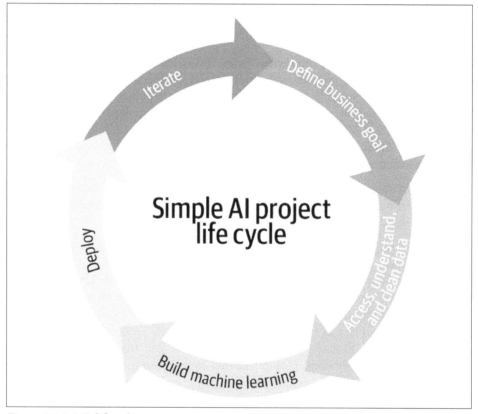

Figure 11-1. ML lifecycle

The speed at which you can iterate through the ML lifecycle affects how fast you can put your work to practical use. For example, an implemented model can become outdated due to a change in underlying data. In that case, you will need to revisit past work and build upon it again.

Examples of challenges that can show up during a machine learning project's lifecycle are:

Lack of reproducibility
> Data scientists on the same team may not be able to reproduce each other's results even if the code and parameters have been tracked. This can be a result of the execution environment (system configuration or library dependencies) being different.

Lack of standardization of models
> Different teams may use different libraries and different conventions for storing machine learning models. This can become a problem when sharing work across teams.

Trying to structure your work while going through the ML lifecycle can quickly become overwhelming. In light of such challenges, multiple open source and proprietary platforms are available to help. One leading open source platform is MLflow, which we will introduce in the upcoming section.

MLflow

MLflow is an open source platform for managing the end-to-end machine learning lifecycle. It helps us reproduce and share experiments, manage models, and deploy models for end users. In addition to a REST API and CLI, it also provides APIs for Python, R, and Java/Scala.

It has four main components, as shown in Figure 11-2:

MLflow Tracking
> This component records parameters, metrics, code versions, models, and artifacts such as plots and text.

MLflow Projects
> This component provides you with a reusable, reproducible format to share with other data scientists or transfer to production. It helps you manage the model training process.

MLflow Models
> This component enables you to package models to deploy to a variety of model serving and inference platforms. It provides a consistent API for loading and applying models, regardless of the underlying library used to build the model.

MLflow Registry
> This component enables you to collaboratively keep track of model lineage, model versions, stage transitions, and annotations in a central store.

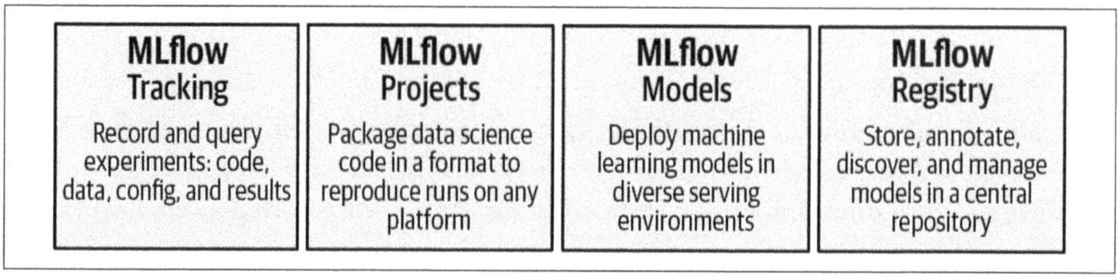

MLflow Tracking	**MLflow** Projects	**MLflow** Models	**MLflow** Registry
Record and query experiments: code, data, config, and results	Package data science code in a format to reproduce runs on any platform	Deploy machine learning models in diverse serving environments	Store, annotate, discover, and manage models in a central repository

Figure 11-2. MLflow components

Let's install MLflow. It's straightforward to do so using pip:

```
$ pip3 install mlflow
```

That's it!

MLflow integrates with many popular machine learning frameworks such as Spark, TensorFlow, PyTorch, and others. We will be using its native support for Spark over the next few sections. Importing the Spark-specific MLflow component is as easy as running `import mlflow.spark`.

In the next section, we'll introduce MLflow Tracking and add it to our decision tree code from Chapter 4.

Experiment Tracking

A typical machine learning project involves experimenting with several algorithms and models to solve a problem. The associated datasets, hyperparameters, and metrics need to be tracked. Typically, experiment tracking is done using makeshift tools such as spreadsheets and can be inefficient or, worse, unreliable.

MLflow Tracking is an API and UI for logging parameters, code versions, metrics, and artifacts when running your machine learning code and for later visualizing the results. You can use MLflow Tracking in any environment (for example, a standalone script or a notebook) to log results to local files or to a server and then compare multiple runs. It is library-agnostic and integrates with multiple frameworks.

MLflow Tracking is organized around the concept of *runs*, which are executions of some piece of data science code. MLflow Tracking provides a UI that lets you visualize, search, and compare runs, as well as download run artifacts or metadata for analysis in other tools. It contains the following key features:

- Experiment-based run listing and comparison

- Searching for runs by parameter or metric value
- Visualizing run metrics
- Downloading run results

Let's add MLflow Tracking to our decision tree code in the PySpark shell. It's assumed that you have downloaded the Covtype dataset (*https://oreil.ly/0xyky*) and are familiar with it. The Covtype dataset is available online as a compressed CSV-format data file, *covtype.data.gz*, and accompanying info file, *covtype.info*.

Start `pyspark-shell`. As mentioned previously, building decision trees can be resource intensive. If you have the memory, specify `--driver-memory 8g` or similar.

We start by preparing the data and machine learning pipeline:

```
from pyspark.ml import Pipeline
from pyspark.sql.functions import col
from pyspark.sql.types import DoubleType
from pyspark.ml.feature import VectorAssembler
from pyspark.ml.classification import DecisionTreeClassifier

data_without_header = spark.read.option("inferSchema", True).\
                                  option("header", False).\
                                  csv("data/covtype.data")

colnames = ["Elevation", "Aspect", "Slope",
            "Horizontal_Distance_To_Hydrology",
            "Vertical_Distance_To_Hydrology",
            "Horizontal_Distance_To_Roadways",
            "Hillshade_9am", "Hillshade_Noon",
            "Hillshade_3pm", "Horizontal_Distance_To_Fire_Points"] + \
[f"Wilderness_Area_{i}" for i in range(4)] + \
[f"Soil_Type_{i}" for i in range(40)] + \
["Cover_Type"]

data = data_without_header.toDF(*colnames).\
                            withColumn("Cover_Type",
                                       col("Cover_Type").\
                                       cast(DoubleType()))

(train_data, test_data) = data.randomSplit([0.9, 0.1])

input_cols = colnames[:-1]
vector_assembler = VectorAssembler(inputCols=input_cols,outputCol="featureVector")

classifier = DecisionTreeClassifier(seed = 1234,
                                    labelCol="Cover_Type",
                                    featuresCol="featureVector",
                                    predictionCol="prediction")

pipeline = Pipeline(stages=[vector_assembler, classifier])
```

To start logging with MLflow, we start a run using `mlflow.start_run`. We will use a `with` clause to automatically end the run at the end of the block:

```
import mlflow
import mlflow.spark
import pandas as pd
from pyspark.ml.evaluation import MulticlassClassificationEvaluator

with mlflow.start_run(run_name="decision-tree"):
    # Log param: max_depth
    mlflow.log_param("max_depth", classifier.getMaxDepth())
    # Log model
    pipeline_model = pipeline.fit(train_data)
    mlflow.spark.log_model(pipeline_model, "model")
    # Log metrics: Accuracy and F1
    pred_df = pipeline_model.transform(test_data)
    evaluator = MulticlassClassificationEvaluator(labelCol="Cover_Type",
                                                  predictionCol="prediction")
    accuracy = evaluator.setMetricName("accuracy").evaluate(pred_df)
    f1 = evaluator.setMetricName("f1").evaluate(pred_df)
    mlflow.log_metrics({"accuracy": accuracy, "f1": f1})
    # Log artifact: feature importance scores
    tree_model = pipeline_model.stages[-1]
    feature_importance_df = (pd.DataFrame(list(
                                    zip(vector_assembler.getInputCols(),
                                        tree_model.featureImportances)),
                                columns=["feature", "importance"])
                    .sort_values(by="importance", ascending=False))
    feature_importance_df.to_csv("feature-importance.csv", index=False)
    mlflow.log_artifact("feature-importance.csv")
```

We can now access our experiment data via the tracking UI. Start it by running the `mlflow ui` command. By default it starts on port 5000. You can use the `-p <port_name>` option to change the default port. Once you have successfully started the UI, go to *http://localhost:5000/*. You will see a UI as shown in Figure 11-3. You can search across all the runs, filter for those that meet particular criteria, compare runs side by side, etc. If you wish, you can also export the contents as a CSV file to analyze locally. Click the run in the UI named `decision-tree`.

	⌂ Start Time	Duration	Run Name	User	Source	Version	Models	accuracy	f1	r2	max_depth
☐	⏱ 1 minute ago	30.1s	decision-tree	analytical-m...	-	-	⚡ spark	0.701	0.684	-	5
☐	⏱ 5 months ago	41.3s	random-forest	analytical-m...	ipykernel_l...	-	⚡ spark	-	-	0.228	5

Figure 11-3. MLflow UI 1

When viewing an individual run, as shown in Figure 11-4, you'll notice that MLflow stores all the corresponding parameters, metrics, etc. You can add notes about this run in free text, as well as tags.

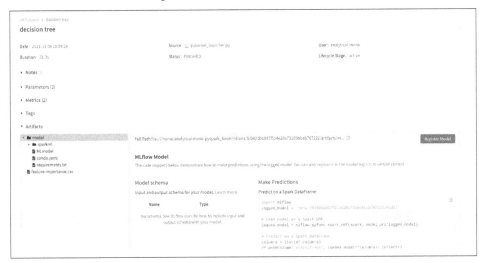

Figure 11-4. MLflow UI 2

We are now able to track and reproduce our experiments. Let's now discuss managing our models using MLflow.

Managing and Serving ML Models

An MLflow Model is a standard format for packaging machine learning models that can be used in a variety of downstream tools—for example, real-time serving through a REST API or batch inference on Apache Spark. The format defines a convention that lets you save a model in different "flavors" that can be understood by different libraries.

Flavors are the key concept that makes MLflow Models powerful. They make it possible to write tools that work with models from any ML library without having to integrate each tool with each library. MLflow defines several "standard" flavors that all of its built-in deployment tools support, such as a "Python function" flavor that describes how to run the model as a Python function. However, libraries can also define and use other flavors. For example, MLflow's `mlflow.sklearn` library allows loading models back as a scikit-learn `Pipeline` object for use in code that is aware of scikit-learn, or as a generic Python function for use in tools that just need to apply the model (for example, the `mlflow.sagemaker` tool for deploying models to Amazon SageMaker).

An MLflow Model is a directory containing a set of files. We had earlier logged our model using the `log_model` API. This created a file called *MLmodel*. Open the decision-tree run and scroll down to the "Artifacts" section. Check out the *MLmodel* file. Its contents should be similar to what's depicted in Figure 11-5.

```
artifact_path: model
flavors:
  python_function:
    data: sparkml
    env: conda.yaml
    loader_module: mlflow.spark
    python_version: 3.6.12
  spark:
    model_data: sparkml
    pyspark_version: 3.0.1
run_id: 0433bb047f514e28a73109bbab767222
utc_time_created: '2021-11-06 12:34:27.758915'
```

Figure 11-5. MLflow Model

The file captures our model's metadata, signature, and flavors. The Model signature defines the schema of a model's inputs and outputs.

Our model file has two flavors: python_function and spark. The python_function flavor enables MLflow's model deployment and serving tools to work with any Python model regardless of which ML library trained the model. As a result, any Python model can be easily productionalized in a variety of runtime environments.

The spark model flavor enables exporting Spark MLlib models as MLflow Models. For example, to make predictions on a Spark DataFrame using the logged model:

```
import mlflow

run_id = "0433bb047f514e28a73109bbab767222"  ❶
logged_model = f'runs:/{run_id}/model'  ❷

# Load model as a Spark UDF.
loaded_model = mlflow.spark.load_model(model_uri=logged_model)

# Predict on a Spark DataFrame.
preds = loaded_model.transform(test_data)
preds.select('Cover_Type', 'rawPrediction', 'probability', 'prediction').\
        show(1, vertical=True)
...
-RECORD 0----------------------------
 Cover_Type    | 6.0
 rawPrediction | [0.0,0.0,605.0,15...
 probability   | [0.0,0.0,0.024462...
 prediction    | 3.0
only showing top 1 row
```

❶ This ID can be obtained from the tracking UI in the relevant *MLmodel* file.

❷ We use Python f-strings for adding the relevant run ID.

We can also use the `mlflow serve` command-line tool to serve the model corresponding to a particular run ID.

```
$ mlflow models serve --model-uri runs:/0433bb047f514e28a73109bbab767222/model \
    -p 7000

...

2021/11/13 12:13:49 INFO mlflow.models.cli: Selected backend for...
2021/11/13 12:13:52 INFO mlflow.utils.conda: === Creating conda ...
Collecting package metadata (repodata.json): done
Solving environment: done ...
```

You have successfully deployed your model as a REST API!

We can now use this endpoint to perform inference. Let's prepare and send a request to the endpoint to see it in action. We'll use the `requests` library to do this. Install it using pip first if you don't yet have it:

```
pip3 install requests
```

Now we'll send a request containing a JSON object in a pandas-split orientation to the model server.

```python
import requests

host = '0.0.0.0'
port = '7001'

url = f'http://{host}:{port}/invocations'

headers = {
    'Content-Type': 'application/json;',
    'format': 'pandas-split';
}

http_data = '{"columns":["Elevation","Aspect","Slope", \
    "Horizontal_Distance_To_Hydrology", \
    "Vertical_Distance_To_Hydrology","Horizontal_Distance_To_Roadways", \
    "Hillshade_9am","Hillshade_Noon","Hillshade_3pm",\
    "Horizontal_Distance_To_Fire_Points",\
    "Wilderness_Area_0","Wilderness_Area_1","Wilderness_Area_2",\
    "Wilderness_Area_3","Soil_Type_0","Soil_Type_1","Soil_Type_2",\
    "Soil_Type_3","Soil_Type_4","Soil_Type_5","Soil_Type_6",\
    "Soil_Type_7","Soil_Type_8","Soil_Type_9","Soil_Type_10",\
    "Soil_Type_11","Soil_Type_12","Soil_Type_13",\
    "Soil_Type_14","Soil_Type_15","Soil_Type_16",\
    "Soil_Type_17","Soil_Type_18","Soil_Type_19",\
```

```
"Soil_Type_20","Soil_Type_21","Soil_Type_22",\
"Soil_Type_23","Soil_Type_24","Soil_Type_25",\
"Soil_Type_26","Soil_Type_27","Soil_Type_28",\
"Soil_Type_29","Soil_Type_30","Soil_Type_31",\
"Soil_Type_32","Soil_Type_33","Soil_Type_34",\
"Soil_Type_35","Soil_Type_36","Soil_Type_37",\
"Soil_Type_38","Soil_Type_39","Cover_Type"],\
"index":[0],\
"data":[[2596,51,3,258,0,510,221,232,148,6279,1,\
        0,0,0,0,0,0,0,0,0,0,0,0,0,0,0,0,0,0,0,\
        0,0,0,0,0,0,0,0,0,0,0,0,1,0,0,0,0,0,0,0,0,0,0,0,5.0]]'\

r = requests.post(url=url, headers=headers, data=http_data)

print(f'Predictions: {r.text}')
...
Predictions: [2.0]
```

We not only loaded a saved model but also deployed it as a REST API and performed inference in real time!

Let us now learn how to create an MLflow Project for the work we have done so far.

Creating and Using MLflow Projects

MLflow Projects is a standard format for reusable and reproducible packaging. It's a self-contained unit that bundles all the machine code and dependencies required to execute a machine learning workflow and enables you to produce a particular model run on any system or environment. MLflow Projects includes an API and command-line tools for running projects. It can also be used to chain projects together into workflows.

Each project is simply a directory of files, or a Git repository, containing your code. MLflow can run some projects based on a convention for placing files in this directory (for example, a *conda.yml* file is treated as a Conda environment), but you can describe your project in more detail by adding an MLproject file, which is a YAML-formatted text file.

MLflow currently supports the following project environments: Conda environment, Docker container environment, and system environment. By default, MLflow uses the system path to find and run the Conda binary.

Creating a basic MLflow project is straightforward. The required steps are listed in Figure 11-6.

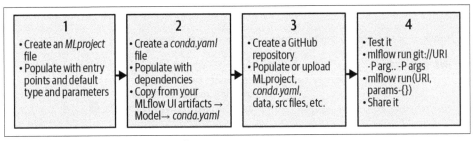

1	2	3	4
• Create an *MLproject* file • Populate with entry points and default type and parameters	• Create a *conda.yaml* file • Populate with dependencies • Copy from your MLflow UI artifacts → Model→ *conda.yaml*	• Create a GitHub repository • Populate or upload MLproject, *conda.yaml*, data, src files, etc.	• Test it • mlflow run git://URI -P arg.. -P args • mlflow run(URI, params-{}) • Share it

Figure 11-6. How to build an MLflow Project

We will start by creating our project directory named *decision_tree_project*:

```
mkdir decision_tree_project
cd decision_tree_project
```

Next, we'll first create an MLproject file:

```
name: decision_tree_project

conda_env: conda.yml

entry_points:
  main:
    command: "python train.py"
```

We now need our *conda.yml* file. We can get this from the MLflow UI introduced in a previous section. Go inside the decision-tree run that we previously saw. Scroll down to the Artifacts, click the conda YAML file, and copy its contents into *conda.yml* in our project directory:

```
channels:
- conda-forge
dependencies:
- python=3.6.12
- pip
- pip:
  - mlflow
  - pyspark==3.2.1
  - scipy==1.5.3
name: mlflow-env
```

We will now create the Python script that will be used to train a decision tree model upon the MLflow project being executed. For this, we'll use the code from a previous section:

```
from pyspark.sql import SparkSession
from pyspark.ml import Pipeline
from pyspark.sql.functions import col
from pyspark.sql.types import DoubleType
from pyspark.ml.feature import VectorAssembler
from pyspark.ml.classification import DecisionTreeClassifier
```

```python
from pyspark.ml.evaluation import MulticlassClassificationEvaluator

spark = SparkSession.builder.appName("App").getOrCreate()

def main():
    data_without_header = spark.read.option("inferSchema", True).\
                                option("header", False).\
                                csv("../data/covtype.data") ❶

    colnames = ["Elevation", "Aspect", "Slope",
                "Horizontal_Distance_To_Hydrology",
                "Vertical_Distance_To_Hydrology",
                "Horizontal_Distance_To_Roadways",
                "Hillshade_9am", "Hillshade_Noon",
                "Hillshade_3pm",
                "Horizontal_Distance_To_Fire_Points"] + \
    [f"Wilderness_Area_{i}" for i in range(4)] + \
    [f"Soil_Type_{i}" for i in range(40)] + \
    ["Cover_Type"]

    data = data_without_header.toDF(*colnames).\
                            withColumn("Cover_Type",
                                    col("Cover_Type").\
                                    cast(DoubleType()))

    (train_data, test_data) = data.randomSplit([0.9, 0.1])

    input_cols = colnames[:-1]
    vector_assembler = VectorAssembler(inputCols=input_cols,
                            outputCol="featureVector")

    classifier = DecisionTreeClassifier(seed = 1234,
                                    labelCol="Cover_Type",
                                    featuresCol="featureVector",
                                    predictionCol="prediction")

    pipeline = Pipeline(stages=[vector_assembler, classifier])

    pipeline_model = pipeline.fit(train_data)
    # Log metrics: Accuracy and F1
    pred_df = pipeline_model.transform(test_data)
    evaluator = MulticlassClassificationEvaluator(labelCol="Cover_Type",
                                        predictionCol="prediction")
    accuracy = evaluator.setMetricName("accuracy").evaluate(pred_df)
    f1 = evaluator.setMetricName("f1").evaluate(pred_df)
    print({"accuracy": accuracy, "f1": f1})


if __name__ == "__main__":
    main()
```

❶ Data is assumed to be one directory level above the MLflow project directory being executed.

Data can also be included inside an MLflow project. In this case, we don't do so because of the large size. In such a case, data can be shared using cloud storage such as AWS S3 or GCS.

You can simulate how it will work for a collaborator locally before sharing, too. We do that using the `mlflow run` command.

```
mlflow run decision_tree_project
...
[...]
{'accuracy': 0.6988990605087336, 'f1': 0.6805617730220171}
```

We now have a reproducible MLflow project. We can upload it to a GitHub repository and share it with a collaborator who will be able to reproduce our work.

Where to Go from Here

This chapter introduced the MLflow project and guided you through its implementation for a straightforward project. There is a lot to explore within the MLflow project itself. You can find more information in the official docs (*https://mlflow.org*). There are other tools out there that can serve as alternatives as well. These include open source projects, such as Metaflow and Kubeflow, as well as proprietary offerings by big cloud providers including Amazon SageMaker and the Databricks platform.

Of course, tools are only part of the solution to the challenges that a real-world machine learning project offers. Processes need to be defined by the people working on any project. We hope that you will build upon the foundations offered in this chapter and contribute to successful machine learning projects in the wild.

Index

About the Authors

Akash Tandon is cofounder and CTO of Looppanel. Previously, he worked as a senior data engineer at Atlan.

Sandy Ryza leads development of the Dagster project and is a committer on Apache Spark.

Uri Laserson is founder and CTO of Patch Biosciences. Previously, he worked on big data and genomics at Cloudera.

Sean Owen, a principal solutions architect focusing on machine learning and data science at Databricks, is an Apache Spark committer and PMC member.

Josh Wills is a software engineer at WeaveGrid and the former head of data engineering at Slack.

Colophon

The animal on the cover of *Advanced Analytics with PySpark* is an Atlantic mudskipper (*Periophthalmus barbarus*), an amphibious fish most commonly found in mangrove swamps and mudflats on Africa's west coast.

This mudskipper is olive-brown in color and often has blue markings. Strong pectoral fins allow easy movement on land and in water. Its frog-like eyes allow it to hunt while remaining mostly submerged in mud or water.

Atlantic mudskippers are ambush predators, feeding on small insects and crustaceans using water suction created by expanding their head. Male members of the species are territorial and create mud ridges to delineate zones of approximately 10 square feet.

While the Atlantic mudskipper is listed as Least Concern by the IUCN, many of the animals on O'Reilly covers are endangered; all of them are important to the world.

The cover illustration is by Karen Montgomery, based on an antique line engraving from Johnson's *Natural History*. The cover fonts are Gilroy Semibold and Guardian Sans. The text font is Adobe Minion Pro; the heading font is Adobe Myriad Condensed; and the code font is Dalton Maag's Ubuntu Mono.

O'REILLY®

Learn from experts.
Become one yourself.

Books | Live online courses
Instant Answers | Virtual events
Videos | Interactive learning

Get started at oreilly.com.

Milton Keynes UK
Ingram Content Group UK Ltd.
UKHW020943200624
444457UK00007BA/89